W9-BHH-165

MARATHON

JEFF GALLOWAY

Copyright ©1996 by Jeff Galloway

All rights reserved. No part of this publication may be reproduced or transmitted in any form or by any means, electronic or mechanical, including photocopy, recording, or any information storage and retrieval systems without the written permission of the publisher.

Library of Congress Cataloging in Publication Data

Galloway, Jeff, 1945-
Marathon!

1. Running. 2. Running-Training. 3. Fitness-Health. 4. Sports-Fiction. I. Title

ISBN: 0-9647187-1-5

Grateful thanks to Zoila Harmouche for layout and graphic design
        ...to Carol Miller for proofreading and project coordination
        ...to Amy Reis for research
        ...to Michele Langevin for research
        ...to Brennan and Westin Galloway for ideas and feedback
        ...to Barbara Galloway for recipes and support
        ...to Elliott Galloway for giving me a vision of what I can be when I grow up
        ...to Kitty Galloway for support and inspiration

Third Printing: May 1998

Printed in the United States of America

Phidippides Publication
4651 Roswell Road, Suite I-802
Atlanta GA 30342
www.jeffgalloway.com

TABLE OF CONTENTS

TABLE OF CONTENTS

THE NEXT FITNESS GENERATION

RUNNING AWAY FROM ALIENATION

BELIEF ENVIRONMENT

PHIDIPPIDES...THE FIRST MARATHONER DIDN'T KNOW WHAT HE HAD STARTED

THERE *IS* A BETTER SHOE

A JANUARY 1ST MARATHON RESOLUTION

SETTING UP THE MARATHON PROGRAM

WALK BREAKS?

FRAMING THE MARATHON EXPERIENCE

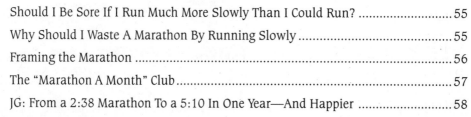

A FASTER MARATHON

HILLS BUILD STRENGTH

SPEED *PLAY*

THE BLOOD SUGAR EFFECT

THE ENERGY CRISIS

THE INSPIRATION OF THE MARATHON...AND THE GROUP

THE POWER OF REHEARSAL

IN ONE YEAR.....

THE MARATHON SHUFFLE

HIGH PERFORMANCE SHUFFLING

HILL *PLAY*

IT'S TOO COLD

WHY WASTE THE MARATHON ON THOSE UNDER 40!

HEART RATE MONITORS IN A MARATHON PROGRAM

THE MARATHON FAT FURNACE

INTRODUCTION
WHY....THE MARATHON?

*F*irst, the migration became a race.

It must have started in a very innocent way. Picture a "tribe" of our ancestors walking and running together to gather food, to move to a better environment, or to flee from predators. The primitive ego of one competitive individual drives him or her to pass the others and move into the lead.

The concept of sport was born as we transformed exertion needed for survival into an activity which could be appreciated in its own right toward the pursuit of excellence. The ancient Greeks brought this idea to its highest ancient expression through the Olympic Games. So highly respected were these events that even the normally independent and bellicose Greek states would cease fighting during the competitions. Indeed, historic Greek events were chronologically dated according to most recent Olympiade.

The blame or praise for the re-emergence of sport as a major factor in our society can be tied to the Modern Olympic Games. In all probability, running today would be a much smaller activity, linked directly to a track, were it not for Baron Pierre de Coubertin, who insisted on having a race held mostly outside the stadium. The Baron recognized the selfless act of a Greek messenger/soldier who courageously ran the news of the Greek victory over the Persians into Athens and died. Inside this book, you'll find an interpretation of the history of Phidippides; we could be running 260 miles in "the marathon" if we commemorated the journey which he probably made.

In North America, the Olympics were originally appreciated for sport and not used as inspiration for personal exercise goals. For the first half of the 20th century, heart disease was almost unheard of, and most citizens performed many hours of exertion each day in their work. The glamour events were held on the track, among competitors who were primarily college students or grads. Marathoners were mostly blue-collar workers and were mostly ignored. But a group in New England was inspired by the point-to-point race on the course of the ancient Greek messenger. Legend has it that at least part of the original Boston Marathon course was run along the route of Paul Revere.

A growing number of North American cities wanted to have their own version of the Patriot's Day race in Beantown. The proliferation of local road races continued to be a primarily blue-collar activity until the age of Cooper and Shorter. By 1968, very few citizens performed any significant daily exertion. In that year, Dr. Kenneth Cooper published Aerobics and shook up the medical establishment by warning that exercise could reduce the growing epidemic of heart disease. The number of deaths from heart disease has gone down each year since.

When a Yale grad failed to win a medal in the 1972 Olympic 10K, he decided to go for it in the only other event for which he had qualified: the marathon. After Frank Shorter won that race, many commentators noted that he had "invented the marathon" for white-collar opinion leaders. In fact, a growing number of college athletes and grads had migrated away from the track and into the marathon during the '60's. Shorter became the articulate spokesperson of this new generation of runners.

For many of the participants in the first running boom (1976-83), the marathon was sport. The physical and mental benefits of fitness were as important as their finishing time. Many of these "first-wavers" burned out from too many races, run slower than they thought they were capable.

After a gradual reduction of marathoners during the middle '80's, a second running boom was born. During the previous decade, media and medical authorities had created the awareness that we should be exercising. Yet since the decline of the first running boom, obesity in the U.S. has increased from about 25 percent to 37 percent of the adult population.

Leading the crest of the second running wave are the new marathoners, to whom this book is dedicated. These folks in their 30's, 40's, 50's and 60's have produced the greatest number of marathoners in history—about three times that of the first wave. Growing at the rate of over 30 percent a year, marathoning has become the fastest growing exertion activity today.

For most of the members of this new wave, finishing time is of no consequence. The average performance in some marathons today is often 45 minutes slower than it was for the average marathon finisher of the first wave. To train for the marathon is to go into battle against the lack of respon-

sibility most North Americans feel for their own health. To finish is to win!

Over a million people will struggle for the motivation to break away from a sedentary lifestyle and train for a marathon this year. As we are challenged to increase endurance and prepare for a marathon, we experience the same type of attitude boost, exhilaration and mental formatting enjoyed by our forbears during constant migrations. The physical enhancements, natural relaxants and improved mind-body communication developed by our ancient ancestors allow us to increase creativity, improve our problem-solving and enjoy greater quality in our 21st century lives.

Finally....the race has gone back to the migration.

A2

BEFORE YOU TAKE
THOSE FIRST STEPS...

*T*here are very few people who should not exercise because of cardiovascular, structural, muscular, or other problems. It is very important to ensure that you are not in this risk category.

- Before beginning any exercise, diet or other improvement program, be sure to have yourself and the program evaluated by specialists in the areas you are pursuing.

- The advice in this book is offered as such—advice from one exerciser to another. It is not meant to be a prescription and should be evaluated as noted above and below.

- Specific structures and problems of individuals may require program modifications.

- In each area, find specialists who are also knowledgeable about the positive and other effects of exercise and running.

- Ask several respected leaders in the fitness community for recommendations of specialists.

- Always back off any exercise or program when you feel any risk of injury or health.

- The benefits come from regular exercise and steady adherence to a long-term program.

- Never radically increase the amount of exercise or drastically change diet and other health elements.

- Joining a group helps motivation.

- Have FUN and you'll want to continue.

A3

SETTING UP *YOUR* MARATHON PROGRAM

A PROGRAM FOR THOSE WHO HAVE JOBS, FAMILIES, AND.....A LIFE

We recognize that you have many other aspects of your life which are more important than the marathon. This program allows you to fit your training into a very busy schedule and "do it all." The achievement of completing a marathon training program and finishing the marathon will be your treasure for the rest of your life. It is my pleasure to announce that you don't have to significantly alter your work or family life, every week, to accomplish this.

The schedules which follow are the latest evolution in a minimal mileage, low-impact training routine which has been used successfully by an estimated 100,000 marathoners since 1978. By looking further at the chapter on "Setting Up The Marathon Training Program" in this book and following all of the medical and safety guidelines, you'll have an enjoyable time in the marathon itself.

MINIMUM: THREE DAYS A WEEK

You'll need a minimum of three days a week: a long run run and two other sessions of at least 30 minutes each. If you're already doing more than that, you may continue for a while at your current amount of exercise until the long runs go beyond 15 miles.

SLOW LONG RUNS

Because the participants in this program run the long ones slowly, they recover quickly, can enjoy the rest of the day and family/social activities, and can be productive at work the next day. Slow runs bestow the same endurance as fast runs for the same distance. Your long ones will be done every other weekend until the long one reaches 18. At that point, the long one shifts to every third weekend. By increasing the long one up to 26 miles you teach the body and mind together exactly what it needs to do in the marathon itself.

WALK BREAKS

By inserting one to two-minute walk breaks into the long runs from the beginning of each long one, you'll shift off the main running muscles and keep them resilient. This has allowed beginners to finish a marathon in six months and has opened up the exhilaration of the marathon finish line experience to almost everyone. Many runners have posted their personal best marathon times because the walk breaks conserve their most important marathon resource: the leg muscles.

FUN

Together, our mission is to have fun in our exertion. Individually, we can feel the relaxation effects of the physical journey, the more significant effects of the attitude-boosting mechanisms and mental focus enhancers. By hooking up with another person or a group you will find a gentle and playful spirit with the warmth of friendships based on gutteral bonding and respect.

Inside, you'll find many other proven ways to have fun as you burn fat. So.....get out there and play!

A5

BEGINNER PROGRAM

Week #	Mon	Tue	Wed	Thu	Fri	Sat	Sun
1.	walk 30 min	run/walk 30min	walk 30 min	run/walk 30 min	walk 30 min	off	3-4 run/walk
2.	walk 30 min	run/walk 30min	walk 30 min	run/walk 30 min	walk 30 min	off	4-5 run/walk
3.	walk 30 min	run/walk 30min	walk 30 min	run/walk 30 min	walk 30 min	off	5-6 run/walk
4.	walk 30 min	run/walk 30min	walk 30 min	run/walk 30 min	walk 30 min	off	6-7 run/walk
5.	walk 30 min	run/walk 30min	walk 30 min	run/walk 30 min	walk 30 min	off	7-8 run/walk
6.	walk 30 min	run/walk 30min	walk 30 min	run/walk 30 min	walk 30 min	off	8-9 mi
7.	walk 30 min	run/walk 30min	walk 30 min	run/walk 30 min	walk 30 min	off	9-10 mi
8.	walk 30 min	run/walk 30min	walk 30 min	run/walk 30 min	walk 30 min	off	10-11 mi
9.	walk 30 min	run/walk 30min	walk 30 min	run/walk 30 min	walk 30 min	off	11-12 mi
10.	walk 30 min	run/walk 30min	walk 30 min	run/walk 30 min	walk 30 min	off	6 mi
11.	walk 30 min	run/walk 30min	walk 30 min	run/walk 30 min	walk 30 min	off	13-14 mi
12.	walk 30 min	run/walk 30min	walk 30 min	run/walk 30 min	walk 30 min	off	7 mi
13.	walk 30 min	run/walk 30min	walk 30 min	run/walk 30 min	walk 30 min	off	15-16 mi
14.	walk 30 min	run/walk 30min	walk 30 min	run/walk 30 min	walk 30 min	off	7 mi
15.	walk 30 min	run/walk 30min	walk 30 min	run/walk 30 min	walk 30 min	off	17-18 mi
16.	walk 30 min	run/walk 30min	walk 30 min	run/walk 30 min	walk 30 min	off	8 mi
17	walk 30 min	run/walk 30min	walk 30 min	run/walk 30 min	walk 30 min	off	19-20 mi
18.	walk 30 min	run/walk 30min	walk 30 min	run/walk 30 min	walk 30 min	off	8-9 mi
19.	walk 30 min	run/walk 30min	walk 30 min	run/walk 30 min	walk 30 min	off	8-9 mi
20.	walk 30 min	run/walk 30min	walk 30 min	run/walk 30 min	walk 30 min	off	22-23 mi
21.	walk 30 min	run/walk 30min	walk 30 min	run/walk 30 min	walk 30 min	off	8-10 mi
22.	walk 30 min	run/walk 30min	walk 30 min	run/walk 30 min	walk 30 min	off	8-10 mi
23.	walk 30 min	run/walk 30min	walk 30 min	run/walk 30 min	walk 30 min	off	24-26 mi
24.	walk 30 min	run/walk 30min	walk 30 min	run/walk 30 min	walk 30 min	off	8-10 mi
25.	walk 30 min	run/walk 30min	walk 30 min	run/walk 30 min	walk 30 min	off	8-10 mi
26.	walk 30 min	off	walk 30 min	off	walk 30 min	off	**The Marathon**
27.	walk 45 min	run/walk 45 min	walk 30-60 min	run/walk 40 min	walk 30-60 min	off	7-10 mi run/walk
28.	walk 45 min	run/walk 45 min	walk 30-60 min	run/walk 45 min	walk 30-60 min	off	9-15 mi run/walk
29.	walk 45 min	run/walk 45 min	walk 30-60 min	run/walk 45 min	walk 30-60 min	off	12-20 mi run/walk

FROM JEFF GALLOWAY'S MARATHON! 1-800-200-2771

- Stay conversational on all of your exercise sessions. This means that you should be exerting yourself at a low enough level that you could talk. It's okay to take deep breaths between sentences, but you don't want to "huff and puff" between every word.

- For the first few weeks, you will be doing more walking than running. On every "run/walk" day, walk for 2-3 minutes and jog 1-2 minutes. Every 3-4 weeks you may evaluate how you're feeling. If you want to increase the running, start by taking a 3-minute walk with a 2-minute run. Many of our beginners don't get further than this. Advanced beginners progress to a maximum of running for 2 minutes and walking for 2 minutes.

- Be sure to do the running portion slow enough at the beginning of every run (especially the long one) so that you'll feel tired but strong at the end. This conservatism will allow you to recover faster.

- Don't wait to take walk breaks! By alternating walking and running from the beginning, you speed recovery without losing any of the endurance effect of the long one.

- Best results will be achieved when you increase the long one to 26 miles. If your last one is only 24 miles, you must run slowly and take a few more walking breaks during the first 5 and 10 miles of the marathon itself.

- As the runs get longer, be sure to keep your blood sugar boosted by eating a PowerBar (or equivalent) about an hour before exercise and pieces of a PowerBar (or equivalent) during the second half of the long run or marathon. Drink water continuously before and during exercise and with all food. Gradually introduce your system to the nutrients on your long runs.

- Above all, HAVE FUN!

A7

A8

"TO FINISH" PROGRAM

Week #	Mon	Tue	Wed	Thu	Fri	Sat	Sun
1.	walk/XT 40 min	run 30-45 min	walk or XT	run 30-45 min	walk or XT	off	3 mi easy
2.	walk/XT 40 min	run 30-45 min	walk or XT	run 30-45 min	walk or XT	off	4 mi
3.	walk/XT 40 min	run 30-45 min	walk or XT	run 30-45 min	walk or XT	off	5 mi
4.	walk/XT 40 min	run 30-45 min	walk or XT	run 30-45 min	walk or XT	off	6 mi
5.	walk/XT 40 min	run 30-45 min	walk or XT	run 30-45 min	walk or XT	off	7 mi
6.	walk/XT 40 min	run 30-45 min	walk or XT	run 30-45 min	walk or XT	off	8 mi
7.	walk/XT 40 min	run 30-45 min	walk or XT	run 30-45 min	walk or XT	off	9 mi
8.	walk/XT 40 min	run 30-45 min	walk or XT	run 30-45 min	walk or XT	off	10 mi
9.	walk/XT 40 min	run 30-45 min	walk or XT	run 30-45 min	walk or XT	off	11-12 mi
10.	walk/XT 40 min	run 30-45 min	walk or XT	run 30-45 min	walk or XT	off	6 mi
11.	walk/XT 40 min	run 30-45 min	walk or XT	run 30-45 min	walk or XT	off	13-14 mi
12.	walk/XT 40 min	run 30-45 min	walk or XT	run 30-45 min	walk or XT	off	7 mi
13.	walk/XT 40 min	run 30-45 min	walk or XT	run 30-45 min	walk or XT	off	15-16
14.	walk/XT 40 min	run 30-45 min	walk or XT	run 30-45 min	walk or XT	off	8 mi
15.	walk/XT 40 min	run 30-45 min	walk or XT	run 30-45 min	walk or XT	off	17-18
16.	walk/XT 40 min	run 30-45 min	walk or XT	run 30-45 min	walk or XT	off	8-10 mi
17	walk/XT 40 min	run 30-45 min	walk or XT	run 30-45 min	walk or XT	off	19-20
18.	walk/XT 40 min	run 30-45 min	walk or XT	run 30-45 min	walk or XT	off	5K race or 8-10
19.	walk/XT 40 min	run 30-45 min	walk or XT	run 30-45 min	walk or XT	off	8-9 mi
20.	walk/XT 40 min	run 30-45 min	walk or XT	run 30-45 min	walk or XT	off	22-23
21.	walk/XT 40 min	run 30-45 min	walk or XT	run 30-45 min	walk or XT	off	5K race or 8-10
22.	walk/XT 40 min	run 30-45 min	walk or XT	run 30-45 min	walk or XT	off	8-10 mi
23.	walk/XT 40 min	run 30-45 min	walk or XT	run 30-45 min	walk or XT	off	24-26 mi
24.	walk/XT 40 min	run 30-45 min	walk or XT	run 30-45 min	walk or XT	off	5K race or 8-10
25.	walk/XT 40 min	run 30-45 min	walk or XT	run 30-45 min	walk or XT	off	8-10 mi
26.	run 40 min	off	run 30 min	off	run/walk 30 min	off	**The Marathon**
27.	walk 45 min	run/walk 45 min	walk 30-60 min	run/walk 45 min	walk 30-60 min	off	7-10 mi run/walk
28.	walk 45 min	run/walk 45 min	walk 30-60 min	run/walk 45 min	walk 30-60 min	off	9-15 mi run/walk
29.	walk 45 min	run/walk 45 min	walk 30-60 min	run/walk 45 min	walk 30-60 min	off	12-20 mi run/walk

FROM JEFF GALLOWAY'S MARATHON! 1-800-200-2771

- Every other day you can cross-train instead of walking. Cross-country ski machines, water running, cycling, and any other mode which you find fun and interesting (but non-pounding) will improve overall fitness.

- Stay conversational on all of your exercise sessions. This means that you should be exerting yourself at a low enough level that you could talk. It's okay to take deep breaths between sentences, but you don't want to "huff and puff" between every word.

- Be sure to do the running portion slow enough at the beginning of every run (especially the long one) so that you'll feel tired but strong at the end. This conservatism will allow you to recover faster.

- Don't wait to take walk breaks! By alternating walking and running from the beginning, you speed recovery without losing any of the endurance effect of the long one.

- As the runs get longer, be sure to keep your blood sugar boosted by eating a PowerBar (or equivalent) about an hour before exercise and pieces of a PowerBar (or equivalent) during the second half of the long run or marathon. Drink water continuously before and during exercise and with all food. Gradually introduce your system to the nutrients on your long runs.

- Best results will be achieved when you increase the long one to 26 miles. If your last one is only 24 miles, you must run slowly and take a few more walking breaks during the first 5 and 10 miles of the marathon itself.

- Above all, HAVE FUN!

A9

A10

TIME GOAL MARATHON: 4:40

Week #	Mon	Tue	Wed	Thu	Fri	Sat	Sun
1.	XT	40-50 min	20-30 min	XT	40-50 min	off	4-6 hills (5-7 mi)
2.	XT	40-50 min	20-30 min	XT	40-50 min	off	5K race (6-7 mi)
3.	XT	40-50 min	20-30 min	XT	40-50 min	off	7-8 hills (7-8 mi)
4.	XT	40-50 min	20-30 min	XT	40-50 min	off	9-10 hills (8-9 mi)
5.	XT	45-50 min	25-35 min	XT	45-50 min	off	5K race (9-10 mi)
6.	XT	45-50 min	25-35 min	XT	45-50 min	off	3-4 x 1 mi (11 mi)
7.	XT	45-50 min	25-35 min	XT	45-50 min	off	4-5 x 1 mi (8 mi)
8.	XT	45-50 min	25-35 min	XT	45-50 min	off	5-6 x 1 mi (13 mi)
9.	XT	45-50 min	25-35 min	XT	45-50 min	off	5K race (6 mi)
10.	XT	45-55 min	25-40 min	XT	45-55 min	off	15-16 mi easy
11.	XT	45-55 min	25-40 min	XT	45-55 min	off	5K race (6 mi)
12.	XT	45-55 min	25-40 min	XT	45-55 min	off	17-18 mi easy
13.	XT	45-55 min	25-40 min	XT	45-55 min	off	5-6 x1 mi
14.	XT	45-55 min	25-40 min	XT	45-55 min	off	19-20 mi easy
15.	XT	45-55 min	25-40 min	XT	45-55 min	off	5K race (10 mi)
16.	XT	45-55 min	25-40 min	XT	45-55 min	off	5 x1 mi
17.	XT	45-55 min	25-40 min	XT	45-55 min	off	22-23 mi easy
18.	XT	45-55 min	25-40 min	XT	45-55 min	off	5K race
19.	XT	45-55 min	25-40 min	XT	45-55 min	off	4 x 1 mi
20.	XT	45-55 min	25-40 min	XT	45-55 min	off	24-26 mi easy
21.	XT	45-55 min	25-40 min	XT	45-55 min	off	5K race
22.	XT	45-55 min	25-40 min	XT	45-55 min	off	3-4 x 1 mi
23.	XT	45-55 min	25-40 min	XT	45-55 min	off	27-28 mi easy
24.	XT	45-55 min	25-40 min	XT	45-55 min	off	5K or 3 x 1 mi
25.	XT	40-45 min	20-25 min	XT	40-45 min	off	3 x 1 mi
26.	run 40 min	off	run 30 min	off	run 30 min	off	**The Marathon**
27.	walk 45 min	run/walk 30 min	walk 30-60 min	run/walk 40 min	walk 30-60 min	off	7-10 mi run/walk
28.	walk 45 min	run/walk 45 min	walk 30-60 min	run/walk 45 min	walk 30-60 min	off	9-15 mi run/walk
29.	walk 45 min	run/walk 45 min	walk 30-60 min	run/walk 45 min	walk 30-60 min	off	12-20 mirun/walk

- breaks in the marathon. If you're unrealistically optimistic in predicting your marathon goal pace, you'll run the mile repeats too fast and risk overtraining and injury. So if this pace causes you to breathe heavily, shift to a slower pace and adjust your marathon goal accordingly. Be sure to walk (don't jog) between mile repeats for at least 4 minutes.

- 5K races help you predict a realistic goal in the marathon. Take your performance times on accurately measured courses, and use the "Predicting Race Performance" chart in Galloway's Book On Running. The more races you have, the more accurate your prediction will be. Adjust your mile repeat sessions accordingly.

- Marathon pace running can be done on two other days during the week (Wednesday and Friday). After a slow warm-up, followed by 4-8 acceleration GLIDERS, run 1-3 miles at the marathon pace your 5K races are predicting. This tells you what it's like to run at marathon goal pace. Make sure that you've recovered from the weekend run, and break up the paced miles with slow jogging between.

- The pace of the Tuesday run should be at least one minute per mile slower than marathon goal pace and slower if you're still tired from the weekend session. You may also do a few acceleration-GLIDERS on this day, but be careful. Never hesitate to slow down on the Tuesday, Wednesday and Friday runs.

- You have some flexibility on the number of minutes to be run during the week. Never increase the amount more than 10 percent above what you have been doing the week before. Don't hesitate to cut back on some of these days if you're feeling tired from the (hopefully) playful but tiring weekend.

- After hill and speed sessions and 5K races you'll see the total mileage recommendation for the day in parentheses. This can be accumulated by adding up the warm-up, the warm-down, hill distance, and any other running during the session.

- On the XT (cross-training) days you can swim, run in the water, use exercise machines such as rowing, cross-country ski, and cycle. Don't use the stair machines. If you miss one of these XT days, don't worry.

- Run the long ones at least 2 minutes per mile slower than you could run that same distance on that day (adjust for heat, humidity, hills, etc.). By running slower, you'll speed recovery and reduce the chance of injury.

- Take a one-minute walk break every 3-5 minutes from the beginning of every long run. On the first few long ones, you may run 5 minutes between breaks. But when the long one reaches 18 miles (and further) shift to a one-minute break every 3 minutes. These breaks shift the use of the muscles before they get over-fatigued. You'll have better muscle response late in the run and will recover faster. There is NO reduction of endurance when you take walk breaks.

- Early in the schedule, hill play is recommended on the weekend. Do not sprint. After a relaxed warm-up, do 4-8 accelerations. Then run each hill at about 10K race pace. Keep feet low to the ground and avoid tension in the leg muscles (especially the hamstring). Run up and over the top of the hill, and walk down. Walk more before the next hill if you need more recovery.

- Follow the same warm-up procedure for mile repeats. For a time goal of 4:40, run each mile repeat in10:15. This prepares you for the pace you'll be running between walk

TIME GOAL MARATHON: 4:20

Week #	Mon	Tue	Wed	Thu	Fri	Sat	Sun
1.	XT	40-50 min	20-30 min	XT	40-50 min	off	4-6 hills (5-7 mi)
2.	XT	40-50 min	20-30 min	XT	40-50 min	off	5K race (6-7 mi)
3.	XT	40-50 min	20-30 min	XT	40-50 min	off	7-8 hills (7-8 mi)
4.	XT	40-50 min	20-30 min	XT	40-50 min	off	9-10 hills (8-9 mi)
5.	XT	45-50 min	25-35 min	XT	45-50 min	off	5K race (9-10 mi)
6.	XT	45-50 min	25-35 min	XT	45-50 min	off	3-4 x 1 mi (11 mi)
7.	XT	45-50 min	25-35 min	XT	45-50 min	off	4-5 x 1 mi (8 mi)
8.	XT	45-50 min	25-35 min	XT	45-50 min	off	5-6 x 1 mi (13mi)
9.	XT	45-50 min	25-35 min	XT	45-50 min	off	5K race (6 mi)
10.	XT	45-55 min	25-40 min	XT	45-55 min	off	15-16 mi easy
11.	XT	45-55 min	25-40 min	XT	45-55 min	off	5K race (9 mi)
12.	XT	45-55 min	25-40 min	XT	45-55 min	off	17-18 mi easy
13.	XT	45-55 min	25-40 min	XT	45-55 min	off	6-7 x 1 mi
14.	XT	45-55 min	25-40 min	XT	45-55 min	off	19-20 mi easy
15.	XT	45-55 min	25-40 min	XT	45-55 min	off	5K race (10 mi)
16.	XT	45-55 min	25-40 min	XT	45-55 min	off	6 x1 mi
17.	XT	45-55 min	25-40 min	XT	45-55 min	off	22-23 mi easy
18.	XT	45-55 min	25-40 min	XT	45-55 min	off	5K race
19.	XT	45-55 min	25-40 min	XT	45-55 min	off	5 x 1 mi
20.	XT	45-55 min	25-40 min	XT	45-55 min	off	24-26 mi easy
21.	XT	45-55 min	25-40 min	XT	45-55 min	off	5K race
22.	XT	45-55 min	25-40 min	XT	45-55 min	off	3-5 x 1 mi
23.	XT	45-55 min	25-40 min	XT	45-55 min	off	27-28 mi easy
24.	XT	45-55 min	25-40 min	XT	45-55 min	off	5K or 3 x 1 mi
25.	XT	40-45 min	20-25 min	XT	40-45 min	off	3 x 1 mi
26.	run 40 min	off	run 30 min	off	run 30 min	off	**The Marathon**
27.	walk 45 min	run/walk 30 min	walk 30-60 min	run/walk 45 min	walk 30-60 min	off	7-10 mi run/walk
28.	walk 45 min	run/walk 45 min	walk 30-60 min	run/walk 45 min	walk 30-60 min	off	9-15 mi run/walk
29.	walk 45 min	run/walk 45 min	walk 30-60 min	run/walk 45 min	walk 30-60 min	off	12-20 mi run/walk

- the marathon. If you're unrealistically optimistic in predicting your marathon goal pace, you'll run the mile repeats too fast and risk overtraining and injury. So if this pace causes you to breathe heavily, shift to a slower pace and adjust your marathon goal accordingly. Be sure to walk (don't jog) between mile repeats for at least 4 minutes.

- 5K races help you predict a realistic goal in the marathon. Take your performance times on accurately measured courses, and use the "Predicting Race Performance" chart in Galloway's Book On Running. The more races you have, the more accurate your prediction will be. Adjust your mile repeat sessions accordingly.

- Marathon pace running can be done on two other days during the week (Wednesday and Friday). After a slow warm-up followed by 4-8 acceleration GLIDERS, run 1-3 miles at the marathon pace your 5K races are predicting. This tells you what it's like to run at marathon goal pace. Make sure that you've recovered from the weekend run, and break up the paced miles with slow jogging between.

- The pace of the Tuesday run should be at least one minute per mile slower than marathon goal pace and slower if you're still tired from the weekend session. You may also do a few acceleration-GLIDERS on this day, but be careful. Never hesitate to slow down on the Tuesday, Wednesday and Friday runs.

- You have some flexibility on the number of minutes to be run during the week. Never increase the amount more than 10 percent above what you have been doing the week before. Don't hesitate to cut back on some of these days if you're feeling tired from the (hopefully) playful but tiring weekend.

- After hill and speed sessions and 5K races you'll see the total mileage recommendation for the day in parentheses. This can be accumulated by adding up the warm-up, the warm-down, hill distance, and any other running during the session.

- On the XT (cross-training) days you can swim, run in the water, use exercise machines such as rowing, cross-country ski, and cycle. Don't use the stair machines. If you miss one of these XT days, don't worry.

- Run the long ones at least 2 minutes per mile slower than you could run that same distance on that day (adjust for heat, humidity, hills, etc.). By running slower, you'll speed recovery and reduce the chance of injury.

- Take a one-minute walkbreak every 4-6 minutes from the beginning of every long run. On the first few long ones, you may run 6 minutes between breaks. But when the long one reaches 18 miles (and further) shift to a one-minute break every 4 minutes. These breaks shift the use of the muscles before they get over-fatigued. You'll have better muscle response late in the run and will recover faster. There is NO reduction of endurance when you take walk breaks.

- Early in the schedule, hill play is recommended on the weekend. Do not sprint. After a relaxed warm-up, do 4-8 accelerations. Then run each hill at about 10K race pace. Keep feet low to the ground and avoid tension in the leg muscles (especially the hamstring). Run up and over the top of the hill, and walk down. Walk more before the next hill if you need more recovery.

- Follow the same warm-up procedure for mile repeats. For a time goal of 4:20, run each mile repeat in 9:30. This prepares you for the pace you'll be running between walk breaks in

Time Goal Marathon: 4 Hours

A14

Week #	Mon	Tue	Wed	Thu	Fri	Sat	Sun
1.	XT	40-50 min	20-30 min	XT	40-50 min	off	4-6 hills (5-7 mi)
2.	XT	40-50 min	20-30 min	XT	40-50 min	off	5K race (6-7 mi)
3.	XT	40-50 min	20-30 min	XT	40-50 min	off	7-8 hills (7-8 mi)
4.	XT	40-50 min	20-30 min	XT	40-50 min	off	9-10 hills (8-9 mi)
5.	XT	45-50 min	25-35 min	XT	45-50 min	off	5K race (9-10 mi)
6.	XT	45-50 min	25-35 min	XT	45-50 min	off	3-5 x 1mi (11 mi)
7.	XT	45-50 min	25-35 min	XT	45-50 min	off	5K race (8 mi)
8.	XT	45-50 min	25-35 min	XT	45-50 min	off	5-7 x 1mi(14mi)
9.	XT	45-50 min	25-35 min	XT	45-50 min	off	5K race (7 mi)
10.	XT	45-55 min	25-40 min	XT	45-55 min	off	15-16 mi easy
11.	XT	45-55 min	25-40 min	XT	45-55 min	off	5K race (9 mi)
12.	XT	45-55 min	25-40 min	XT	45-55 min	off	17-18 mi easy
13.	XT	45-55 min	25-40 min	XT	45-55 min	off	6-8 x 1mi
14.	XT	45-55 min	25-40 min	XT	45-55 min	off	19-20 mi easy
15.	XT	45-55 min	25-40 min	XT	45-55 min	off	5K race (10 mi)
16.	XT	45-55 min	25-40 min	XT	45-55 min	off	6-8 x 1mi
17.	XT	45-55 min	25-40 min	XT	45-55 min	off	22-23 mi easy
18.	XT	45-55 min	25-40 min	XT	45-55 min	off	5K race
19.	XT	45-55 min	25-40 min	XT	45-55 min	off	4-6 x 1 mi
20.	XT	45-55 min	25-40 min	XT	45-55 min	off	25-26 mi easy
21.	XT	45-55 min	25-40 min	XT	45-55 min	off	5K race
22.	XT	45-55 min	25-40 min	XT	45-55 min	off	3-5 x 1 mi
23.	XT	45-55 min	25-40 min	XT	45-55 min	off	27-28 mi easy
24.	XT	45-55 min	25-40 min	XT	45-55 min	off	5K or 4 x 1mi
25.	XT	40-45 min	20-25 min	XT	40-45 min	off	4 x 1 mi
26.	run 40 min	off	run 30 min	off	run 30 min	off	**The Marathon**
27.	walk 45 min	run/walk 30 min	walk 30-60 min	run/walk 40 min	walk 30-60 min	off	7-10 run/walk
28.	walk 45 min	run/walk 45 min	walk 30-60 min	run/walk 45 min	walk 30-60 min	off	9-15 mi run/walk
29.	walk 45 min	run/walk 45 min	walk 30-60 min	run/walk 45 min	walk 30-60 min	off	12-20 mi run/walk

- After hill and speed sessions and 5K races you'll see the total mileage recommendation for the day in parentheses. This can be accumulated by adding up the warm-up, the warm-down, hill distance, and any other running during the session.

- On the XT (cross-training) days you can swim, run in the water, use exercise machines such as rowing, cross-country ski, and cycle. Don't use the stair machines. If you miss one of these XT days, don't worry.

- Run the long ones at least 2 minutes per mile slower than you could run that same distance on that day (adjust for heat, humidity, hills, etc.). By running slower, you'll speed recovery and reduce the chance of injury.

- Take a one-minute walk-break every 4-6 minutes from the beginning of every long run. On the first few long ones, you may run 6 minutes between breaks. But when the long one reaches 18 miles (and further) shift to a one-minute break every 4 minutes. These breaks shift the use of the muscles before they get over-fatigued. You'll have better muscle response late in the run and will recover faster. There is NO reduction of endurance when you take walk breaks.

- Early in the schedule, hill play is recommended on the weekend. Do not sprint. After a relaxed warm-up, do 4-8 accelerations. Then run each hill at about 10K race pace. Keep feet low to the ground, avoid tension in the leg muscles (especially the hamstring). Run up and over the top of the hill, and walk down. Walk more before the next hill if you need more recovery.

- Follow the same warm-up procedure for mile repeats. For a time goal of 4 hours, run each mile repeat in 8:40. This prepares you for the pace you'll be running between walk

- breaks in the marathon. If you're unrealistically optimistic in predicting your marathon goal pace, you'll run the mile repeats too fast and risk overtraining and injury. So if this pace causes you to breathe heavily, shift to a slower pace and adjust your marathon goal accordingly. Be sure to walk (don't jog) between mile repeats for at least 4 minutes.

- 5K races help you predict a realistic goal in the marathon. Take your performance times on accurately measured courses, and use the "Predicting Race Performance" chart in Galloway's Book On Running. The more races you have, the more accurate your prediction will be. Adjust your mile repeat sessions accordingly.

- Marathon pace running can be done on two other days during the week (Wednesday and Friday). After a slow warm-up followed by 4-8 acceleration GLIDERS, run 1-3 miles at the marathon pace your 5K races are predicting. This tells you what it's like to run at marathon goal pace. Make sure that you've recovered from the weekend run, and break up the paced miles with slow jogging between.

- The pace of the Tuesday run should be at least one minute per mile slower than marathon goal pace and slower if you're still tired from the weekend session. You may also do a few acceleration-GLIDERS on this day, but be careful. Never hesitate to slow down on the Tuesday, Wednesday and Friday runs.

- You have some flexibility on the number of minutes to be run during the week. Never increase the amount more than 10 percent above what you have been doing the week before. Don't hesitate to cut back on some of these days if you're feeling tired from the (hopefully) playful but tiring weekend.

TIME GOAL MARATHON: 3:45

A16

Week #	Mon	Tue	Wed	Thu	Fri	Sat	Sun
1.	XT	40-50 min	20-30 min	XT	40-50 min	off	4-6 hills (5-7 mi)
2.	XT	40-50 min	20-30 min	XT	40-50 min	off	5K race (6-7 mi)
3.	XT	40-50 min	20-30 min	XT	40-50 min	off	7-8 hills (7-8 mi)
4.	XT	40-50 min	20-30 min	XT	40-50 min	off	9-10 hills (8-9 mi)
5.	XT	45-50 min	25-35 min	XT	45-50 min	off	5K race (9-10 mi)
6.	XT	45-50 min	25-35 min	XT	45-50 min	off	3-5 x 1mi (12 mi)
7.	XT	45-50 min	25-35 min	XT	45-50 min	off	4-6 x 1mi (8 mi)
8.	XT	45-50 min	25-35 min	XT	45-50 min	off	5-7x 1mi (14 mi)
9.	XT	45-50 min	25-35 min	XT	45-50 min	off	5K race (7 mi)
10.	XT	45-55 min	25-40 min	XT	45-55 min	off	15-16 mi easy
11.	XT	45-55 min	25-40 min	XT	45-55 min	off	5K race (9 mi)
12.	XT	45-55 min	25-40 min	XT	45-55 min	off	17-18 mi easy
13.	XT	45-55 min	25-40 min	XT	45-55 min	off	6-8 x 1 mi
14.	XT	45-55 min	25-40 min	XT	45-55 min	off	19-20 mi easy
15.	XT	45-55 min	25-40 min	XT	45-55 min	off	5K race (10 mi)
16.	XT	45-55 min	25-40 min	XT	45-55 min	off	7-9 x 1 mi
17.	XT	45-55 min	25-40 min	XT	45-55 min	off	22-23 mi easy
18.	XT	45-55 min	25-40 min	XT	45-55 min	off	5K race
19.	XT	45-55 min	25-40 min	XT	45-55 min	off	5-7 x 1 mi
20.	XT	45-55 min	25-40 min	XT	45-55 min	off	25-26 mi easy
21.	XT	45-55 min	25-40 min	XT	45-55 min	off	5K race
22.	XT	45-55 min	25-40 min	XT	45-55 min	off	4-6 x 1 mi
23.	XT	45-55 min	25-40 min	XT	45-55 min	off	28-29 mi easy
24.	XT	45-55 min	25-40 min	XT	45-55 min	off	5K or 4 x 1 mi
25.	XT	40-45 min	20-25 min	XT	40-45 min	off	4-5 x 1 mi
26.	run 40 min	off	run 30 min	off	run 30 min	off	**The Marathon**
27.	walk 45 min	run/walk 30 min	walk 30-60 min	run/walk 40 min	walk 30-60 min	off	7-10 mi run/walk
28.	walk 45 min	run/walk 45 min	walk 30-60 min	run/walk 45 min	walk 30-60 min	off	9-15mi run/walk
29.	walk 45 min	run/walk 45 min	walk 30-60 min	run/walk 45 min	walk 30-60 min	off	12-20 mi run/walk

A17

- After hill and speed sessions and 5K races you'll see the total mileage recommendation for the day in parentheses. This can be accumulated by adding up the warm-up, the warm-down, hill distance, and any other running during the session.

- On the XT (cross-training) days you can swim, run in the water, use exercise machines such as rowing, cross-country ski, and cycle. Don't use the stair machines. If you miss one of these XT days, don't worry.

- Run the long ones at least 2 minutes per mile slower than you could run that same distance on that day (adjust for heat, humidity, hills, etc.). By running slower, you'll speed recovery and reduce the chance of injury.

- Take a one-minute walk-break every 4-6 minutes from the beginning of every long run. On the first few long ones, you may run 6 minutes between breaks. But when the long one reaches 18 miles (and further) shift to a one-minute break every 4 minutes. These breaks shift the use of the muscles before they get over-fatigued. You'll have better muscle response late in the run and will recover faster. There is NO reduction of endurance when you take walk breaks.

- Early in the schedule, hill play is recommended on the weekend. Do not sprint. After a relaxed warm-up, do 4-8 accelerations. Then run each hill at about 10K race pace. Keep feet low to the ground and avoid tension in the leg muscles (especially the hamstring). Run up and over the top of the hill and walk down. Walk more before the next hill if you need more recovery.

- Follow the same warm-up procedure for mile repeats. For a time goal of 3:45, run each mile repeat in 8:05. This prepares you for the pace you'll be running between walk breaks in the marathon. If you're unrealistically optimistic in predicting your marathon goal pace, you'll run the mile repeats too fast and risk overtraining and injury. So if this pace causes you to breathe heavily, shift to a slower pace, and adjust your marathon goal accordingly. Be sure to walk (don't jog) between mile repeats for at least 4 minutes.

- 5K races help you predict a realistic goal in the marathon. Take your performance times on accurately measured courses, and use the "Predicting Race Performance" chart in Galloway's Book On Running. The more races you have, the more accurate your prediction will be. Adjust your mile repeat sessions accordingly.

- Marathon pace running can be done on two other days during the week (Wednesday and Friday). After a slow warm-up, followed by 4-8 acceleration GLIDERS, run 1-3 miles at the marathon pace your 5K races are predicting. This tells you what it's like to run at marathon goal pace. Make sure that you've recovered from the weekend run and break up the paced miles with slow jogging between.

- The pace of the Tuesday run should be at least one minute per mile slower than marathon goal pace and slower if you're still tired from the weekend session. You may also do a few acceleration-GLIDERS on this day, but be careful. Never hesitate to slow down on the Tuesday, Wednesday and Friday runs.

- You have some flexibility on the number of minutes to be run during the week. Never increase the amount more than 10 percent above what you have been doing the week before. Don't hesitate to cut back on some of these days if you're feeling tired from the (hopefully) playful but tiring weekend.

Time Goal Marathon: 3:30

A18

Week #	Mon	Tue	Wed	Thu	Fri	Sat	Sun
1.	XT	40-60 min	20-30 min	XT	40-60 min	off	4-6 hills (5-7 mi)
2.	XT	40-60 min	20-30 min	XT	40-60 min	off	5K race (6-7 mi)
3.	XT	40-60 min	20-30 min	XT	40-60 min	off	7-8 hills (7-8 mi)
4.	XT	40-60 min	20-30 min	XT	40-60 min	off	9-10 hills (8-9 mi)
5.	XT	45-60 min	25-35 min	XT	45-60 min	off	5K race (9-10 mi)
6.	XT	45-60 min	25-35 min	XT	45-60 min	off	3-5 x 1mi (12 mi)
7.	XT	45-60 min	25-35 min	XT	45-60 min	off	5K race (8 mi)
8.	XT	45-60 min	25-35 min	XT	45-60 min	off	6-8 x 1mi (14 mi)
9.	XT	45-60 min	25-35 min	XT	45-60 min	off	5K race (8 mi)
10.	XT	45-65 min	25-40 min	XT	45-65 min	off	15-16 mi easy
11.	XT	45-65 min	25-40 min	XT	45-65 min	off	5K race (9 mi)
12.	XT	45-65 min	25-40 min	XT	45-65 min	off	17-18 mi easy
13.	XT	45-65 min	25-40 min	XT	45-65 min	off	7-9 x1 mi
14.	XT	45-65 min	25-40 min	XT	45-65 min	off	19-20 mi easy
15.	XT	45-65 min	25-40 min	XT	45-65 min	off	5K race (10 mi)
16.	XT	45-65 min	25-40 min	XT	45-65 min	off	8-10 x 1 mi
17.	XT	45-65 min	25-40 min	XT	45-65 min	off	22-23 mi easy
18.	XT	45-65 min	25-40 min	XT	45-65 min	off	5K race
19.	XT	45-65 min	25-40 min	XT	45-65 min	off	5-7 x 1 mi
20.	XT	45-65 min	25-40 min	XT	45-65 min	off	25-26 mi easy
21.	XT	45-65 min	25-40 min	XT	45-65 min	off	5K race
22.	XT	45-65 min	25-40 min	XT	45-65 min	off	4-6 x 1 mi
23.	XT	45-65 min	25-40 min	XT	45-65 min	off	28-29 mi easy
24.	XT	45-55 min	25-40 min	XT	45-55 min	off	5K or 4 x 1 mi
25.	XT	40-45 min	20-25 min	XT	40-45 min	off	4-5 x 1 mi
26.	run 40 min	off	run 30 min	off	run 30 min	off	**The Marathon**
27.	walk 45 min	run/walk 30 min	walk 30-60 min	run/walk 45 min	walk 30-60 min	off	7-10 mi run/walk
28.	walk 45 min	run/walk 45 min	walk 30-60 min	run/walk 45 min	walk 30-60 min	off	9-15 mi run/walk
29.	walk 45 min	run/walk 45 min	walk 30-60 min	run/walk 45 min	walk 30-60 min	off	12-20 mi run/walk

- After hill and speed sessions and 5K races you'll see the total mileage recommendation for the day in parentheses. This can be accumulated by adding up the warm-up, the warm-down, hill distance, and any other running during the session.

- On the XT (cross-training) days you can swim, run in the water, use exercise machines such as rowing, cross-country ski, and cycle. Don't use the stair machines. If you miss one of these XT days, don't worry.

- Run the long ones at least 2 minutes per mile slower than you could run that same distance on that day (adjust for heat, humidity, hills, etc.). By running slower, you'll speed recovery and reduce the chance of injury.

- Take a one-minute walk break every 4-6 minutes from the beginning of every long run. On the first few long ones, you may run 6 minutes between breaks. But when the long one reaches 18 miles (and further) shift to a one-minute break every 4 minutes. These breaks shift the use of the muscles before they get over-fatigued. You'll have better muscle response late in the run and will recover faster. There is NO reduction of endurance when you take walk breaks.

- Early in the schedule, hill play is recommended on the weekend. Do not sprint. After a relaxed warm-up, do 4-8 accelerations. Then run each hill at about 10K race pace. Keep feet low to the ground and avoid tension in the leg muscles (especially the hamstring). Run up and over the top of the hill, and walk down. Walk more before the next hill if you need more recovery.

- Follow the same warm-up procedure for mile repeats. For a time goal of 3:30, run each mile repeat in 7:40. This prepares you for the pace you'll be running between walk breaks in the marathon. If you're unrealistically optimistic in predicting your marathon goal pace, you'll run the mile repeats too fast and risk overtraining and injury. So if this pace causes you to breathe heavily, shift to a slower pace and adjust your marathon goal accordingly. Be sure to walk (don't jog) between mile repeats for at least 4 minutes.

- 5K races help you predict a realistic goal in the marathon. Take your performance times on accurately measured courses, and use the "Predicting Race Performance" chart in Galloway's Book On Running. The more races you have, the more accurate your prediction will be. Adjust your mile repeat sessions accordingly.

- Marathon pace running can be done on two other days during the week (Wednesday and Friday). After a slow warm-up followed by 4-8 acceleration GLIDERS, run 1-3 miles at the marathon pace your 5K races are predicting. This tells you what it's like to run at marathon goal pace. Make sure that you've recovered from the weekend run and break up the paced miles with slow jogging between.

- The pace of the Tuesday run should be at least one minute per mile slower than marathon goal pace and slower if you're still tired from the weekend session. You may also do a few acceleration-GLIDERS on this day, but be careful. Never hesitate to slow down on the Tuesday, Wednesday and Friday runs.

- You have some flexibility on the number of minutes to be run during the week. Never increase the amount more than 10 percent above what you have been doing the week before. Don't hesitate to cut back on some of these days if you're feeling tired from the (hopefully) playful but tiring weekend.

A19

A20

Time Goal Marathon: 3:15

Week #	Mon	Tue	Wed	Thu	Fri	Sat	Sun
1.	XT or 3 easy	40-55 min	20-50 min	XT	40-55 min	off	4-6 hills (5-7 mi)
2.	XT or 3 easy	40-55 min	20-50 min	XT	40-55 min	off	5K race (6-7 mi)
3.	XT or 3 easy	40-55 min	20-50 min	XT	40-55 min	off	7-8 hills (7-8 mi)
4.	XT or 3 easy	40-65 min	20-50 min	XT	40-55 min	off	9-10 hills (8-9 mi)
5.	XT or 3 easy	45-70 min	25-55 min	XT	45-50 min	off	5K race (9-10 mi)
6.	XT or 3 easy	45-70 min	25-55 min	XT	45-70 min	off	3-5 x 1mi (12 mi)
7.	XT or 3 easy	45-70 min	25-55 min	XT	45-70 min	off	5K race (8 mi)
8.	XT or 4 easy	45-70 min	25-55 min	XT	45-70 min	off	6-8 x 1mi (14 mi)
9.	XT or 4 easy	45-70 min	25-55 min	XT	45-70 min	off	5Krace (8mi)
10.	XT or 4 easy	45-75 min	25-60 min	XT	45-75 min	off	15-16 mi easy
11.	XT or 4 easy	45-75 min	25-60 min	XT	45-75 min	off	5K race (9 mi)
12.	XT or 4 easy	45-75 min	25-60 min	XT	45-75 min	off	17-18 mi easy
13.	XT or 4 easy	45-75 min	25-60 min	XT	45-75 min	off	7-9 x1mi
14.	XT or 4 easy	45-75 min	25-60 min	XT	45-75 min	off	19-20 mi easy
15.	XT or 4 easy	45-75 min	25-60 min	XT	45-75 min	off	5K race (10 mi)
16.	XT or 4 easy	45-75 min	25-60 min	XT	45-75 min	off	9-11x1mi
17.	XT or 4 easy	45-75 min	25-60 min	XT	45-75 min	off	22-23 mi easy
18.	XT or 4 easy	45-75 min	25-60 min	XT	45-75 min	off	5K race
19.	XT or 4 easy	45-75 min	25-60 min	XT	45-75 min	off	5-8 x 1mi
20.	XT or 4 easy	45-75 min	25-60 min	XT	45-75 min	off	25-26 mi easy
21.	XT or 4 easy	45-75 min	25-60 min	XT	45-75 min	off	5K race
22.	XT or 4 easy	45-75 min	25-60 min	XT	45-75 min	off	5-8 x 1 mi
23.	XT or 4 easy	45-75 min	25-60 min	XT	45-75 min	off	28-29 mi easy
24.	XT	45-55 min	25-50 min	XT	45-55 min	off	5K or 4 x 1mi
25.	XT	40 min	20-35 min	XT	40 min	off	4-6 x 1 mi
26.	run 40 min	off	run 30 min	off	run 30 min	off	**The Marathon**
27.	XT 45 min	run/walk 30 min	XT 30-60 min	run/walk 40 min	XT 30-60 min	off	7-10 mi run/walk
28.	XT 45 min	run/walk 45 min	XT 30-60 min	run/walk 45 min	XT 30-60 min	off	9-15 mi run/walk
29.	XT 45 min	run/walk 45 min	XT 30-60 min	run/walk 45 min	XT 30-60 min		12-20 mi run/walk

From Jeff Galloway's MARATHON! 1-800-200-2771

- the marathon. If you're unrealistically optimistic in predicting your marathon goal pace, you'll run the mile repeats too fast and risk overtraining and injury. So if this pace causes you to breathe heavily, shift to a slower pace and adjust your marathon goal accordingly. Be sure to walk (don't jog) between mile repeats for at least 3 minutes.

- 5K races help you predict a realistic goal in the marathon. Take your performance times on accurately measured courses, and use the "Predicting Race Performance" chart in Galloway's Book On Running. The more races you have, the more accurate your prediction will be. Adjust your mile repeat sessions accordingly.

- Marathon pace running can be done on two other days during the week (Wednesday and Friday). After a slow warm-up followed by 4-8 acceleration GLIDERS, run 1-3 miles at the marathon pace your 5K races are predicting. This tells you what it's like to run at marathon goal pace. Make sure that you've recovered from the weekend run and break up the paced miles with slow jogging between.

- The pace of the Tuesday run should be at least one minute per mile slower than marathon goal pace and slower if you're still tired from the weekend session. You may also do a few acceleration-GLIDERS on this day, but be careful. Never hesitate to slow down on the Tuesday, Wednesday and Friday runs.

- You have some flexibility on the number of minutes to be run during the week. Never increase the amount more than 10 percent above what you have been doing the week before. Don't hesitate to cut back on some of these days if you're feeling tired from the (hopefully) playful but tiring weekend.

- After hill and speed sessions and 5K races you'll see the total mileage recommendation for the day in parentheses. This can be accumulated by adding up the warm-up, the warm-down, hill distance, and any other running during the session.

- On the XT (cross-training) days you can swim, run in the water, use exercise machines such as rowing, cross-country ski, and cycle. Don't use the stair machines. If you miss one of these XT days, don't worry.

- Run the long ones at least 2 minutes per mile slower than you could run that same distance on that day (adjust for heat, humidity, hills, etc.). By running slower, you'll speed recovery and reduce the chance of injury.

- Take a one-minute walk-break every 5-7 minutes from the beginning of of every long run. On the first few long ones, you may run 7 minutes between breaks. But when the long one reaches 18 miles (and further), shift to a one-minute break every minutes. These breaks shift the use of the muscles before they get over-fatigued. You'll have better muscle response late in the run and will recover faster. There is NO reduction of endurance when you take walk breaks.

- Early in the schedule, hill play is recommended on the weekend. Do not sprint. After a relaxed warm-up, do 4-8 accelerations. Then run each hill at about 10K race pace. Keep feet low to the ground, avoid tension in the leg muscles (especially the hamstring). Run up and over the top of the hill, and walk down. Walk more before the next hill if you need more recovery.

- Follow the same warm-up procedure for mile repeats. For a time goal of 3:15, run each mile repeat in 7:05 This prepares you for the pace you'll be running between walk breaks in

A21

TIME GOAL MARATHON: 2:59

Week #	Mon	Tue	Wed	Thu	Fri	Sat	Sun
1.	XT or 3 easy	40-55 min	20-50 min	XT	40-55 min	off	4-6 hills (5-7 mi)
2.	XT or 3 easy	40-60 min	20-50 min	XT	40-60 min	off	5K race (6-7 mi)
3.	XT or 3 easy	40-65 min	20-50 min	XT	40-60 min	off	7-8 hills (7-8 mi)
4.	XT or 3 easy	40-65 min	20-50 min	XT	40-60 min	off	9-10 hills (8-9 mi)
5.	XT or 3 easy	45-75 min	25-55 min	XT	45-65 min	off	5K race (9-10 mi)
6.	XT or 3 easy	45-80 min	25-55 min	XT	45-65 min	off	5-7 x 1mi (12 mi)
7.	XT or 3 easy	45-80 min	25-55 min	XT	45-70 min	off	5K race (8 mi)
8.	XT or 4 easy	45-80 min	25-55 min	XT	45-75 min	off	6-8 x 1mi (14 mi)
9.	XT or 4 easy	45-80 min	25-55 min	XT	45-80 min	off	7-9 x 1mi (10 mi)
10.	XT or 4 easy	45-85 min	25-60 min	XT	45-80 min	off	15-16 mi easy
11.	XT or 4 easy	45-85 min	25-60 min	XT	45-85 min	off	5K race (9 mi)
12.	XT or 4 easy	45-85 min	25-60 min	XT	45-85 min	off	17-18 mi easy
13.	XT or 4 easy	45-85 min	25-60 min	XT	45-85 min	off	9-11 x1 mi
14.	XT or 4 easy	45-85 min	25-60 min	XT	45-85 min	off	19-20 mi easy
15.	XT or 4 easy	45-85 min	25-60 min	XT	45-85 min	off	5K race (10 mi)
16.	XT or 4 easy	45-85 min	25-60 min	XT	45-85 min	off	10-12 x1 mi
17.	XT or 4 easy	45-85 min	25-60 min	XT	45-85 min	off	22-23 mi easy
18.	XT or 4 easy	45-85 min	25-60 min	XT	45-85 min	off	5K race
19.	XT or easy	45-85 min	25-60 min	XT	45-85 min	off	5-8 x 1 mi
20.	XT or 4 easy	45-85 min	25-60 min	XT	45-85 min	off	25-26 mi easy
21.	XT or 4 easy	45-85 min	25-60 min	XT	45-85 min	off	5K race
22.	XT or easy	45-85 min	25-60 min	XT	45-85 min	off	5-8 x 1 mi
23.	XT or 4 easy	45-75 min	25-60 min	XT	45-75 min	off	28-30 mi easy
24.	XT	45-55 min	25-50 min	XT	45-55 min	off	5K or 4 x 1 mi
25.	XT	40 min	20-35 min	XT	40 min	off	4-6 x 1 mi
26.	run 40 min	off	run 30 min	off	run 30 min	off	**The Marathon**
27.	XT 45 min	run/walk 30 min	XT 30-60 min	run/walk 40 min	XT 30-60 min	off	7-10 mi run/walk
28.	XT 45 min	run/walk 45 min	XT 30-60 min	run/walk 45 min	XT 30-60 min	off	9-15 mi run/walk
29.	XT 45 min	run/walk 45 min	XT 30-60 min	run/walk 45 min	XT 30-60 min	off	12-20 mi run/walk

- fast and risk overtraining and injury. So if this pace causes you to breathe heavily, shift to a slower pace and adjust your marathon goal accordingly. Be sure to walk (don't jog) between mile repeats for at least 4 minutes.

- 5K races help you predict a realistic goal in the marathon. Take your performance times on accurately measured courses, and use the "Predicting Race Performance" chart in Galloway's Book On Running. The more races you have, the more accurate your prediction will be. Adjust your mile repeat sessions accordingly.

- Marathon pace running can be done on two other days during the week (Wednesday and Friday). After a slow warm-up followed by 4-8 acceleration GLIDERS, run 1-3 miles at the marathon pace your 5K races are predicting. This tells you what it's like to run at marathon goal pace. Make sure that you've recovered from the weekend run and break up the paced miles with slow jogging between. Hopefully your legs will feel good enough to do 1-2 of these marathon pace miles on the Wednesday and Friday before your marathon (unless the marathon is on Saturday and then shift to Tuesday and Thursday).

- The pace of the Tuesday run should be at least one minute per mile slower than marathon goal pace and slower if you're still tired from the weekend session. You may also do a few acceleration-GLIDERS on this day, but be careful. Never hesitate to slow down on the Tuesday, Wednesday and Friday runs.

- You have some flexibility on the number of minutes to be run during the week. Never increase the amount more than 10 percent above what you have been doing the week before. Don't hesitate to cut back on some of these days if you're feeling tired from the (hopefully) playful but tiring weekend.

- After hill and speed sessions and 5K races you'll see the total mileage recommendation for the day in parentheses. This can be accumulated by adding up the warm-up, the warm-down, hill distance, and any other running during the session.

- On the XT (cross-training) days you can swim, run in the water, use exercise machines such as rowing, cross-country ski, and cycle. Don't use the stair machines. If you miss one of these XT days, don't worry.

- Run the long ones at least 2 minutes per mile slower than you could run that same distance on that day (adjust for heat, humidity, hills, etc.). By running slower, you'll speed recovery and reduce the chance of injury.

- Take a one-minute walk-break every 8-10 minutes from the beginning of every long run. On the first few long ones, you may run 10 minutes between breaks. But when the long one reaches 18 miles (and further), shift to a one-minute break about every mile. These breaks shift the use of the muscles before they get over-fatigued. You'll have better muscle response late in the run and will recover faster. There is NO reduction of endurance when you take walk breaks.

- Early in the schedule, hill play is recommended on the weekend. Do not sprint. After a relaxed warm-up, do 4-8 accelerations. Then run each hill at about 10K race pace. Keep feet low to the ground and avoid tension in the leg muscles (especially the hamstring). Run up and over the top of the hill, and walk down. Walk more before the next hill if you need more recovery.

- Follow the same warm-up procedure for mile repeats. For a time goal of 2:59, run each mile repeat in 6:32. This prepares you for the pace you'll be running between walk breaks in the marathon. If you're unrealistically optimistic in predicting your marathon goal pace, you'll run the mile repeats too

A23

Time Goal Marathon: 2:39

Week #	Mon	Tue	Wed	Thu	Fri	Sat	Sun
1.	XT or 3 easy	40-55 min	20-50min	XT	40-55 min	off	4-6 hills (5-7 mi)
2.	XT or 3 easy	40-60 min	20-50min	XT	40-60 min	off	5K race (6-7 mi)
3.	XT or 3 easy	40-65 min	20-50min	XT	40-60 min	off	7-8 hills (7-8 mi)
4.	XT or 3 easy	40-65 min	20-50min	XT	40-60 min	off	9-10 hills (8-9 mi)
5.	XT or 3 easy	45-75 min	25-55min	XT	45-65 min	off	5K race (9-10 mi)
6.	XT or 3 easy	45-80 min	25-55min	XT	45-65 min	off	5-7 x 1mi (11 mi)
7.	XT or 3 easy	45-80 min	25-55min	XT	45-70 min	off	5K race (8 mi)
8.	XT or 4 easy	45-80 min	25-55min	XT	45-75 min	off	6-8 x 1mi (13 mi)
9.	XT or 4 easy	45-80 min	25-55min	XT	45-80 min	off	8-10x 1mi (12 mi)
10.	XT or 4 easy	45-85 min	25-60min	XT	45-80 min	off	15-16 mi easy
11.	XT or 4 easy	45-85 min	25-60min	XT	45-85 min	off	5K race (9 mi)
12.	XT or 4 easy	45-85 min	25-60min	XT	45-85 min	off	17-18 mi easy
13.	XT or 4 easy	45-85 min	25-60min	XT	45-85 min	off	10-11 x1 mi
14.	XT or 4 easy	45-85 min	25-60min	XT	45-85 min	off	19-20 mi easy
15.	XT or 4 easy	45-85 min	25-60min	XT	45-85 min	off	5K race (10 mi)
16.	XT or 4 easy	45-85 min	25-60min	XT	45-85 min	off	11-13 x1 mi
17.	XT or 4 easy	45-85 min	25-60min	XT	45-85 min	off	22-23 mi easy
18.	XT or 4 easy	45-85 min	25-60min	XT	45-85 min	off	5K race
19.	XT or 4 easy	45-85 min	25-60min	XT	45-85 min	off	5-8 x 1 mi
20.	XT or 4 easy	45-85 min	25-60min	XT	45-85 min	off	25-26 mi easy
21.	XT or 4 easy	45-85 min	25-60min	XT	45-85 min	off	5K race
22.	XT or 4 easy	45-85 min	25-60min	XT	45-85 min	off	5-8 x 1 mi
23.	XT or 4 easy	45-75 min	25-60min	XT	45-75 min	off	28-30 mi easy
24.	XT	45-55 min	25-50min	XT	45-55 min	off	5K or 4 x 1 mi
25.	XT	40 min	20-35min	XT	40 min	off	4-6 x 1 mi
26.	run 40 min	off	run 30 min	off	run 30 min	off	**The Marathon**
27.	XT 45 min	run/walk 40 min	XT 30-60 min	run/walk 40 min	XT 30-60 min	off	7-10 mi run/walk
28.	XT 45 min	run/walk 45 min	XT 30-60 min	run/walk 45 min	XT 30-60 min	off	9-15 mi run/walk
29.	XT 45 min	run/walk 45 min	XT 30-60 min	run/walk 45 min	XT 30-60 min	off	12-20 mi run/walk

A24

- For the first few weeks, you will be doing more walking than running. On every "walk-run" day, walk for 2-3 minutes and jog 1-2 minutes. Every 3-4 weeks you may evaluate how you're feeling. If you want to increase the running, start by taking a 3 minute walk with a 2 minute run. Many of our beginners don't get further than this. Advanced beginners progress to a maximum of running for 2 minutes and walking for 2 minutes.

- After hill and speed sessions and 5K races you'll see the total mileage recommendation for the day in parentheses. This can be accumulated by adding up the warm-up, the warm-down, hill distance, and any other running during the session.

- On the XT (cross-training) days you can swim, run in the water, use exercise machines such as rowing, cross-country ski, and cycle. Don't use the stair machines. If you miss one of these XT days, don't worry.

- Run the long ones at least 2 minutes per mile slower than you could run that same distance on that day (adjust for heat, humidity, hills, etc.). By running slower, you'll speed recovery and reduce the chance of injury.

- Take a one minute walk break every 8-10 minutes from the beginning of every long run. On the first few long ones, you may run 10 minutes between breaks. But when the long one reaches 18 miles (and further) shift to a one-minute break about every mile. These breaks shift the use of the muscles before they get over-fatigued. You'll have better muscle response late in the run and will recover faster. There is NO reduction of endurance when you take walk breaks.

- Early in the schedule, hill play is recommended on the weekend. Do not sprint. After a relaxed warm-up, do 4-8 accelerations. Then run each hill at about 10K race pace. Keep feet low to the ground and avoid tension in the leg muscles (especially the hamstring). Run up and over the top of the hill, and walk down. Walk more before the next hill if you need more recovery.

- Follow the same warm-up procedure for mile repeats. For a time goal of 2:39, run each mile repeat in 5:40. This prepares you for the pace you'll be running between walk breaks in the marathon. If you're unrealistically optimistic in predicting your marathon goal pace, you'll run the mile repeats too fast and risk overtraining and injury. So if this pace causes you to breathe heavily, shift to a slower pace and adjust your marathon goal accordingly. Be sure to walk (don't jog) between mile repeats for at least 4 minutes.

- 5K races help you predict a realistic goal in the marathon. Take your performance times on accurately measured courses, and use the "Predicting Race Performance" chart in Galloway's Book On Running. The more races you have, the more accurate your prediction will be. Adjust your mile repeat sessions accordingly.

- Marathon pace running can be done on two other days during the week (Wednesday and Friday). After a slow warm-up, followed by 4-8 acceleration GLIDERS, run 1-3 miles at the marathon pace your 5K races are predicting. This tells you what it's like to run at marathon goal pace. Make sure that you've recovered from the weekend run and break up the paced miles with slow jogging between. Hopefully, your legs will feel good enough to do 1-2 of these marathon pace miles on the Wednesday and Friday before your marathon (unless the marathon is on Saturday and then shift to Tuesday and Thursday).

- The pace of the Tuesday run should be at least one minute per mile slower than marathon goal pace and slower if you're still tired from the weekend session. You may also do a few acceleration-GLIDERS on this day, but be careful. Never hesitate to slow down on the Tuesday, Wednesday and Friday runs.

- You have some flexibility on the number of minutes to be run during the week. Never increase the amount more than 10 percent above what you have been doing the week before. Don't hesitate to cut back on some of these days if you're feeling tired from the (hopefully) playful but tiring weekend.

A25

BELIEVING GETS YOU MORE THAN HALFWAY THERE

*I*t was the end of the day and motivation was low, but the stack on her desk was high with folders marked "confidential psychological profiles." She couldn't believe that

the thought really crossed her mind, but she was hoping that the phone would ring. And it did.

"Doctor Suzi's support line....Do you understand that this is a toll call? Okay, what's the problem?....So your boss smokes and there's only one other smoker in the office. What type of responsibility do you feel here?....Well, a female friend of mine never said a word, but when anyone came into her office with a cigarette, she took out her long-nosed scissors and snipped it off, catching the ashes in a pot held underneath. She never had to do this for anyone twice. She explained that she was allergic to

smoke and would throw up on people after breathing a small amount. Believe me, that got their attention.

"I can't help you with office regulations, but this is a clear-cut case of responsibility. Your boss is playing irresponsibly with the health of the employees in the office and needs to be confronted with that. Have you met with him as individuals or as a group? ....Well then, you should take that step to show him how strongly you feel. The government of the United States has determined that secondhand smoke causes cancer and other death-producing diseases. Well, if he doesn't act, then *his* bosses should know. This is a serious long-term health problem that he needs to address ....What do you mean 'at the same time you feel sorry for him?' Now *you've* got the problem. You must take responsibility for *your* health, and that means taking action against your boss' smoking in the office. Okay, you can do it!

"Doctor Suzi's support line. Do you know that you're paying for this call? Go ahead. ....This isn't a love counseling service. Well, okay, if it involves someone that you're working with. She's pulling you into the stockroom? Come on, that doesn't happen. So you want to know how to deal with the co-worker who caught you and is blackmailing you to get some shady things done at work? First, what do you think is your responsibility—to all parties? ....Well, you're paying for my opinion so I'll tell you that this is an honesty case. Truth is the best ally

1

you have....Yea, you report to your boss and say that this, um, incident happened, and that it won't happen again. Well, if you don't want to take some responsibility and give this up, I can't help you.

"Doctor Suzi's supp....Yes, this is Dr. Suzi, and this must be Crazy Jim. You're one of maybe two people I know who speak with that abrasive Brooklyn accent. So what is it now? What type of crazy client do you want me to say 'couldn't help himself, Judge, he's just out of his mind.'

"My *shrink* practice is doing well, Jim, in spite of the necessary shift away from governmental entitlement business and Medicare/Medicaid. The income is okay, but I'm missing something....No, not that. I really felt great last spring and summer as I prepared for the Peachtree. Once I got into it, my spirit was engaged and I.... just.... felt better in other areas. I need another goal that gets me mobilized. I'm ready, but I don't know what form it will take.

"Yes, you were right. You predicted that I'd drop my regular fitness after Peachtree. There were some other reasons, but you were right.

"You're having focus problems, too? The one who is always so targeted on the next 'cause'....the next protest? Well, *I* would be worried about that also—any change in thought patterns and motivation lapse that significant....at your age! So you're telling me that you haven't been doing any regular exercise but you're going to do the New York Marathon this year? You need therapy. Let's see....I've got an appointment open tomorrow....

"Yes, I still hold those 'getting back into focus' sessions. I'm actually expanding my group work because of the government cutbacks. It's either that or supervise a continual stream of HMO patients on drug

therapy, and they're worse than your 'public defender' clients.

"Okay, meet me at Phidippides Sports. We're actually gathering in a back room at the bagel shop around the corner. But *my* motivation starts with the buying of a new pair of shoes. It's the American way: Buy something, then you're committed.

"Sure, you'll find it in the research!

"I'm looking forward to this new class too— *I* need the group support for *my* exercise. Okay, see you a week from next Wednesday."

Near Athens, Greece

"So tell me, Tom, what's getting you down about finalizing your teaching outline for your class tomorrow?"

"Sam, I've taught this team-building course a hundred times. But each time I have to sell it and evaluate it to a different corporate audience. I wish I could use the same approach each time, but each class is different and forces me to develop a new approach, with different exercises. In addition, I was just told that the CEO of the world's largest computer company is going to attend."

"Am I reading you correctly, Tom? You originally thought that you'd have a better chance of changing behaviors if you didn't have to work through a 'boss structure' in these team-building sessions. Now that you're the boss, you're finding that there's another side of the 'boss world?' Significant diversions of time and responsibilities, not to mention *stress...*"

"I was too optimistic. I really believed that I could get the attention of these young people and open up to them this wonderful new lifestyle, which they would suddenly absorb and follow to the letter. Now I'm facing reality...and responsibility. In order to get these future corporate decision makers to make the lifestyle changes I feel are needed, I've probably put too much on myself trying to teach them in a week how to mentally focus like a world-class athlete. I still know that it's possible, but I'm losing my confidence. I'm just not sure."

A philosophical look came over Sam's face.

"I should be dead now. I had a 50 percent chance of living after having the heart attack on the plane back from Boston in March. I was one of them, Tom. I had no idea of how good you can feel and how well your mind and body work together until I did it....and got out there three times a week with you and Suzi. But when I tried to get this message instilled in my college students, they nodded their heads, verbalized the concepts, and passed the tests. But only one or two actually took up forward motion exercise as a lifestyle activity."

"But in one particular senior Anthropology project there were more skeptics. From the first day of class, they couldn't emphathize....couldn't get inside the mindset of ancient man at the various stages of development. So, for extra credit, I set up a personal migration project—a walking/ running program for each of them. These former couch potatoes have all reported back to me that they've become exercisers. Several wrote outstanding papers about the teamwork and support mechanisms based upon the interplay of group dynamics and exercise. It was not planned but became my most successful teaching experience in over two decades. The good chemistry started as a challenge, for me and them, during the first meeting of the group when they started questioning me."

Tom thought for a moment and then the light seemed to come on. "Let the experience do the teaching. When we run and walk together, in all of my groups, the folks just start opening up. They share experiences and talk about the team-building issues from class. They get to know personalities and learn to respect one another. Instead of being worried about a new approach, I should just make sure that their exertion experience is a good one—and talk about the concepts while moving....at least part of every class."

"That uplifting feeling that follows exertion is universal," said Sam. "It's one of the few easily accessible experiences which directly connect you to the ancient nerve endings....which were probably 'plugged in' the same way ours are....starting from the first time our most ancient ancestors moved forward together in the upright position."

Tom and Sam took their last sips of coffee and headed out the door. As they got into a good, exertive walk along the scenic little harbor, Tom's thoughts were still on the class, which began in less than 24 hours. "I need to give the group a goal—something that would keep them challenged both individually and as a team....like Peachtree was for Suzi, you and me."

"Speaking about Suzi," asked Sam. "What do you hear from her?" as they headed up the rugged but walkable trails.

"I miss seeing her," Tom said and paused to accurately express how he felt. "As we went through the Peachtree program, we seemed to pull some positive energy from one another and I miss that."

"I never could figure out whether you two were dating or not," said Sam.

"We didn't either, and I guess it's over now."

"I don't think it is."

"Why do you say that?"

"Because you're talking about her the way you're talking about her."

Atlanta, Georgia, USA

"Hello....yes, this is Dr. Suzi....excuse me, but could you tell me your name? Oh, Sarah, you had me fooled again. You've maintained your college tradition of disguising your voice. Where are you calling from? Well, when is your plane? I can drive out and see you.

"Oh....so not on this trip. No, there's nothing going on in my love life. How about yours?

"No, nothing ever came of that. He's over in Greece now anyway.

"Sure, I'd love to talk with your sister. So she's just in a lull now? Just tell her to give me a ring!

"You, the perpetual jock, would ask about my exercise. Things were going so well as of last summer and then I just drifted off. I need another goal. It's strange...I went from being the queen of the couch a year ago to feeling now that training for a 5K or a 10K like Peachtree isn't enough. I'm ready for a challenge that forces me to dig deep.

"No! A marathon is too far. I can't see myself doing anything extreme like that. Maybe your sister Laura and I can get one another energized around some goal. It's worth a try.

"Okay....whatever you say. I'll wait for her call. I'll think about your challenge in the Vancouver International Marathon for next year.

"Go and get your plane, but give me a chance to see you during your next layover, roommate!"

Back in Greece

Tom was walking steadily now along the path overlooking the cozy inlet and town which had been used by humans for at least 4000 years.

"Sam, I keep coming back to my program which starts tomorrow. It's all outlined, my presentations are all in place—but I need a way to get them energized....to bond with this project of team-building....a lifestyle focus experience in the first hour."

"What about challenging them with a goal of completing the marathon?"

Tom thought for a moment and then started talking through his thoughts with Sam: "These are young men and women who have been selected by their companies as potential leaders in their various areas. I told them that they would have to accept a physical challenge project. Their companies want them to have a series of annual team-building experiences with their peers in other companies. I sold this to management as a team-builder, a challenge, and an introduction to the healthy lifestyle needed for top performance in the 21st century.

Goals: Team-Building Exertion

Each participant will:

- develop bonding with other leaders through a series of significant personal challenges

- develop a network of young corporate leaders based upon respect

- experience (and adopt) an energy-giving, healthy lifestyle which improves attitude and productivity

- maintain the major components which affect long-term health

"I want them to come out of this knowing how to pull resources from inside—and from one another. The companies involved signed off on the concept of offering the marathon as a goal, as long as I offered a choice of other goals.

"In the interviews, I realized that these young executives are very average young adults when it comes to health and fitness. Each knows he or she should be exercising and eating foods that are more healthy, but almost all have been eating poorly and have not been active. Many didn't exercise much as kids....you know....the TV babysitter generation. When we were going through the school system, Sam, there was a reasonably good physical education program of three or four days each week and playground after school. Things have changed. Many of these folks went to schools where physical education was considered a 'frill' and wasn't taught. Schools and recreation centers have limited their free play because of liability. These 25 to 30 year-old kids are victims of the budget and litigation crunch in education."

Sam: "Tom, you were a great athlete. You should be inspirational in getting people to exercise."

Tom: "I've always had trouble getting people motivated because I found, *personally*, that the experience generates its own motivation. I've had the hardest time understanding why others can't just get out there. It seems so obvious that they'll feel so much better."

Sam: "I agree, Tom, once you get them doing something, once they get into the flow of very easy forward motion exercise three times a week, the experience becomes its own reward. But I'm speaking as one who had the hardest time setting up my belief environment."

Tom: "Only recently have I come to understand the reasoning behind having a back-up support structure in place to get folks through the first few months when most lose motivation."

"It's more than that, Tom. The 'belief environment' takes the various motivational components inside and mobilizes them, connects them as a team. Before my heart attack, I was like the young people you're about to work with. I could get my body out there for several weeks, but I was lazy and didn't try to focus or format my mind. You know what helped me most? That session which Suzi dragged us to...."

"You mean the one with that hippie type guy?"

"Yes. He organized the mental issues so that I could focus on each area. My conclusion about the effect on me is based upon his ability to connect me now with where I want to be....one, three and five years from now. After I made that organization, I had the structure of a mental training program. Now, when I spend a little time each week focusing on my belief environment, I stay motivated all week and have less of a tendency to drift away....to the couch."

[For more information on the Belief Environment and mental focus, see Return of the Tribes to Peachtree Street, pp. 29-35.]

Because Tom had become "hooked" on exercise at an early age, he was still having to struggle with a way to bring this into the lives of others. "If I'm out there on the roads, the energy which I generate keeps me motivated. The glow from my last run makes me crave the feeling of exertion in my next one. I need to communicate this to my class."

Tom: "Say, what's the latest on your heart condition, Sam?"

5

"As long as I'm getting out the door, everything is fine. Dr. Life gave me a thorough check-up and testing protocol before he let me get on the plane over here. But I have to go back to my mental exercises and tie everything together to keep it. I envy your awareness level that allows you to intuitively enjoy running as its own reward. Most of us need three support systems:

♦ group support of fellow exercisers

♦ mental focusing exercise—for our individual belief environment

♦ a meaningful and challenging goal

"That's it, Sam!" Tom said as he shifted thoughts back to his corporate program. "I need to encourage—and not dictate—that these young people shoot for a marathon. Of course, I'll offer other goals, but the marathon is such a good example of a meaningful goal."

"Yea, it'll scare them to death! But maybe that's what *I* need, Tom, the impossible dream of the marathon.....to get me to feel totally energized again."

Tom: "If you really want it, the marathon can be more than a dream. It could be your physical vision for this year. When I got back into running after you had your heart attack, I had the most focused mental period of my life, thanks to my former competitive rival Dylan. He not only challenged me by saying that I'd never become competitive again but was very abrasive about it. Over a three-month period, I molded the vision of my return to fitness performance on every run, during the clinics, and even during my choice of foods.

"Every time I ate a PowerBar, for example, I imagined feeling energized as I pushed up the hills on Peachtree Street. The challenge became a vision, which I kept filling in,

Tom's Running Resume'

■ He worked hard in high school track, running the mile, but never made it to the state championships.

■ In college, he moved up to three-mile and six-mile competition. He showed promise but there were no great performances.

■ After college, when no one else gave him a chance (not even his wife at the time), Tom thought that he could make himself into one of the top U.S. distance runners. He focused on this goal, steadily raised his performances, and qualified for the U.S. Olympic Trials.

■ But he failed to enjoy each great improvement. After each performance, he immediately shifted to the next level of improvement, expecting himself to to do better.

■ In 1980, Tom was one of the "long shot" candidates for making the Olympic Team. "Everybody knew that Tony Sandoval and Bill Rodgers would almost certainly claim the first and second spots. There were 10 of us that had an almost equal chance at the third position, depending upon the weather, etc."

■ When the U.S. boycotted the 1980 Olympics, Tom lost his goal and his drive and totally quit running for an extended period.

■ He drifted in and out of training in the early 80's, was divorced, and began a career of putting on fitness activities for businesses.

■ From 1986-9, Tom got back into running but became injured repeatedly before improvement could take hold.

- From 1990-95, he came out of retirement about every six months but couldn't achieve to expectations fast enough and dropped out with injury or frustration each time.

- Last spring, while helping Sam and Suzi to get a program started for the Peachtree Road Race, Tom slowed down and realized the satisfaction and attitude boost that he had intuitively received from running but had never articulated because of his preoccupation with performance.

- Tom's son Chris moved back into town and began running again. Father and son trained together, off and on, leading up to Peachtree.

- A former rival told Tom that he would never regain his competitive drive. This got Tom's competitive juices flowing again, but he pushed too hard and became injured. By re-learning to enjoy his transcendental sessions with Sam and Suzi, he "got back in the saddle" and regained perspective. With his injury healed, he trained with Chris and got to know his son for the first time.

- At Peachtree, Tom ran the best race of his life at 42 and his best Peachtree time: 30:01.

- Most importantly, he savored it and appreciated a single performance for the first time in his life.

[For more background on Tom, Chris, Sam and Suzi, see Return of the Tribes to Peachtree Street.]

Making your *Dream* into a *Vision*

Dream: Images

- often of fantasy, as the dreams during sleep

- which have no direct connection to your experience

- of specific items or experiences you'd like—but don't have a behavioral plan to take you from the present to your dream

Vision: A series of images which

- give a clear vision of the final result including the behaviors

- break down the change process into a series of behavioral changes

- give a vision of behaviors at each step along the way

- directly attach to behaviors you want to change

- start with a behavior that has been done in the recent past

- continue through a series of improvement experiences to the goal behavior

- fill in the future experience with the eating behaviors, the exercise behaviors, etc. which are necessary to make it happen

- a clear image of the final behavior...in all aspects

[For more on *vision* and *dream*, see Return of the Tribes to Peachtree Street, pp.28-29.]

7

mentally, with hundreds of behavioral changes and fine-tuning. The mental behavior picture became very complete and very real. It got me engaged, inside and out.

Challenges which are meaningful will keep the motivation flowing."

Sam: "Tell me again how you got to the

point that your motivation just kept flowing when you didn't have a goal?"

Tom: "I'm just beginning, after over 20 years of running, to realize that I don't have to have a time goal or a high finish place to justify my running. It's hard to shift gears, but it's a lot more fun when running is its own reward. If I run slowly enough at the beginning of most of my runs now, I enjoy each one and look forward to the next one. I picked this up at a Galloway clinic.

"You see, Sam, I had always tied achievement and performance in races and workouts to the good feelings that came out of my runs: the attitude boost, the feeling of accomplishment, the stress release, and now the overwhelming transcendental quality of it. Only last spring, when I became injured, did I back off, run with you and Suzi, and realize that these good and satisfying feelings came from exertion, even at a very slow pace. How ironic, when I took away all hope of competition, I was able to rebound in every way and run my best Peachtree ever."

Sam: "You're saying that it took going back to the pace of the turtle to allow you to rebuild and then run the pace of the hare.

"I know, cognitively, that I can tap into the reward system; it's the energy to get started which is missing. Suzi really helped us with her 'quick motivational fixes' last spring."

Tom: "She has such a creative guilt delivery system, along with her research and the 'boosters.' I just enjoyed calling her at the end of a hard day to get her usually aggravated reaction. But she always came through."

Sam: "The physical reward system has been in place for millions of years. Our ancestors were ruled almost exclusively by the physical need and reward of exercise—they had to stay active in order to survive: to

8

Jeff Galloway: Starting slowly can make almost any run an enjoyable experience

This past year has been my best year of running—*and my slowest*. More than three years ago, I shifted from an every-other-day running program to running two days out of three. To minimize over-training injury, I slowed down all of my runs. During this period, I've had almost no need to take time off for repair of aches, pains or worse.

Prior to this slowdown, I had been starting my runs on slow days at 7-7:30 minutes per mile. When I shifted into "slow" gear, the pace became about 9-10 minutes per mile. Yes, even though I still run some 10K races at 5:30 pace, I start virtually all of my daily runs at about 10 minutes per mile and feel great because of it.

The unexpected benefit of this extra slow start has been an early shift into the right brain. Much sooner than usual, I found my mind wandering into creative journeys of all types. When the body is not under the usual stress of starting exercise at "normal" pace, it will relax, and your left brain doesn't have to respond to stress with its usual stream of negative messages.

Most folks go too fast in the beginning of a run because their pacing instincts take over. It's easy to go too fast before the body is warmed up because the biomechanics of running form allow us to move along very efficiently at a pace that is too fast for the muscles, the energy resources, and the cardiovascular system. A gentle warm-up will gradually introduce the muscles and all of your systems to exercise at the same time.

When in doubt, run slower at the beginning. You'll increase your enjoyment without significantly lowering the training effect or the fat-burning.

find new food sources, avoid predators, etc. Our bodies are programmed to reward us when we do our endurance activity."

Tom: "But we are so *mental* now. Sam, don't you think our preoccupation with the logical focus of our left brain causes problems?"

Sam: "Over the past 100,000 years or so, we've developed this complex mental and emotional network which is increasingly separated from the benefits of exercise. To put it into Darwinian terms, our survival, at least through about age 60, is no longer directly related to our ability to move forward and live a healthy lifestyle."

Tom: "Suzi's friend, the hippie guy, really had some great ideas in setting up the 'belief environment.' True confessions....I just didn't buy into it at first. But his concepts were strong and kept coming back

to me. When I thought about it, I realized that the better athletes have had a regular mental program, usually intuitive. I guess we have to set up the mental framework first, in order to keep the body, mind and spirit on track."

Sam: "I know you weren't that impressed with him at first, but corporate America is. He does contract programs for Home Depot, Motorola, you name it. He's tapped into a good, basic series of steps which help you go directly back into the 'wiring': a simple but powerful focusing and reward system which is kept on track by forward motion activity."

As the two approached the top of the hill, Tom asked Sam about his work in Greece, questioning whether the ancient Greeks really appreciated sport and fitness. Sam admitted that in his collegiate studies, he

Sam's Exercise Background

- He tried football in eighth grade but developed a knee injury that still bothers him.

- He barely passed high school Physical Education.

- He made fun of college athletes.

- For most of his adult life, Sam did no exercise at all.

- On an archeological field project three years ago, Sam had trouble climbing 200 meters up a hill to a newly discovered site, even though the incline and altitude weren't very significant.

- For three years, he walked two or three times a week, one to two miles each time.

- Eight months ago, Sam had a heart attack on an airplane, sitting next to Tom and Suzi.

- A successful angioplasty operation gave Sam another chance.

- He used the Peachtree Road Race as his goal, exercising very regularly with Tom and Suzi.

- Since Peachtree, the motivation for exercise hasn't been high for Sam, whose work environment has changed.

- Currently he walks twice weekly for 20 to 30 minutes, with some one to two-minute jogging breaks.

10

Sam's Evolutionary Beliefs

1. Human beings are programmed to improve in ways that enhance their survival.

2. For millions of years, forward motion was necessary for survival, and a series of layers of benefits and internal connections were developed inside us to intuitively "nag us" into exercise and to reward us for doing so.

3. Even as we have evolved away from needing exercise for survival, virtually all of the benefits and connections are still there.

4. When we take a few weeks to reintroduce ourselves to the enjoyment of easy exercise, we can connect to these positive reinforcements, which are a significant evolutionary benefit passed on by ancient ancestors.

5. The exercise experience lifts us out of a growing aggravation, frustration, and depression which is a direct result of modern busy life: alienation, lack of logical organization, loss of appreciation for morality.

6. The experience of moving forward is so basic to the human psyche that it gives us an overall feeling of security, of taking action, of getting back to at least one experience during which you know what you're doing and that what you're doing is good for you.

7. We are continuing to evolve. If we really get into the endurance experience we can make innovations which will enhance our enjoyment of exercise and connect these benefits with productivity in other areas of our lives.

8. As our lifestyles have become more sedentary, a growing number of humans have responded to an intuitive need to return to our exertive roots. We need the recreational exertion to be more alive: keeping the cardiovascular system healthy and the mind/body connections working directly and with greater energy.

Suzi's List: Mental Benefits of Exercise

A series of internal rewards are experienced by individuals who regularly engage in forward-moving, endurance exertion.

- Natural relaxants, endorphins, are released, which give relief to the muscles being used.

- Mid-brain relaxants, which give a feeling of well-being to the whole system after exercise, are also released.

- Regular activity activates other centers, making attitude-enhancing connections which produce positive messages from many areas of the body.

- A central connection point for the spirit where these positive feelings are tied together gives one a feeling of satisfaction and accomplishment.

- Brain activity is enhanced, showing coordinated positive patterns after exercise.

- The "junk" (neurosis and psychosis aggravators) is pushed out to the side so that it doesn't cause trouble.

- The connections between the parts of your brain that you need for your primary activities (work, family, relaxation, etc.) are enhanced.

- The connections between the various sections of your body to keep mind and body and the various components in communication are enhanced. As they stay in touch, one can achieve better utilization of resources and overall balance for greater enjoyment of life.

had the hardest time articulating why the Greeks set aside such a high place in the public status hierarchy to their athletes. "Like many hard-core academics, I felt that they had gotten off track in their almost worship of these physical performers. But when you look closely, you can see three levels of appreciation for sport and exercise:

- the ego's quest for pure achievement

- the inner satisfaction of doing one's best

- the rewards from just getting out there

Sam: "Surely there were individuals and small cults through the ages which had developed this awareness. But the Greeks were different in that, for the first time in history, these qualities were appreciated by the civilization as a whole. Athletes became an expression of the quest of the spirit, and this is what gave meaning to the original,

ancient Olympics, which lasted more than a thousand years!"

"But, Sam, how did this relate to man's development, his evolution as a runner-walker?"

"The Greeks didn't understand it at the time, but their appreciation of recreational fitness was a bridge in human development of man. In earlier times, man *had* to move and exert himself to survive. The Greeks were the first major civilization to appreciate exertion as something worthy of respect by itself and worth the long hours and effort invested for the personal development which became the result.

"The organization of society and the specialization of labor had occurred in other great civilizations before the Greeks. But the Greeks, particularly in Athens, were able to appreciate and use leisure time, recognizing

11

What is a Belief Environment?

1. A series of beliefs which completely surround and support your behavioral goal

To do the marathon you believe that the experience is beneficial to you in many ways. You will

- develop the resources to respond to a positive challenge

- increase discipline and maintain a regular exercise program for four to six months

- find connections to internal capabilities

- learn how to dig a little deeper when the going gets tough

- do what is reasonably possible to support the goal (eating, sleeping, scheduling, etc.)

- pull out of yourself a growing series of changes

2. And the belief that you can make the following behavioral commitments:

- get out and do the exercise, three times a week

- eat lower-fat foods leading up to exercise

- generally learn to like the taste of foods lower in fat

- maintain a set of positive mental exercises which keep you on track

- make lifestyle changes in eating, regular exercise and in self-motivation—which will stick

that the individual should spend the discretionary time doing what he or she thought was important. Above all, athletes were celebrated. Possibly, this is due to the giving of meaning and respect to exertion, which had always been a survival activity."

"Yea," said Tom, "You can see by the prevalence of the running motif on vases, in literature, etc. that the Greeks elevated running into an expression of the human spirit of which they were proud and then into a form which would be preserved for eternity."

Sam: "It was not just acceptable for athletes to take time off from work, study, etc. to train for the Olympics; it was publicly appreciated. Cities would spend resources to send their athletes to a training camp before the Olympic Games. Just to go to the Olympics was a great honor and bestowed respect on the athlete's family and city.

"What they started has prevailed. With all its problems, there's still a healthy appreciation of the modern Olympic games and the spirit of the athletes. But we've taken it too far with the over-emphasis on pro sports."

Tom: "I used to think that all of the pro sports stuff was unnecessary and overdone. But getting back to the Greeks, athletes give dramatic expression and meaning to the triumph of the human spirit. For maybe a million generations, humans have been faced with failure, defeat, complete fatigue, pain, suffering, and have been able to dig down deeper and rebound."

"So you're saying," noted Sam, "that the public looks up to the struggle and triumph of the athlete. The competitor hangs in there, past the time when many would give up, endures adversity, and digs down deeper inside, often without knowing that the resources are there. Finally, even in defeat,

he or she is rewarded by often unexpected creativity and strength."

Tom: "Yes. It reconfirms in all of us that there are sources inside which we haven't tapped yet. The athlete's triumph directly connects to our spirit—saying that we as average humans can respond to the constant challenges of our daily lives."

Sam: "The Greeks certainly recognized this. And now, so do a growing number of North Americans. To see so many average people moving off the couch and on to the roads is inspiring to me: from watching to participating. For the first time in history, a significant percentage of average humans like myself are putting themselves to the real physical tests. I guess we're becoming athletes."

Tom: "That's certainly what's propelled the dramatic increase in marathoners: over 30 percent increase per year. And the times are up to an hour slower than they were 15 years ago. The new generation of marathoners is not in it for fast times but to reach the finish line and complete the satisfaction circle which just keeps going."

Sam: "The Greeks embraced the up-and-down nature of the human experience: tragedy and comedy were interwoven. A city which was victorious and exuberant one year could be enslaved the next. In this period of flux, they searched for concepts and values which could give inner meaning, and they embraced their heroes.

"The Greek concept of the hero can reach its greatest expression with athletes. Here's a civilization which elevated athletes to a peak because of their spirit and dedication and encouraged anyone to take part in exertive sports whether they achieved or not. Modern day marathoners are probably the best modern expression of the Greek hero."

12

The Satisfaction/ Accomplishment Circle:

Dissatisfaction with being inactive

Receives a unique sense of accomplishment, self esteem Develops inner discipline, changes lifestyle Continues/Gets a program started

Learns that there is strength inside

Receives significant benefits, attitude boost, etc.

Struggles, overcomes challenges

13

Tom: "Even better, we are able to become our own heroes. Instead of living through the success of someone else, we can take control and steer our feelings of self-esteem where we want them to go and have at least a little insulation from the uncontrollable forces around us."

Sam: "Yes....and experience the calming and strength-giving sense of accomplishment by just getting out and exercising....just by reaching the finish line."

Tom: "You mean we don't have to live vicariously through the success or failure of some genetic marvel who slam dunks or breaks a few bones on his way to the goal line."

Tom continues: "Being on these trails which could have been used by the original Greek athletes and hearing you talk of the spirit of the Greek athlete....I feel it inside. As we crest this hill and see the same view of the Aegean probably seen by Phidippides, I'm inspired to do another marathon—and do it well!"

Sam: "That is probably the greatest power of exertion: it bestows its own simple reward. We can feel the same dedication, the same clear and clean energized feelings as received by Phidippides and by the ancient athletes. And it's self-generating. We can feel as good as our ancient granddaddies did as they overcame fear and anxiety by moving forward to new trails, strange environments and unknown challenges. As I speak, *I'm* getting inspired again. *I* may even try that marathon thing."

"If you do it, so will I."

"It's a deal."

THE NEXT FITNESS GENERATION

*T*he slightly abrasive voice went directly to the point: "I volunteered for this project because it was supposed to help my networking and other business skills, but you're just talking about running or walking a marathon. I'd rather get on with the components which will enhance my career. No offense to you, but I'm not sure that our companies are getting their money's worth by your talking about the marathon."

The 43 year-old paused before answering the 28 year-old. The instructor glanced out the window at the beautiful panorama of rugged hillsides meeting the Aegean Sea. After watching the gentle waves of clear water roll onto the secluded beach, he gently but directly looked at the questioner and answered.

"Your companies selected you for—and you volunteered to participate in—this 12-month program. While we are targeting the goal of finishing a marathon, half-marathon, or 10K, the personal lifestyle changes you make are up to you. I have seen the results of this program both in individual enhancement and benefit to the company. Your companies have also assured me that if any of you wish to withdraw from the program within the first two days, you can do so with no negative consequences to your career or otherwise."

The inquiring mind responded: "Yes, I was told that I would have to do some physical

training and to organize a group at my worksite, but let me read from the memo which was attached to my sign-up form: 'This program has been shown to help the

participant expand capacities for personal and corporate goal setting, while learning and using the dynamics of team-building. Due to the goal, and the long-range program, you'll help others and yourself to set up a high performance lifestyle to lower stress, improve attitude, and enjoy the satisfaction of being more productive.' You haven't mentioned anything about those other components mentioned in the memo."

"Your questioning is beneficial for all of us, Mr. Green, and I'm not going to try to convert you. But, the basis for this program emerged from research and interviews with key top executives concerning the most influential experiences in molding their lives. The one experience that kept popping up during the 25 to 35 year-old period which which had a life-changing and lasting effect was the training for and completion of a marathon. Remember, you can listen and consider all of this for 48 hours before deciding whether to stay or not. We only want those who are committed to the program to stay after that."

The CEO who had been sitting in the shadows in the back of the room broke in at this point.

"I appreciate your concern for maximizing the investment which your companies are making in this program. I can speak for almost every other CEO of the companies represented here....and that is significant, because over the years, we have agreed on very few things, very few. The almost unanimous decision to put this program together was based upon the fact that all of us concur that people are our greatest resource, and you young leader candidates are our solid gold capital for the future. Of all the training programs we looked at which involved team-building and networking, this marathon training program offered more levels of benefit: health care reduction, attitude enhancement, productivity improvement, team and network building, and happier people.

"I speak from experience on this one. As an executive, you will struggle through repeated challenges and reach points when you don't feel you can take it or respond and produce. Training for a marathon will put you through a series of tests which produce changes inside that will make you a better executive and a better person. In the marathon program, as in life, everyone gets into situations when he or she doesn't feel strong enough. It happens to me several times a day. But you dig deeper and you learn the process of reaching down and somehow pulling out the strength and

creativity to solve problems and go on. Without my daily fitness, I wouldn't be as productive as I am. Your confidence, problem-solving skills, and ability to deal with adversity—all will be significantly enhanced through this program.

"The bottom line in this program is the satisfaction which you will receive. Believe me, there are very, very few satisfying elements of corporate life. As you complete the program and approach the finish line of the marathon (or whichever event you choose), you will have sidestepped or overcome a series of confrontations and self doubts which would stop most people in your companies. The result is a feeling of achievement and accomplishment which you don't get in any other experience. The other CEO's and I have seen that this pattern gives you a better attitude, allows you to overcome adversity better, and bestows a sense of confidence which makes our companies better. In short, we believe in you because you believe in yourself through experiences like this."

The CEO had to go out on a hike around the Plain of Marathon and turned the program back over to Tom with an endorsement. "We've used dozens of programs like this and have looked at hundreds of others. This marathon training program has given the best return on our personnel investment that we have seen."

"Please enlighten me on how training for a marathon can make a difference in corporate behavior," Green continued with his questions.

The instructor looked beyond the students to the clouds rolling in over the rocky hills and continued: "The marathon is significant enough as a challenge to get your attention and is more likely to motivate you to get out there to exercise and eat correctly than a goal which is less demanding. The signifi-

15

The Executive Marathon Team

You have been selected to join an elite group of young executives in key industries. This goal-oriented program has helped hundreds of corporate leaders improve team-building and networking skills both inside and outside the company. You'll be establishing a non-business communication venue, while helping others and yourself to set up a lifestyle health and fitness program at your company.

This program has been shown to help the participant expand capacities for personal and corporate goalsetting, while learning and using the dynamics of team-building. Due to the goal, and the long-range program, you'll help others and yourself to set up a high performance lifestyle to lower stress, improve attitude and enjoy the satisfaction of increased productivity.

1. The one-week training program is held just outside Athens, Greece. Here you'll learn about the concepts of training and team-building and start your program which begins with a walk and run up to the top of a local mountain, overlooking the beautiful Aegean Sea. One year from now, you'll return to finish the marathon (or any race of your choice), which follows the original marathon course into the original stadium of the modern Olympic Games, practically in the shadow of the Acropolis.

2. After your training in Athens, you'll return to set up a program at your worksite, which will prepare even beginning exercisers to finish a marathon. This responsibility is not an enormous consumer of your work time and will be done in addition to your other responsibilities. Each week your group will meet for fitness on Tuesday, Thursday and Sunday mornings. Exercise groups will be divided into sub-groups, based upon conditioning and background.

3. You'll have the back-up support of the *Achievement In Motion* team throughout. We're only a phone call away.

16

cant series of challenges requires each to continually dig deep and develop resources from mind and spirit. You'll have the chance to develop the use of the creative and intuitive right side of your brain.

"Mr. Green, you'll see research that shows that for every hour you spend in aerobic, endurance exercise, you get back at least an hour and a half of productivity through increased energy, and better focus. How's that for return on investment?

"But that's just a side effect. As part of the requirement for coming here, you are to immerse yourself in group exertion as a team-building exercise, get to know your fellow participants here and stay in touch afterward. Many lifelong friendships and networks will be established here.

"As you take this format back to your workplace, you'll develop and improve your own leadership skills. You'll be recruiting people from every division of your company and from all levels of management and staffing. This network establishes a communication vehicle outside the normal stresses and strains of company business. Finally, your evaluation of work in this project will be based upon the success of the program at your worksite, particularly the selection and training of a new company leader who is at least as enthusiastic and supportive as you are going to be."

Matt Green was still not buying into the program: "No disrespect intended, but I just wanted to be on the record that this time could be better spent working on business skills and information."

"Your bottom line this week," the lean instructor continued, "is to make it up to the top of that mountain you see up there."

Most of the 28- to 35-year olds were instantly challenged as they looked at the

Benefits of Group Marathon Training

1. Marathoners develop "focus skills" which improve work and personal relationships.

2. The group support produces a positive social setting each week.

3. Self-esteem rises with the accomplishment of longer and longer runs.

4. Participants develop great respect for each member of the group.

5. With improved health and fitness, participants are more productive in other areas.

6. This internalizes the components of the healthy lifestyle: regular exercise, lower fat nutrition and positive mental attitude.

rugged hill which grew into a small mountain and dominated the beautiful and dramatic scene framed in the giant picture window. It got their attention.

"If you take responsibility for your own understanding of this project, you'll develop the fitness and technique this week to complete that climb with no trouble. And you will have started your marathon training in the process. You'll also improve your team-building skills as you are giving yourself a unique and satisfying experience."

"Let me tell you that not all CEOs are behind this," Green inserted. "Mine feels skeptical like me and is going to evaluate this strictly by the numbers. He's tracking those who are involved in this program by productivity, sales and efficiency. We'll see."

Green continued. "Okay, let's say we come back here 15 to 20 years from now and everyone says what they're doing and how exercise has affected their career. What will be the result in your mind?"

After a few seconds of formatting his thoughts, the marathon leader gave his version of the future.

"Those who got into the program and learned to enjoy the transcendental and restorative quality of exercise will make statements such as these:

'I feel that I have some control over my attitude and therefore my career.'

'I might have progressed faster up the corporate ladder if I had spent my 30 to 45 minutes a day in career building, but I doubt it. I was more mentally alert and productive from exercise and made up more than an hour of productivity.'

'I'm successful and I'm happy. My creativity keeps getting better.'

Those who didn't get involved will have a different set of statements:

'I'm one of the highest ranking persons in my company at my age, but I feel burned out.'

'My boss tells me that I'm one of the most effective managers in the company, but I'm not well liked by my staff or my peers. That comes with the territory, I'm sure.'

'Happiness....that's not important to me in my career. I need to achieve.'"

As he dismissed the class for lunch, the instructor walked up to a slightly over-weight 53-year old who had just slipped into the rear of the conference room. "How am I doing, Professor Sam?"

"You're the professor here—and a very effective one indeed. You learn so much working with young adults because they know everything, don't they, Tom?"

17

RUNNING AWAY FROM ALIENATION

"*S*o how is my old roomie doing, Laura?"

"Well, Suzi, sister Sarah sends her greetings from Lake Tahoe where she is marketing director for a ski lodge and has even learned to ski."

"That's a switch. In college, Sarah hated the concept of skiing—thought it too commercial and trendy. As she is one who is not likely to change, I'll bet that a man is involved in her sudden interest in the slopes."

"Actually, she went to a running camp there and loved the area. The lodge HQ for the running camp needed someone with her background...and, yes, there was this local ski instructor..."

"I know. The rest is history. She was always the active one. Tell her to come and visit sometime so that I can reciprocate out there."

"Sarah is still running—and still into challenges. She told me that her challenge to you is still good: to do the Vancouver Marathon. She'll pay your entry fee. Of course, she did tell me that before you chose your college classes you counted how many steps it took to get to the classroom. Is that really true?"

"I'll have to think about that one. Actually, if you'll keep a secret, we could have some fun with this. I've actually started to do some exercise and know of a very low impact way to do that 26-mile thing. But I can tell, Laura, that you would like to get on

with our chat so let's go. Sarah told me that you've been going through some rough times and might enjoy talking every once in a while. I'd welcome that."

"I know that Sarah put you up to this, and sometimes I resent my older sister trying to take care of me. But in this case something told me that it was the right thing to do. I'm past the point of needing a good talk."

"You mentioned over the phone that you were increasingly feeling left out of things. Is that at work? In a relationship?"

Laura thought for a few awkward seconds and struggled to respond. "My job has become more impersonal."

"This is always strange, but, please, just tell me anything you want."

After an awkward silence, Suzi followed up: "Look, I just would like to hear about your job, Laura, or what you're doing in this big city after growing up in Fort Walton Beach, Florida."

That seemed to send a small gleam to Laura's eyes, and she started with her move to the big city to be with her high school sweetheart. "This is the first time I've admitted how much I really miss Fort Walton. But I could never go back and live there."

As Laura told childhood stories and Suzi reciprocated, both felt the security of sharing. Laura's increased confidence propelled her into her problems at work.

"I got a good job—a much better one than my boyfriend—and that started the trouble. I'm certainly paid well enough, but there is no fulfillment. Through three consolidations, the company has kept me—they've actually given me the responsibilities of several other people whose jobs were 'terminated.' With the help of several software systems and our mainframe, I'm doing the job that took four people to do just three years ago. As our company has gone through a shift to computerized systems, I interact so seldom with other people. Maybe that causes you to lose some of the 'human touch' or something."

"Can I ask what is happening between you and your high school sweetheart?"

"That's easy—nothing. He left me for a woman we both knew in high school. It's hard to describe how I feel about that."

Laura was surprised when Suzi laughed and then explained how Suzi's former roommate had moved out only to move in with her former "significant other" less than a year ago.

"I don't know why I feel this way, but I just don't seem to be in control of things. I long for something permanent and positive in my life. I have a good place to live, a good job, all the creature comforts I need, but I'm just not happy. At this stage of my life, I expected to feel more control. Sometimes I want to pack my bags and go back to the simple life of the Florida Panhandle, but I keep from doing it because I know I couldn't stand the slow pace of things once I settled in."

Suzi knew it was her time to say something, but she gathered her thoughts for a moment.

"Whether you talk this out with me or with someone else, you're doing the right thing by addressing your feelings. I can tell that you have all the components you need to be as happy as you can be—to hold the alienation at a distance. You just need an activity that gets you in touch with yourself regularly, in a positive way.

"Too many people build their lives around their relationships. When interpersonal problems develop, they don't have enough to fall back on or the right combination of stress release activities to help. One of the best things you can do is to find an activity which boosts your spirits and which will also help you enjoy being yourself.

"Alienation is the malaise of the 90's. A friend, an anthropologist, believes that humans have some very primitive tribal instincts which need a positive form of expression. I've tried to resist agreeing with him, but *my* instincts tell me he's right. To put it into a computer analogy, we're wired

19

with circuits that need natural connections to other human beings. When these circuits are not regularly used, we start to feel disconnected, because we *are* disconnecting from our roots. Unfortunately, the direction of the 21st century lifestyle is headed toward more dependence upon machines and away from human interaction."

"How do other people deal with this alienation?"

"I went through this earlier this year when I experienced my *man problems* and conducted myself in a classic non-productive pattern: spend money on a buying spree."

Laura laughed, "Men buy the big toys, like cars boats and motorcycles. That's what my honey did. And put it on my credit card!"

Suzi: "And women just buy and buy and buy. I should know: I spent six months paying off my credit card bills from a six-hour weekend binge!"

"But it's good for the U.S. economy," added Laura.

"And certainly good for my business. I have two clients who come in almost exclusively due to the depression/shop cycle: When depressed, go shopping which builds up debt which creates more depression which brings them into my office. Laura, have you ever tried getting into exercise?"

"Yes, I purchased a cross country ski machine, thinking that its presence in the living room would get me into shape. It hasn't."

"You mean you have to use it to get the benefits," joked Suzi.

"I'm just not physical. Sarah got all the athletic genes in our family."

"Let's show her—let's challenge her to that marathon."

The S & L (Suzi & Laura) Marathon Pre-Conditioning Program

1. Tuesday and Thursday—30 to 45 minutes of walking five minutes and jogging one minute

2. Saturday—Start with three miles and increase by half a mile per week. Walk five minutes and jog one minute.

3. Optional: Walk as you can on the other days.

4. Avoid muscle soreness and burnout by easing into exercise. Don't increase dramatically your total amount of exercise or the strenuous part of the exercise.

5. The jogging should be very slow—never get into "huffing and puffing." Stay conversational.

[For more information, see Galloway's Book On Running, pp.32-36, and Return of the Tribes to Peachtree Street, pp.36-38.]

6. If you are adapting well to the exercise and want to decrease the walking, here's a formula: After two weeks, you could walk four minutes and jog one minute. Every two weeks thereafter, you could reduce the walk by one minute until you're doing two minutes of walking and one minute of jogging. Two weeks later, you could increase the jogging to two minutes (so that you're walking two minutes and jogging two minutes).

Again, remember that you never want to push too hard. When in doubt, drop back for a session or two or stay at the level where you feel comfortable.

20

BELIEF ENVIRONMENT

*T*om surveyed his young executive marathon team about their exercise-related motivation problems. The results backed up the replies from participants in a wide range

of groups with which Tom had worked:

- ◆ About 80 percent said that it was difficult to get out the door:

    - too tired after work

    - too tired early in the morning

    - just "too tired"

    - no time to exercise

- ◆ About 50 percent had trouble sticking with a program for three weeks or more:

    - Over-exercised early and burned out

    - Under-exercised and didn't fully experience the attitude boost

    - The excitement of a 'new' program wore off

    - Tried to do too much, couldn't do it, and cutting back seemed like defeat

    - Couldn't keep the exercise session inserted into a busy schedule

    - Depended upon a friend to exercise instead of pulling out the self-discipline

As the various individuals told stories about their own failed attempts at staying motivated, the session became more open and fun. But when the talk turned to proven methods for sticking with a training program, only a few mentioned rewards: ice cream, new clothes, health club membership, etc. Tom felt the group consciousness moving toward the need for an overall structure or concept and asked them how strongly they believed in their ability to stay personally motivated. But first, he congratulated most of them for choosing the marathon as their goal.

"I know that many of you question whether you have the discipline, focus and inner

Constructing Your Motivation Book

Keep a notebook with separate sections for the following:

1. Verbalize your goals in completing the marathon.

2. Inventory your resources

   ability to improve focus

   ability to improve concentration

   ability to respond to challenges

   ability to dig down deep when under stress

   ability to get the job done...sometimes not knowing how you actually did it

   other abilities and capabilities (list)

3. Inventory your past experiences where you have been successful under pressure.

4. List your behaviors and accomplishments which continue to reinforce your positive momentum.

5. List the motivational and other items you need more work on.

6. Work these up into a belief exercise.

7. As the program progresses, modify this belief exercise to mold your improved attitude, reinforce progress and focus your belief.

8. Keep adding the many positive thoughts and accomplishments.

You'll add items to this notebook as you go. But your overall goal is to internalize all of the items in your environment, using the notebook for reinforcement and fine-tuning. Your beliefs allow you to find your resources, which lead you to positive behaviors, which strengthen your beliefs, which bring out better resources, which produce more consistent and positive behaviors.

strength to get through the program and then do the marathon. Well, it's there. Your ancient ancestors lived and died to develop this for you. As you go through the normal series of doubts, before and during exercise, realize that everyone gets them: feelings that you're just too tired, that exercise is going to be uncomfortable, etc. Your forebears went through these feelings constantly and developed mechanisms for going on. Simply stated, you must 'gut it out.' Once out the door, the motivation and rewards will flow out.

"What you're doing is constructing an environment of beliefs about your inner resources, what you want to do, and how to connect the two to get the program on track. First, you must start writing your own book."

They talked about goals which were appropriate for this program. Several of the guys

Tom: Specific goal achievement will probably *not* give you the satisfaction you anticipate

As Tom prepared for the 1980 Olympic Trials, he knew that he was ready for improvement. Under the suggestion of a sports psythologist he had met, Tom set up a series of six goals leading up to the Olympic Trials. He had already done the first one. Each successive goal got more difficult. Each time goal or place finish he projected would have been a dream only three years before, but he was reaching the physical peak of his life. The pace picked up faster than he could assimilate.

The qualifying race for the Olympic Trials was on a course he had run before. Leading up to the race he mentally rehearsed it over and over again. In all of this, Tom assumed that he would be satisfied with the fulfillment of each of these goals, especially the qualification for the Olympic Trials.

22

who had done some running at different stages of their lives mentioned specific marathon times which they would like to achieve. Others talked about goals which involved specific experiences: the wearing of the marathon T-shirt or the framing of the marathon medal on their wall. Tom volunteered that he had lost focus after the Olympic trials because his goals were too specific. Specific goals leave little flexibility and set you up for negative left brain messages and the chance of backing yourself into a "failure corner."

Tom recommended general goals. "Instead of going for a specific time in a marathon or even focusing on the finish line of a marathon, look beyond. Picture yourself enjoying fitness and finding it a natural part of your life. Feel the increased confidence as you continue to stay active, modify attitude, and mold your vision of the future.

"You may not have the ability to run a marathon faster than four hours, but you definitely have the power to create attitudes which will last long past the marathon. The goal of becoming one who has a positive, enjoyable and energetic fitness lifestyle is much more important than any level of performance. All of you are 10 years ahead of me.... that's how long it took me to realize this!

"The most powerful force for keeping you on track is your belief environment. Your responses to the survey indicate that each of you has a belief environment about exercise. Unfortunately, the common theme for most of you is negative: that you can't stick with exercise, that it hurts, etc. Each one of you can turn this around and construct a new, positive series of beliefs, which you affirm with each slow and positive exercise session. With the strength which you will draw from yourselves, one another and

23

But Tom noted four problems with this process:

1. If he didn't achieve the specific goal (finished back two or three places or was off 10 or 12 seconds), he had some feelings of failure, regardless of how he had mentally prepared for a less than perfect outcome. This sometimes interrupted his focus when he needed to move mentally to the next goal.

2. When he did achieve the goal, there was no enjoyment. He immediately shifted to the next goal and the pressures which it could bring.

3. Because he set up very specific goals, his left brain gave him a stream of negative messages after speed sessions or minor races that didn't go well. ("You're not

going to do what you projected. Why put yourself through this?").

4. When he performed to capacity and qualified for the Olympic Trials, he had run the race of his life. Unfortunately, he had mentally rehearsed a time goal which was 25 seconds faster. This took the edge off his performance.

Tom now believes that he set up goals which were too specific. He should have rehearsed the feelings of satisfaction and achievement from each performance (and not a specific time or place). Furthermore, he should have continually filled in his belief environment with visions that he was gaining confidence, was making connections with his inner resources, and was feeling an overall increase in positive momentum for more improvement.

from the groups which you will be establishing in your workplace, you'll set up a solid and progressive momentum inside and outside.

"We all have a belief environment and have the capability to mold it by connecting to the many isolated sources of strength inside. You may be using some or many of the abilities independently now. When we embark on a continuous challenge, the separate power sources work as a team. As you use them, you will intuitively discover new ones. Soon, you won't even have to search for them.

"One of the most powerful effects of running, and especially training for a marathon, is the self esteem and self identification you realize as you connect up your resources of strength. All of the capabilities were there before; the challenge of marathon training pulls them together and forces you to keep them accessible and to put them to use. Human beings are designed to respond to challenges. We're set up to improve in almost every way from meaningful, creative challenges like the marathon.

"We don't have to dwell on this very long, but by being aware of your BE (Belief Environment) from the beginning, you can speed up the process and benefit from the increased capabilities. This helps train the creative, right side of your brain to intuitively make these connections.

"Your belief environment helps to mobilize the inner resources into an internal strength structure, a connection of resources which

- automatically shifts from one to the other and back again to keep the motivation going

- gives a steady, back-up feeling of support when engaged (with mental and physical activity)

- keeps you on 'automatic pilot'—physically moving forward even when you doubt your capabilities

- connects with the extra energy stores which are always in reserve

- mobilizes alternative muscle connections which give an extra push when you feel like you can't go on

- keeps a continuous stream of positive motivation—especially when significant negative experiences occur

- reaches down for motivation when it is really running low

- through practice gives early warning signs to anticipate motivational lapses and take action before they become major lapses

- monitors and conserves resources

- intuitively stops you and alerts you if you're under a health threat

- intuitively seeks and challenges the components of your vision, molding it and making it more responsive and usable—for you

- makes regular connection with this inner structure

- through mental rehearsal, develops an instant "reflex" response from your internal strength resources and helps you learn to engage the specific components which are needed

"Each push you make through doubt, discomfort and lack of belief in yourself helps you strengthen your overall BE and the efficiency of response of your resources.

"Your belief environment is a response of the spirit which engages the intuitive and imaginative qualities of your right brain. This quiet side of your head manages and organizes how you deal with stress and personal challenges in a similar way that the nervous system manages the skeleton and the exercising muscles. At first, the personal challenges, mistakes and lessons

Belief Exercise

"I believe in my ability to make the changes."

"I know that there will be struggles, but I believe in my ability to get through them."

"I believe in my creative capacity to find fun in the experience."

"I know that there will be challenges which will force me to evaluate each part of my belief environment, making it more realistic, responsive and meaningful to the specific experience for which I'm challenged."

"By believing that I will respond to these creative challenges, I am making many intuitive changes occur inside me which will engage my resources and make the change process more efficient."

"By immersing myself into the belief environment, I am becoming part of the improvement process which will improve all areas of my life."

[Taken and modified from Jeff Galloway's Return of the Tribes, p. 29.]

"Many who begin our marathon program say that their goal marathon will be the first and last. A significant percentage, however, come back year after year—using the marathon to get the attention of their physical, mental and spirit systems and keep them at a high level of readiness. After several marathons, the process becomes very smooth and comfortable, but the challenge never goes away—and that's good!"

Tom was almost thinking that his favorite student Matt Green had left, until a raspy voice penetrated the room: "This sounds like a lot of the stuff I've heard from inspirational speakers which management sends us young executives to hear."

"Beliefs can help you do anything and do it better. The dramatic effect of this belief environment is based upon the energy you put into your marathon program. You have to struggle against the challenges to build a team of body, mind and spirit, and that's what makes this BE so strong. In other words, Mr. Green, what you put into it, you will get out of it!"

Green: "Those other inspirational speeches haven't done me a bit of good."

Tom: "And this won't help you either unless you use it to become part of the process in training for your marathon."

learned will serve to strengthen this 're-source skeleton' and make it more adaptive to you. By developing a mental focus and rehearsal, we learn to anticipate and avoid problems by taking action before situations become problems.

PHIDIPPIDES...
THE FIRST MARATHONER
DIDN'T KNOW WHAT HE
HAD STARTED

*T*om and Sam made their way up the final half mile to the top of the highest point in the area. It was a magnificent view of the Aegean Sea, and they had to stop and enjoy over 20 miles of visibility in almost every direction.

Sam: "I've been here for three months, walking only along the beach and shoreline. You're here for three days and have discovered an interstate trail system. I had no idea this system was here."

"I couldn't help it, Sam. On my second day here, when nothing was going right with travel arrangements and shipping of materials, I had to find these trails, where the stress release is like a powerful eraser. I've been imagining that Phidippides could have used these same paths."

"You don't have to imagine very much. These are authentic messenger trails," said Sam in between huffs and puffs.

Tom: "I forgot to thank you for telling me about the hotel as a site for my corporate program. And thanks even more for helping to make the arrangements when my American negotiation wasn't getting through."

Sam: "Yes, the Greeks have their own way of doing business."

Tom: "And I'm sure that at least half the problem was that we Americans have our own way."

As they headed toward the ridgeline, Tom slowed the pace of his brisk walk/jog. "Tell me about your newest research, Sam. You said it had something to do with Phidippides."

"The project here in Greece has been funded to study the communication routes of Greece's prehistoric messengers. They were the primary communication system between cities and played a crucial role in the society. But the messengers themselves were not given any significant status in the community.

"Distance running was not considered an athletic event in the ancient Olympics. The 'glamour' events were the sprints. In most Olympiads, the longest run was only one length of the stadium, which was just less than 200 meters. Later, a two-length event also became popular, and, in some Olympiads, an event which was about 5000 meters was run.

"When a young man didn't have a career possibility, he could always become a messenger, which required no skill and drew upon the given endurance potential which each human being possessed."

"Sounds like me when I got out of college," noted Tom, only partially joking.

"Practically anyone could develop the endurance needed by just training and then delivering the messages. There was an

Sam's Professional Background

- For 20 years, Sam was a full professor with tenure at Georgia International University.

- During the past year, long-covered-up University financial problems have been disclosed.

- A new president stepped in to put the University on solid financial ground.

- He cut the number of departments drastically and reduced professors by half.

- Sam's department was cut. He retained his job, but his pay was cut in half.

- Sam's 10-year grant to study migrations of ancient man was given to a crony of the president.

- Crazy Jim did some legal work and got the grant reinstated.

- The National Science Foundation gave the grant directly to Sam.

- With Crazy Jim's help, Sam set up his own foundation and continues the research.

- Sam struggles with his new role, at 53, of business manager, along with his research, etc.

attitude-enhancing qualities of endurance exertion."

As they walked along the ridgeline, Tom and Sam were distracted again by the view. The clouds which covered the sun promoted a silver glow over the surface of the Aegean. The scene included an interesting smattering of islands which seemed to beam a stream of enticing notions: Who lived there? What quaint villages could be found? Were there interesting ruins or artifacts? As the islands seemed artistically arranged into the landscape, they framed and defined the water highways leading to them.

Sam walked over to a pile of rocks near the top of the hill, looking at how they were arranged and other details. "This is the probably the remains of an ancient outpost. Messengers would live here in shifts. The hill was so long that in cases of extreme urgency, a fresh messenger would take over here and deliver it to the next outpost. Lookout positions with a commanding view in all directions, such as this, were important for monitoring ship movement, especially in times of invasion by other countries. The Persians were spotted here hours before the first ship landed on the Plain of Marathon. When a significant ship was spotted, messengers would descend into the town and spread the word. This could literally produce a turnout of the entire population in a few minutes."

"They were the CNN, the CIA and Express Delivery couriers of their day, rolled up into one," noted Tom.

"Only faster than most of their counterparts today (on foot), with fewer blisters."

"Tell me, Sam, do you think Phidippides was the one who ran from Marathon to Athens?"

"It doesn't matter whether he was or wasn't, Tom; he got credit for it."

extensive system of running routes in this area. The ancient messenger-athletes probably used the same trails we're using today. A school was formed in this small harbor town to train messengers—physically, mentally and spiritually, as only the Greeks could do. I've uncovered a few writings (of a later period) from the school records which tell that they got great satisfaction out of their work and had some indication of the powerful psychological and

27

Sam seldom talked about his research or other academic areas but became exuberant as he explained to Tom his recent findings and theories.

He showed how the primitive paths which lead up from the little village of Vouliagmeni were probably the same ones used by the messenger training camp established there beside the hot springs.

"Established about 570 B.C., this camp was designed to train the messenger-athlete as a whole—body, mind and spirit. Phidippides probably trained here. But there was much more going on here than just running messages. This was a major crossroads of ideas and attracted its share of philosophers who would just hang around the town to hear what was going on around their world. You see, the messengers who came through here were a part of all that was happening in Greece. Ideas generated in one part of this civilization would be discussed here and then spread to other regions as these long distance communicators made their deliveries. The messengers were the connecting wire that bound this loose-knit collection of city-states and islands that was ancient Greece.

"The dramatic run and death of Phidippides bestowed heroic status upon those of his occupation. In the flowering of freedom which followed the Battle of Marathon, messengers became the nervous system of the Greek civilization.

When Tom asked how he could trace the influence, Sam referred to records of the camp, which were discovered in excavations in Vouliagmeni. "Normally, such a far-flung empire would see a wide range of levels of development; a traceable idea, for example, would normally take years to make it around the system. But in the Greece of that era, ideas were initiated and cultural events were happening simultaneously in every

The Origin of the Marathon

Phidippides: did he or didn't he?

It all started when the Persians invaded the Greek peninsula in 490 B.C. For several hundred years, the Greeks had developed a unique way of life to the ancient world, one which featured individual freedoms and personal identity. Great civilizations such as Ancient Egypt, Persia and the Fertile Crescent were dictatorships, producing great cities and monuments by, and at the expense of, citizen-slaves.

The aggressive and militaristic Persians landed on the Plain of Marathon, about 25 miles from Athens, determined to conquer the city and enslave the citizens. When intelligence reports reached Athens noting that Persia had more than five times as many soldiers as the Athenians, plans were certainly made to evacuate and burn the city before the invaders came. In a seemingly futile but courageous act, the volunteer Athenian army assembled in the hills above the Plain of Marathon to do battle.

The historical record of this period was passed down in oral reports only to be written down by Herodotus and others more than two centuries later. While the storytelling method of history has been shown to be generally accurate through research and excavation, names and details sometimes became blurred.

region of the Greek world. It was during the period after Phidippides that the role of the messenger changed into that of a communicator, an information processor who collected and discussed concepts. In the process, these guys got in some great exertion. You might call this area a 'concept crossroads.'"

"The experience of the camp here sounds a

Phidippides was mentioned several times in the accounts of the 490 B.C. campaign. When the committee of three generals who commanded the Athenians looked over the massive beachhead of their opponents, they wisely decided to send a messenger to Sparta, to ask for support with troops and supplies. Whereas the Spartans lived by a different philosophy, they certainly would benefit from repelling these hostile non-Greeks.

Phidippides was probably the messenger who ran about 130 miles to Sparta in a day and a half, but that's not all. He spoke so convincingly to the Spartan leadership that they decided to come to the aid of the Athenians but not for 10 days (they were in the middle of an important community ritual).

Phidippides ran back to Marathon the following day and reported to the Athenian leadership, which prepared for immediate attack. Following an innovative battle plan, they descended from the hillsides in a line that was deliberately weak in the center, attacking the massive force of the enemy. The Persians instinctively pounded the strategic center, broke through, and thought they had won. But the Athenian strategists had stacked their fiercest fighters on either side of the center behind their battle line. The invaders were surprised and quickly lost thousands of men. Probably sensing some supernatural force at work, the Persians ran for their ships and sailed away with their survivors.

Historical accounts tell us that a soldier/messenger was then dispatched to Athens to tell of the victory before they burned the city. Tradition has bestowed that honor upon Phidippides, who one assumes was rewarded for valor in battle and exemplary long distance service. He covered the approximately 25 miles and said one magic word to the Athenian leadership: "Nike!" (Victory!). Athens would live, but the wounded and exhausted messenger died.

When events were being considered for inclusion in the first modern Olympic Games in Athens in 1896, a friend of the prime organizer, De Courbertin, suggested that the run of Phidippides be commemorated in a footrace from the Plain of Marathon to the Olympic Stadium. The marathon was born and has been run in every one of the modern Olympic Games.

This distance of about 25 miles was increased in 1908 when the Olympics were held in London. Organizers had already measured the course when the Queen mentioned that she wanted to watch the start. It only took a mention by a queen, in that era, to extend the marathon course, and the extended distance became standard.

A tradition among veteran marathoners when passing the original finish distance at 25 miles is to say "God save the Queen" or something like that. But considering Phidippides' run for reinforcements, today's marathoners are getting off easy—we could be running the equivalent of a 260-mile round trip to Sparta!

lot like that of a modern running vacation," Tom observed.

"Looking out over the same view which was seen by Odysseus and Phidippides, I feel the stirrings of the human spirit—what made the Greek civilization different from what had come before," Sam continued. "Even more invigorating, I feel the desire inside to both challenge myself and open myself up to the new capacities and changes which that may bring about. I'm ready for a marathon."

Sam's Marathon Preparation Program

	Tuesday	Thursday	Sunday
Current:	20-30 min	20-30 min	4 miles (longest in past 2 weeks)

[Sam jogs 2-3 minutes and walks 2-3 minutes on every run]

	Tuesday	Thursday	Sunday
Weeks 1-3:	25-30 min	25-30 min	5 miles
Weeks 4-6:	30-35 min	30-35 min	alternate 6 miles with 4 miles
Weeks 7-10:	35-40 min	35-40 min	alternate 8 miles with 5 miles
Weeks 11+:	35-45 min	35-45 min	increase long run as per schedule and alternate long with 6-8 miles

30

THERE IS
A BETTER SHOE!

*S*am and his wife Bonnie were talking to Tom about the strange look of the newest pair of Nike racing flats when Suzi walked into the store behind them and interrupted

their concentration: "Don't believe him. He's always attracted to a shoe if it looks weird!"

Tom hadn't seen Suzi in over two months and had thought many times about how he was going to react when he saw her. His left brain said that he would greet her as he would a younger sister whom he hadn't seen in a long time. But upon hearing her voice, he instinctively turned around and hugged her. And this wasn't the basic "hug your sister" hug.

"Yea, I'm a Phidippides Running Store junkie," continued Suzi. "I have to come in

every week, even if I haven't run that week to see if there's a new outfit that would be a better match for my shoes. And when they get dirty, a shoe that would better match the outfit. And each week there's usually a group of new ones in each category."

It was New Year's Day, and the store was filled with resolution makers. Some were moving a bit slowly from activities of the night before. Others were filled with the revved-up metabolism which anticipates turning over a new leaf. Even in a store that was consistently positive, this was a high-energy day.

Suzi chatted with both Sam and Tom and received an abbreviated version of the two different perspectives of Greece. Then she quickly told them about Laura, who would be arriving soon to get the first pair of *real* fitness shoes in her life. Tom and Sam promised to be supportive, and they were.

Sam reintroduced Bonnie, who said that she was inspired by the new year to start an exercise program too. She thanked Suzi for inviting her to the informal discussion group at the bagel shop a bit later. Sam joked that with all of his travel he and Bonnie had to schedule a "shoe date" at Phidippides to have some time together.

Laura arrived and seemed very shy and out of her element until they started talking about the prices of the shoes. "I can't believe how much more these shoes cost than my

'Tennie Pump Specials' at the bargain outlet."

Tom explained how the support of a good shoe will make the experience of exercise feel better and reduce the chance of injury. Sam joked that once you made a commitment with your paycheck, you *believe* in the shoe so that you can justify that you're getting your money's worth.

The Phidippides staff person came over to help and worked with Laura and Suzi. Bonnie got into the act but had to be talked out of the pair of shoes she had chosen. Unfortunately, it didn't support her foot, which rolled in too much (over-pronated). "I knew it was too good to be true when I found a *perfect* match for my favorite warmup."

Suzi took a flyer to Laura describing a new course called Fitness 101. Sam and Bonnie became interested as Suzi explained that this was set up for those who were taking their first steps:

"There will be group support, classes on good low-fat food, fat-burning, attitude boosting, etc."

Laura didn't know if she was ready for this, but Suzi was more than just suggesting. Bonnie was afraid that she would be the only beginner in the group, but the store manager assured them that Bonnie could be the "cover child" for the course.

"You need this, Laura," said Bonnie, who was not shy and was beginning to warm up to Sam's fitness friends. "We'll push and pull one another through this thing. You push and I'll pull!"

Suzi and Tom sensed that Laura wasn't sold on this new way of life as they stood outside the store. Tom went to the bagel shop and the three munched as Suzi

Choosing The Right Running Shoe

1. If possible, go to a specialized running shoe store. They are in a better position to know how the running foot works and can match your foot up with a shoe that fits and works.

2. If a specialized running store is not available, see <u>Return of the Tribes,</u> pp. 24-24 and <u>Galloway's Book On Running, pp. 248-259</u>).

3. Find out if you have a floppy or rigid foot. That will determine the type of shoe to get. (See <u>Galloway's Book on Running</u> pp. 251-252.)

4. Take your most worn out shoes with you, and be prepared to spend some time. You're more likely to get a good fit if you take the time to consider several options.

5. Always run and walk in each shoe you're considering. If the store doesn't let you do this, find another store.

confessed. Laura heard the ugly details of how Suzi's former companion of two years, Dylan, dropped her for one of Suzi's own roommates.

The beginnings of emotion began to escape from Laura's face as Suzi described her revenge:

1. Dylan told her that she wouldn't be able to *ever* complete the Peachtree Road Race.

2. Dylan acted as a coach to his new companion (Suzi's sleazy former roommate).

3. The roommate, with a perfect make-up job, passed Suzi early in the race, saying "Now y'all don't run too hard, ya hear?"

4. Suzi passes her back (with mascara running in all directions down "roomie's" face), saying "Now y'all don't run too hard, ya hear?"

5. Dylan publically criticizes his new companion later for getting beaten by Suzi in a fun run. (See Return of the Tribes to Peachtree Street for the whole story.)

Crazy Jim arrived and notified the group that before he took any abuse from them, he needed to get his second cup of coffee. He came back to the table with two cups of coffee, making it clear that both were for him.

Tom: "I haven't seen you recently, James, and I worry when I don't see you for long periods. Last time I lost track of you for a year, you resurfaced with a band of illegal immigrants."

"Alleged illegal immigrants," corrected Jim.

Suzi: "Oh yea, the amigos....the ones you conned me to do profiles on....and no one from the language pool could communicate with them."

"They were native peoples."

"I must say that you won your case because the judge couldn't communicate with them enough to tell if they did it with intent."

Crazy Jim was more subdued than usual, and Suzi thanked him for "working" with the legislature to reinstate some medical psychological services grants for indigents. When Jim volunteered that he was changing careers into computers and software, she seemed stunned.

"I know what you're thinking, Suzi, about my other computer business, but this one is different."

Suzi explained how she did some pro bono work for Jim while she was struggling to set up her practice. Jim volunteered to set up a computer system for her with some machines he found discarded in an alley near a major corporate adversary of his. When they started to work on it, Jim discovered that the company had failed to erase some personnel files which turned out to help him win his case.

"How did your computer finally work?" asked Laura.

"I had to give Jim a key to my office because he only seemed to be able to squeeze it in from 2 to 5 a.m. When it was up and running, about half of the records from client "A" would print out sensitive information from some other client in the database. Fortunately, I never sent any of them out."

"It was a flaw in the software; I promised to fix it," Jim explained.

33

A January 1st Marathon Resolution

*J*im volunteered that his spirit was at an all-time lull, and Tom immediately suspected that it was a woman. "In college, Crazy Jim would take up with the most independent woman on campus and have her waiting on him and then he would dump her. "

Suzi: "Our Jim? I can't imagine....yes, I can."

Tom: "But when that unlikely event occurred—when he became the dump-ee—Jim would sulk around for weeks."

While Jim enjoyed the joking nature of this personal history lesson, he was having a bit of trouble coping with the ability of his friends to predict his behavior patterns.

Jim: "OK, full disclosure."

His woman of six months had left him. He continued to flesh in the story of their relationship which was perfect for his lifestyle: have some fun when the time allowed—even when it was 2 to 4 in the morning. "She was an artist."

She was also half his age (Jim-46) and hurt him most by telling him that he had become a slob. After two weeks of sulking, Jim realized that his lack of physical activity, his gaining of 50 pounds and his growing loss of focus was not making the picture he wanted to see of himself. The young woman had recognized something in him that he had tried to deny.

"I need a challenge and I've decided that it's the New York Marathon. I started a week ago, trying to get geared up for The Peachtree Road Race—but a 10K doesn't

challenge me. The marathon scares me enough to exercise three times every week and even to eat better....I think."

When Laura said that *she* needed a boost of motivation, Dr. Suzi motioned everyone over to the back room in the bagel shop which she had reserved for some privacy. While there was a window on the mall to connect with outdoor activity, the room had a cozy and comfortable feeling to it. Besides, the price was right: the purchase of a dozen bagels and a second (or third) cup of coffee.

As they sat around the tables of the Ansley Mall Bagel shop, Suzi asked each to tell about his or her motivation challenges. Crazy Jim asked in his best New York accent: "Are you sure you're not going to send me a bill for this one?"

Suzi: "You never sent me a bill for your computer work."

Jim: "From what I hear, you paid dearly for it."

Tom said that only a lawyer would worry about that. Suzi, who had had some negative experiences with lawyers, said that

Suzi's Group Guidelines

1. Nothing said in the room leaves the room unless the person saying it wants to talk about it with another member of the group.

2. No judgments are to be made in the room, only observations and personal statements.

3. Feel free to ask anyone else anything, but no one has to answer anything if one does not want to.

4. Dr. Suzi is there as a guide and not as a therapist and may make observations and conclusions which she wouldn't do in therapy.

5. Consider this session to be a frank conversation among helpful friends.

only a lawyer would do that if the tables were turned. Jim joked, saying that he was just asking and that Suzi should put it on his tab. Suzi mumbled that the tab had filled up all her files and had taken up all the available space in her office.

Suzi: "The problem that most of my clients

have is that they don't want to take responsibility for their health habits, their happiness and their lives. Each person blames someone else for their unhappiness and believes that they can't be happy because of the actions or force of that other person. Then when they realize that they need help, they look for a book, a recording, or another person who will give them the continuing push that will change them."

Tom felt the need to lighten things up: "Okay, Suzi, you're saying that we've been bad children and you're not going to give us any more quick-fix motivation tips."

"At least not without putting it on our tab," said Crazy Jim.

"Okay, you guys....and gal. You want a sermon? I'll give you one." She combined the religious background of her two parents—a Yiddish accent with a Southern Baptist sermon. As she stood up, the sound carried over to the main part of the bagel shop. Orthodox bagel buyers began to wonder what was happening in the other room as she loudly stated in tones that any rising TV evangelist would be proud: "Do you believe?" and "There is no future but the belief in responsibility."

After all had had a few laughs, there was a brief silence which begged to be followed by a more serious theme. Laura, who had said not a word, spoke quietly at first, and then with more confidence.

"I have just been thinking about my own situation, and you're right. Every time I feel left out, I blame someone else. What can I do to get out of this?"

Suzi asked what others did when they felt "left out." Jim said that he knew it wasn't the best thing to do, but he would just withdraw from the world and "sulk." Tom felt the need to go for a tough 15 to 18 mile-run over rough terrain. Bonnie volunteered that she hadn't found anything that she couldn't get over with a good shopping spree: "Just give me a credit card with a good limit on it."

Suzi: "One of the best strategies is to take some positive action, doing something which gives you some internal satisfaction and lifts your spirits. It also helps to do something with exertion. I think we're programmed to feel better when we work hard physically. I really hate to admit this, but after going through the struggle to prepare for the Peachtree....I haven't found anything better than walking and running.

"But I know others who walk up a hill or mountain. Others have a vigorous aerobics session, and one friend of mine works like a field hand around her house on yard work. I now believe that the lifting of the spirit is produced by hundreds of little effects of exercise, from the innate security bestowed by breathing deeply and sweating."

"You mean 'glowing'....ladies glow," corrected Bonnie.

Suzi: "I'm proud to say that I sweat...or at least perspire. There's nothing better than the afterglow from a run....when the endorphins are running wild and erasing the pains. But probably the greatest effect is the shifting from the negative logic of the left brain to the intuitive and positive direction of the right brain, energizing your whole body organism to gear up, get moving, move forward, and take care of the things that are happening now."

Laura: "But what should you do when someone has done something bad to you? They are to blame and they have caused you to feel badly."

Suzi: "As long as you continue to blame others for your misfortunes, you will remain

under their control and under the negative spell of the left brain and its negativism. You have the choice: sink back into the negative and stay down or get on with your life, build new positive experiences and become what you do. Do positive things and your life becomes positive."

Sam encouraged Bonnie to ask a question which had obviously been on her mind for a long time. "I've always been the mother of the kids; my life has never seemed to be my own. I'd really like to break out of this."

Suzi thought for a moment before replying, trying to put several thoughts and emotions together to match up with the different needs of the individuals in the room. "Almost everyone believes that the obligations of his or her life has them held hostage. The fact is that we'll find some great rewards when we really dig into our work. It's the satisfaction of expressing the very important occupational side of us, which is constantly seeking meaningful involvement. This doesn't mean just showing up every day but using your mind to solve problems, anticipate and plan, and

Left Brain vs Right Brain

The Left Brain:

This is the logical side of your brain. It has all the excuses, the reasons why you can't do something, the problems, and the people who are to blame for your unhappiness. It is engaged when you're under stress.

The Right Brain:

This the quiet side of your brain, but it is a reservoir of creativity and intuition. When you reduce stress and get under the right brain's control, it can intuitively find creative solutions to almost anything.

mold your area of responsibility into a meaningful experience. In your case, it's the very important work of molding the attitudes, behaviors and *values* of your kids. There's nothing more important than that."

Laura: "What if you're a perfectionist?"

Suzi: "As we become more competent, a bit of the perfectionist comes out in everyone. We should expect ourselves to become better at dealing with details and taking pride in that growth experience. I said 'take pride' and not 'become obsessed.' A perfectionist must get some kind of handle on how to process the increasing details and how he or she projects the perfection on someone else.

"I don't want you to think that exercise is a panacea because it is not. I am using it as a symbol as well as an example of how one piece of life's puzzle can get you going. For women who have a hard time expressing themselves, exercise is especially beneficial. Most women are surprised to find that the journey into exertion, while unsettling at first, is increasingly the best way to get in touch with themselves.

"As you exert yourself, you develop an often unused, gutteral response, which bestows a subtle confidence to say what's bothering you and then to take action and do something about it. We all need this, but women don't get as much 'gutteral experience' as men. You've really made some progress when you can feel something that bothers you, back off, and then say it in a way that will communicate the message while connecting with the other person's feelings."

Bonnie: "Now if I join Laura in this Fitness 101 class, I'll become gutteral and then lose my gut, right?"

Suzi: "Many of the participants will be women who share many of the same feelings and experiences. You'll find great support in the class, but whatever you do to develop your coping strategy for the 21st century, exercise needs to be a part of your program, as does sharing, support giving and support taking."

Jim: "So you have the audacity to empower us to take responsibility for our own happiness."

Suzi: "No, *you're* empowering *yourselves* to be happy."

"As bad as I have felt, emotionally," admitted Jim, "Out of the depths has come an inspiration: to conquer the streets of New York. I'll tell you right away that this scares me, just as it shakes loose some of my long-covered-up intestinal fortitude. I get out the door and it only takes a few minutes on the road to make me feel that I'm counterattacking the 'growing negatives' of getting older, losing vitality, gaining weight. On the days when I take up this challenge, the beginnings of hope and strength come back at the same time."

Sam: "It's part of the human condition to have these ups and downs. The ancient

The Exertion Game

- going to the gentle point of huffing and puffing

- backing off

- easing back into less huffing and puffing

- backing off

- gently finding an exertion level of barely huffing and puffing which can be maintained

The Difference Between a Dream and a Vision

- A dream is an abstract image with no direct connection to reality.

- A vision is an image-experience, organizing behaviors into a pattern which leads to a goal.

Greeks realized that tragedy was constantly interwoven with the challenge, the comedy and the success we experience. What I have regained from my recent incursion into the Greek approach to life is that each of us has the capacity to rebuild from negative experiences, to become stronger than before."

Suzi: "Adversity stimulates growth, but you must set up a plan to manage both."

38

Jim: "And exercise is the best way to manage my way to my New York dream!"

Suzi: "Jim, you've got to change the word 'dream' to the word 'vision'."

The group broke up, planning to meet the following week at the same time. Suzi commended everyone for their openness and their support of one another. She looked each person in the eye and thanked him or her for making the effort to really communicate.

"Well, I guess I'm ready to take responsibility and sign up for Fitness 101," said Laura.

"I still feel almost intimidated by the rest of you—doing the marathon," said Bonnie. "But you know, I managed to break the crust of the Tuscaloosa Junior League when Sam was in grad school. I can do anything after that."

When Suzi asked Laura if she was positive about Fitness 101, the latter again replied: "I guess."

"Laura, you've got to take the word 'guess' out of your exercise vocabulary, okay? Exertion is really responsibility training," she noted. "I kick myself for wasting my patients' time for all these years. Just preaching and talking about 'taking responsibility' almost never works. When you experience the responsibility chain, you give yourself the authority to unlock a vast quantity of good components inside which can make other changes happen."

THE EXERCISE RESPONSIBILITY CHAIN

1. Setting aside time for exercise

2. Getting out and doing it no matter how busy you are

3. Making some changes in food choices

4. Noticing and noting the positive changes in the way you feel

5. Making the exercise a habit

6. Changing your overall dietary plan to coincide with your exercise lifestyle

7. Noting how good you feel and how much more control you have

8. Reinforcing yourself for taking responsibility for your eating and exercise behaviors

Tom: "All of this responsibility is great, but I sure will miss not being able to blame someone else."

Suzi: "That's what we can talk about during our next session: Creative Blaming."

As Tom felt Suzi leaving, he called to her,

explaining that he was assembling his core group of young executives the following week, and he needed someone to talk about *responsibility*. Suzi thought for a moment and said that she could probably do it but wanted to talk it through beforehand. She thought for another minute and suggested meeting at her house at 8 p.m. Tom instantly agreed.

SETTING UP THE MARATHON PROGRAM

1- The weekly long run/walk gets you in shape for the marathon.

2- The other two to four weekly sessions will maintain and fine-tune this endurance.

3- Slower is better: The slower you go on the long ones, the faster you'll recover.

4- Walk breaks every mile, from the beginning, make long ones more fun and speed recovery.

5- On the days you don't run, it's best to walk or perform some other, non-pounding exercise.

40 The organizers were explaining the principles of the Galloway Marathon and telling humorous stories about some unlikely candidates who had had interesting experiences in the program or in the marathon itself. Jim slipped in through the front door of Phidippides Sports and spotted Tom, Suzi and Laura near the heart rate monitor display. He crawled and tiptoed through the crowd to join them, proudly waving his recently acquired application for the New York Marathon.

The room was filled with people who didn't look like marathoners. There was a cross section of body types, most appearing to be average weight or above. Jim, who by profession had become very sensitive to the mood of any gathering of people, was motivated by contagious positive energy fueled by New Year's Resolutions.

"I'd love to plead a case before a jury of these people," Jim whispered to Suzi.

Before Jeff Galloway was introduced, the administrative organizers asked to see how many had just started to exercise during the past 18 months. About 60 percent of the crowd raised their hands. When they asked if there were any general concerns about starting a marathon program or extending endurance in general, several questions seemed to get the interest of most of the crowd.

MEDICAL CLEARANCE

Someone asked about the medical screening required for joining the marathon program. The program director explained that anyone who plans to train for the marathon should first receive clearance from a doctor, preferably one who understands endurance exercise and supports such participation. In fact, the number of people who have problems that would keep them from exercising is tiny, but the doctor's screening and instinct can help direct those few to seek help and avoid exercise-related complications.

LACK OF BACKGROUND

Q: "I tried training for a marathon several times and either got injured or was tired all the time. My wife wants to do this and she's running less than half the distance I was. Shouldn't she build her conditioning up first?"

A: "The highest rate of success in completing a marathon without injury is among those who cover less than 39 miles per week. Your higher mileage probably kept you tired and encouraged injury. The low mileage which we mandate in this program reduces overall fatigue on the joints, tendons, ligaments and bones. By taking walk breaks and building slowly up to 26 miles on the long ones, she should have no trouble with the program and the marathon itself. We've had over 10,000 successful finishers with less than one percent who don't make it through the marathon itself."

IS AGE A FACTOR?

Q: "I'm over 60. I've been running short distances for three years about every other day. I've heard that marathon training can tear down people my age, produce stress fractures....you know."

A: "About 30 percent of our participants are over 50 years of age. As we age, we need more rest between stressful training sessions. By running no more often than three days a week, you'll significantly reduce the residual fatigue which builds up and leads to injury. With walk breaks in every long run, you'll cut down the chance of medical problems to almost nothing. Our 'over 60' participants see the doctor less because they are less likely to add mileage to the program and are better at cutting back or taking an extra day off at the first sign of excess fatigue or overstress. Many active folks like yourself can complete marathons into their 80's, and I've met several marathoners in their 90's. As always, stay in touch with your own capabilities and your doctor."

1. The weekend run/walk builds the endurance necessary to do the marathon. This slow, long one increases by one to two miles every two to three weeks. The maximum length of the long one should build up to 26 miles, three weeks before the marathon.

The Three-Day-A-Week Program

Goal: TO FINISH

Mon	Tue	Wed	Thu	Fri	Sat	Sun
walk 30-60 minutes	run-walk 30 min	walk 30-60 minutes	run-walk 30 min	walk 30-60 minutes	off	long run/ walk

2. During the week, a minimum of two 30-minute sessions will maintain the conditioning gained in the long one. Walk breaks can be placed in these sessions also.

3. On the other, non-running days you can walk or do any non-pounding exercise. Indeed, this type of less stressful exertion will improve overall fitness. Beginning exercisers will need to keep the effort level very low on these alternative exercise days. It's best to do NO exercise at all on the day before the long endurance event (Sunday).

COMPONENTS IN A SYSTEM

Think of your training program as a stereo system. Each exercise session serves as a component designed to produce a specific effect: endurance, maintenance or speed. Endurance is developed and extended by the long run, the speed for faster marathons is produced through repeat mile speed sessions, and the slow runs during the week maintain what you have developed on the weekend. (First-time marathoners shouldn't do the speed sessions but should focus on finishing the marathon feeling good.)

ENDURANCE:

The stamina necessary for the marathon is developed exclusively through increasing the length of the long run. Slower is better. The total focus of the long one is to build endurance .... that's it! Even those who are trying to improve speed are better off by running slowly in the long one: the slower you go, the faster you recover. Endurance is developed through extending the length of the long run whether you go fast or slow. The long one is your most important component, and you can't run it too slowly.

MAINTENANCE:

Slow recovery runs during the week will maintain the endurance and conditioning that you've developed on the long one. Two easy sessions keep the muscles in shape while encouraging recovery: increased blood flow speeds the removal of waste products as well as the replacement of nutrients and damage-repair fluids. You must do BOTH of these 30-minute sessions during the week to avoid struggling each weekend regaining what you developed the previous week.

SPEED:

Those who have run a marathon before and want to improve their times can add a speed component, which is designed only to run a faster marathon. The added *speed* stress will increase the chance of injury but is necessary to raise your performance to a higher level. As long as your goal is realistic, you're taking sufficient rest, and you're running at the pace you can handle, this creative stress will help you improve. By following the program listed below and monitoring your "weak links," you'll minimize the chance of overstress and injury.

BEWARE OF MIXING COMPONENTS

If you try to develop two components in a single session, you'll compromise the effect gained from each.

• *By trying to add speed to the long run*, you'll come away much more tired than you need to be. This "too fast long run fatigue" will not only keep you tired for days and compromise the quality of your speed play or other quality sessions but will also increase the risk of injury. Sometimes the fatigue is so subtle that

42

you don't feel it for two or three long runs. Fatigue will cause the release of stress hormones which mask the sensation of tiredness.

- *If you run too long (or too fast) during speed play sessions*, you'll tend to slow down at the end of the session and reduce progress. Running fast and long in a speed play session will increase dramatically the recovery time needed between sessions and will also increase the chance that you'll have to take a medical vacation from running.

- *Running even a little too fast on your mid-week maintenance days* will slow down recovery and increase residual fatigue. It is crucial to ensure that the pace and duration of those "Tuesday and Thursday" sessions are kept under control. Primary focus on these days should NOT be pace and distance but slow recovery and rehabilitation.

THE LONG RUN CONCEPT

You receive the same endurance from a slow long run as you do from a fast one.

- Twenty miles with walking breaks equals 20 miles fast....in endurance.

- All you're building on long ones is the component of *endurance* so forget about speed.

- Pace from the beginning of the run must be two minutes per mile slower than you *could* run that distance on that day.

- Walk breaks of one to two minutes should be taken every two to eight minutes from the beginning of the run.

- It's not just okay to run slower than two minutes per mile slower than you could run—*it's better!*

BUILDING THE DISTANCE OF THE LONG RUN

Long runs build the specific endurance, conditioning and mental strength to do the marathon, and by doing them slowly, you'll recover faster and enjoy them more. This weekly event starts at a distance which is only slightly longer than you have covered (at one time) in the last two weeks and increases by one to two miles each session. Once this long one reaches 10 miles, it can be scheduled every other week. When the distance reaches 18 to 20 miles, it can be done every third week. By continuing to increase the length to 26 miles, you build the exact endurance necessary to complete the marathon.

"RESERVE" ENDURANCE—FOR TIME-GOAL MARATHONERS

If you've run a marathon and want to go faster, it helps to have at least one long one that pushes beyond 26 miles. This bestows extra endurance, which will help you keep pushing during the latter stages of the marathon itself. On these extra long ones, the recommended pace is three minutes per mile slower than you could run *for that distance on that day*.

ON NON-LONG-RUN WEEKENDS YOU HAVE SEVERAL CHOICES

- You can run a moderate long run (usually 8 to 10 miles, once you've increased to that amount)

- or a 5K road race

- or speed play (if you've run a marathon before and want to improve time).

43

SETTING UP THE MARATHON PROGRAM

The long one must Be SLOW: The slower you run on the long ones.....

- the faster you'll recover afterward

- the better you'll feel throughout the run and at the end

- the lower your chance of injury

- the more you can talk, tell stories, remember stories, and enjoy the group companionship

- the more you increase the chance that endurance will be a positive life experience—for YOU

YOU *MUST* GO INTO THE LONG ONE RESTED:

- Take at least one day off from running the day before the long one.

- Most should refrain from any activity, the day before, which would leave the legs or back tired, tight or sore.

- Light walking the day before the long one is usually fine.

- Some prefer to have two days off from running before the long one.

Jim was feeling very secure about every aspect of the program except for the part about building the long one all the way to 26 miles (three weeks before the marathon itself). He had everything worked out in his mind that the longest distance he would need to run would be 18 miles or so. When Tom tried to explain the reasons behind going further (whispering to avoid bothering the others listening to the speaker), Jim started to argue with him in his own New York way. Jim was convinced that the body would break down when pushing beyond 20 miles. When Tom reached his peak of irritation, he asked a loaded question to the featured speaker who had just asked for questions.

"WHY DO I NEED TO RUN 26 MILES BEFORE THE MARATHON?"

A: "You don't, but our experience tells us that you will have a good experience in the marathon if you do and a negative marathon experience if you don't. You can't expect your body to cover a distance that is significantly longer than it has trained to go without complaining loudly and/or breaking down. By gradually increasing your long one up to 26 miles, you train the body and mind for the specific challenge needed."

"BUT I'VE HEARD THAT GOING BEYOND 20 MILES BREAKS YOU DOWN?"

A: "Only if you do the long one too fast. By going slowly and taking walk breaks, you do no more damage in an increase from 23 to 26 miles than increasing from 18 to 20 miles (or even 12 to 14 miles). Indeed, most whom I've interviewed over the years who train for the marathon using other programs run the long ones too fast and take longer to recover from an 18 to 20-miler than our folks do from their 23 to 26-milers. The slow pace makes all the difference. This gentle increase of two to three miles usually produces only a subtle tiredness as long as you're running those long ones at least two minutes per mile slower than you could run them.

The wonderful advantage which the 26-miler bestows is that by the time you've started the marathon itself, you *know* that you can cover the distance because you *have*! Time goal folks in our program have a reserve endurance because they go up to 28 to 30 miles. Again, the secret in recovering from the long ones, especially when the distance goes beyond 20, is running at least two minutes per mile slower than you could cover the course on that day AND taking the walk breaks early and often."

Laura was fascinated by the session because most of those who were asking questions, indeed most in the room, were like her: had not been exercising much, were over the weight that they wanted to be, and weren't 20 years old. Jim started to say that he was still not convinced, when someone asked a question that caught his interest:

"WHAT IS THE 'THE WALL'?"

A: "Most marathoners who go through our program do not experience the wall. Your endurance limit, or "wall," is the length of your longest endurance session during the past two to three weeks. Through a series of increasingly longer long runs, you can gradually push the wall back. Most folks who maintain our recommended slow pace don't feel anything more than the natural fatigue of going two or three miles further than you did two to three weeks before. Going slowly enough keeps you from breaking down.

"In our program, every other week you'll be running two miles longer than you've run before. When you reach 18 to 20 miles, you'll add three miles to each long one and run it every third week. In a few minutes you'll learn how walking breaks and a slow long run pace will help you recover quickly from these longer and longer runs."

MOVING THE WALL

In the marathon itself, or in any long training run, your 'wall' will start with the distance of your longest run in the past two to three weeks. This can be manipulated, however. If you go faster than you've trained to run, the wall moves closer to the start. If you go slower and take more walking breaks, you'll move the wall closer to the finish (or even beyond it). Those who have done a 26-miler in training and pace themselves in the marathon usually have a very positive experience in the marathon and come back to enjoy many more of them. Time goal runners who have done extra slow 28 to 30-milers prior to the marathon have a high rate of success in the marathon.

OTHER FACTORS

When the distance of the long one exceeds 20 miles, even when running a pace that is only slightly too fast, you'll complicate the recovery process, especially if you're experiencing another major stress. Occasionally, you may be coming down with a virus, etc. during your long run (and not know it). This can dramatically affect the way you feel during and afterward, increasing recovery time. Monitor all of your early warning signs of disease, such as elevated body temperature, elevated pulse rate, etc. (as soon as you are conscious upon awaking in the morning). Use your common sense when facing an unusual feeling of early fatigue and loss of energy and strength and cut the run short if you're concerned. As with all medical problems, stay in touch with a doctor who knows endurance exercise. It's always better to add

45

a little more rest before you've gotten yourself into a major fatigue hole.

BEWARE OF AN INFECTION IN THE LUNGS!

Most runners have been able to continue their training while experiencing a head cold or sore throat. If there is any chance that a virus has spread into your lungs, see a doctor who knows and supports endurance exercise. It's possible for a virus in the lungs to spread into the heart. While rare, this has produced death in some very fit people.

PACING: THE TWO-MINUTE RULE

The pace of the long one should be at least two minutes per mile slower than you could run that same distance on that day. If you run three minutes per mile slower, you'll recover even faster. You receive the same stamina boost from a slow one as you do from a fast one; endurance comes exclusively from the distance of the long one. A slow 26-miler with walking breaks gives the same conditioning effect as a fast 26-miler.

WALK BREAKS

Everyone should take a one to two minute walk break every two to eight minutes *of every long run*. Beginners need the breaks at least every two minutes, and very fit, experienced marathoners should walk at least every eight minutes. The walk can be done very slowly or at any pace desired. [See the next chapter in this book.]

The Walk Break

- Must be taken early to reduce pounding and fatigue

- Must be taken often to allow the primary muscles to recover

- Will also help most marathoners run faster in the marathon itself

NOTE: You must still slow down the overall pace to at least two minutes per mile slower than you could run that distance on that day.

DOESN'T SLOW RUNNING PRODUCE A SLOW RUNNER?

Yes, unless you have some speedplay in your program. But with a regular series of gliders and mile repeats, you can improve marathon speed. Scheduled on non-long-run weekends, these speed sessions allow you to build the endurance-speed needed in the marathon itself. Time goalers can also run segments of their mid-week runs at goal marathon pace, provided they feel recovered from the weekend runs. (See section on speed-play.)

WHAT TYPE OF SPEEDPLAY DO YOU RECOMMEND FOR TIME GOAL RUNNERS?

Those who have completed a marathon before are eligible to join a group of speed-players who will meet about every other week to do timed mile repeats. Each of these *fast* miles is run about 20 seconds faster than you want to run in the race itself. Between each of the fast miles, a walking break of three to six minutes is taken. You'll learn more about this group later when we go over speedplay.

46

WHAT ARE SOME OTHER NON-POUNDING ALTERNATE EXERCISES——AND DO WE *HAVE* TO DO THEM?

On the non-running days, it will help you to do some alternative exercise. Not only will non-pounding activity keep your fat-burning mechanism in tune, but it will also improve the cardiovascular system, give you a good attitude boost and avoid the pounding produced by gravity exercises like running. While marathon completion is based upon the running part of your program, alternative exercise will give you an extra boost of conditioning, extending your overall exercise capacity.

Swimming and light, upper body resistance training can build strength in the postural muscles. Cross country ski machines and running in the water give the legs significant, non-pounding exercise with little chance of overworking them. Cycling, rowing machines and low impact aerobics are also non-pounding but don't bestow any direct benefit to running.

Stair machines can keep the legs from recovering: Don't use these on a non-running day. If you feel that you need some extra strength in the leg muscles and don't have hills which you could *run* in your area, a short routine on the stair machine may serve your purpose as a second exercise session on a mid-week running day. Probably the best fat-burning alternatives to running are cross country skiing machines, rowing and exercise cycling (easy level of each exercise, building up to more than 45 minutes a session).

47

WALK BREAKS?

At this point, Tom noticed that several friends of his, veteran marathoners, were becoming restless. "Those guys are used to running continuously and don't like the idea of taking walk breaks." Jeff Galloway broke in to answer these doubters.

"After 37 years of running—and helping tens of thousands to get into running and improve—I've got some bad news...and some very good news:

The bad news: The human body wasn't designed for running continuously for long distances.

The good news: By alternating running and walking, from the beginning of a run, we can extend our endurance limits dramatically.

- By alternating the use of the primary running muscles, you can become a perpetual forward movement machine, capable (with training and nutrition) of going almost indefinitely.

- Shifting the usage of these key muscle groups (run-walk-run) allows the main propulsion ones (which are doing most of the work when running) to regain resiliency before they reach a significant level of fatigue.

- A 10 to 45-minute time improvement is possible for those who've run a marathon because the primary muscles recover enough on each short break to extend capacity.

- The walk breaks must be taken early and often. If this is done, you'll recover faster and enjoy the long one much more.

- You receive the same endurance from a run with walking breaks as from a continuous run without breaks.

WALK BREAKS:

- Must be taken early enough

- Must be taken often enough

- Will keep muscles resilient and strong to the end

- Will speed up recovery from long runs and the marathon

- Will help you run faster if you're trying for a time goal

- Will reduce the chance of injury

Using Muscles In Different Ways—Starting Early—Keeps Them Resilient

If you use the main running muscles in the same way, step after step, they will fatigue quicker. As the distance gets longer, the fatigue and damage to the muscles increases dramatically. If, however, you shift your usage of the forward motion muscles, you'll extend the capacity of each use of the muscle.

- Beginners take jogging breaks in their walks (one-minute jogs, every five minutes of walking).

- As beginners get in better shape, they may increase the jogging gradually.

- Fitness runners will take a two-minute walk break after two to three minutes of jogging.

- Average runners take walk breaks every three to eight minutes in long runs.

- Advanced runners take walk breaks or "cruise" breaks: a fast shuffle every mile.

Many runners have improved times in marathons and half marathons by taking one-minute walk breaks each mile. This often coincides with the water stops and allows for the water to be ingested instead of being worn with the clothing.

By reducing the intensity of muscle use early in the run (and often), you conserve resources. I believe that this reduction in intensity allows the main running muscles to make adaptations inside so that they can continue to perform at the level you request for much longer than if used continuously.

By shifting back and forth in muscle usage, you increase total capacity by using more of the resources inside the muscles. In races, you'll be able to work harder at the end, with muscles that have more life and capacity. You'll run faster at the end, when you would have slowed down. This is often the difference between achieving a time goal and not.

Walk breaks will also help to speed up recovery time between long runs, races or speed sessions. By building in the recovery breaks early, there is less damage to repair afterward.

Walk breaks will...

....allow those who can only run two miles—to go three or four and feel fine

....help beginners to increase their endurance to 5K, 10K or even the marathon

....bestow the endurance needed for runners of all abilities to go beyond "the wall"

....allow runners over the age of 45 to complete marathons and improve times

....help runners of all ages to improve times because legs are strong at the end

....reduce the chance of injury and over-training to almost nothing

....give time goal runners (<3:30) leg freshness at the end to pick up speed and improve

Thousands of time-goal-oriented veterans have improved their performances by 10, 20, 30 minutes and more by taking the walk breaks early and often. With freshness in the legs at the end, walk breakers can pick up their pace during the last four to eight miles when everyone else is slowing down.

Jeff Galloway's
International Lesson

When I competed internationally, many of the European distance runners who seemed to be my performance equals would run away from me at the end. As I analyzed some of these strategic races, I realized that in the first few miles, the Germans, Finns and Norwegians would seem to slow down every 400 to 800 meters. Mistaking this for a sign of weakness, I pushed the pace and passed them, only to be re-passed during the last mile. With the finish line in sight, my legs were cramping and tight. But my competitors seemed to be relaxed and could increase the pace at the most important part of the race.

When I analyzed the form and leg technique of my competitors during the slowdowns, they seemed to be gliding. Their pace didn't slow down very much, but they relaxed during the short breaks. At the same time, I maintained a strong driving motion throughout. The fast shuffle for 50 to 100 meters didn't let them lose more than 5 to10 meters, which was regained during the next 400 meters. The more experienced competitors were able to shuffle longer and faster, conserving resources for the end of the race.

The gliding and shuffling breaks allowed these European athletes to rest the main driving muscles just enough to reduce fatigue build-up at stategic places in the race. When my muscles started to strain under the continued pushing at the same effort, the Europeans had enough strength and capacity left to increase speed at the end. In some cases I lost to athletes who I'm sure weren't as good as I. But they had the freshness to get a five-meter lead on me with 400 meters to go, and I couldn't catch them.

"Are you saying that I can benefit from a walk break—even though I'm training for a sub-three hour marathon?"

Everyone benefits from walk breaks. They reduce the pounding, enforce the opportunity for water ingestion, and speed up recovery between long ones. Time goal runners will be running 28 to 30-mile long runs before the marathon for maximum performance. The walk breaks help the legs recover in a few days. Because most time goal marathoners will be doing some significant speedplay the following weekend, it is crucial to recover as fast as possible. Walk breaks only help you and have no detrimental effects.

Jeff Galloway related that quite a few runners have used the walk breaks (or glide breaks) to go below the three-hour barrier in the marathon. In one case, a male runner dropped from 3:08 to 2:58 by walking 10 to 20 seconds each mile. A female reported that she improved from 2:58 to 2:53 by taking 30-second glide breaks every mile. She made a five-minute improvement entirely during the last eight miles of the marathon.

"If I've never tried the walk breaks in training runs, would you advise taking them in the marathon?"

They will only help you. After the Marine Corps Marathon last year I was waiting for my bus to the airport when a fellow USMC finisher walked up to me and gave his initial evaluation of the suggestions which I had made at the clinic the evening before.

"When I heard you recommend walk (glide) breaks at the seminar yesterday, I didn't want to even consider it. I don't know why but it just seemed demeaning for a real runner like me to walk like that. You see, I've run 10 marathons with a personal best

Jeff Galloway's Experience

His Choice: A 3:40 marathon *without* **walking breaks...**

or a 3:25 marathon *with* **walking breaks**

Most of you who have time goals will record a faster time, as this gentleman did, if you take the walk breaks early and often.

A friend of mine in his late 40's had been trying for years to run a 3:30 marathon and should have done it, but 3:40 was as fast as he could run. His 5K and 10K performances predicted about 3:25, and he had done plenty of intense training in three different marathon campaigns: high mileage, lots of speedwork, two runs a day, etc.

Finally, he sent in his entry form for my program, only after I told him that if he didn't run below 3:30 in his goal marathon, I'd return his check. Never did I mention the walk breaks because I knew he would say something about 'sissy stuff' and not sign up.

I knew that in the past he had been physically trained (probably overtrained) for his goal and mainly needed to run with a group to slow down his pace on the long one. The group support during speed sessions also helped him enjoy doing mile repeats for the first time in his life.

After the first session he came up to me, irate, and demanded his money back. 'I can't do these walk breaks: they're sissy stuff!' I refused to return his check, reminding him that *a deal was a deal.*

He went through the program, complaining during just about every walk break. Secretly, he told friends in his pace group that he wasn't going to walk during the marathon itself.

On marathon morning, his group leader lined up with him and physically restrained him for one minute each mile...walking. At 18 miles, he looked at my friend and said 'Well, you seem to have just enough life in your legs so run along now!' And he did.

His time was 3:25. He had run 15 minutes faster than he had ever run!

At first, he couldn't believe that he could improve that much while walking every mile. But when he analyzed where he had slowed down in past marathons, it was always in the last six to eight miles. In his recent marathon he kept picking up the pace after 18 and knocked five minutes off his pace in that final segment. He finally admitted that the early and regular 'muscle shifts' left his legs feeling strong and responsive all the way to the finish line.

of 3:57 and have been proud of the fact that I've never walked.

"But after thinking about it overnight, I decided to prove you wrong by doing exactly what you suggested. To tell you the honest truth, I've been sick for the last couple of weeks or so and calculated that I probably couldn't run a *personal best* anyway.

- I walked for a minute every mile and

- Ran at my original goal pace of 3:55 during the running portions.

"By the first half of the marathon, I was behind my goal pace by three minutes. 'Aha,' I said to myself, 'Galloway is going to be wrong. If I'm already three minutes behind at the half, I'll be way behind at the finish.'

"At 20 miles, I was beginning to feel stronger than I had ever felt at that stage of the marathon. I cut out the walk breaks and ran to the finish, except for short breaks at water stops. While tired during the last six miles, I felt good and passed a lot of people, not really aware of my pace.

"I couldn't believe my time at the finish: 3:52—five minutes faster than I had ever run in my life....and after a bad cold! How did that happen?"

"Do I have to take walking breaks at the end of my runs if my legs are tightening up?"

Take them as long as you can because they will speed your recovery. If your legs cramp up at the end when you walk, then just shuffle through the walk breaks. At the end, you want to stay as fluid as you can while still alternating the use of the muscle groups. Cramping at the end tells you to go out slower in the next long run and to work harder to avoid dehydration the day before the run, the morning of the run and during the run itself.

"If I'm already running 20 to 40 minutes without walking, do I need to take walk breaks on my short runs during the week?"

Not on your mid-week runs of 20 to 40 minutes unless you want to. But on your long ones, start taking the walking breaks from the very beginning of the run.

RECOVERY—THE MAIN ISSUE IN A MARATHON PROGRAM

The slower you run, the faster you recover... Yet you receive the same endurance!

Surveys of first-time marathoners have shown that over 50 percent of those who start a marathon training program don't make it to the starting line of their chosen marathon. Even among those "first-timers" who are off and running at the start, a

52

Walk Breaks In The Marathon Itself—How Long and How Often?

Beginning Runners: 2-3 minutes of walking for every 1-2 minutes of jogging

Fitness Runners (who don't race): 1 minute of walking for every 3-4 minutes of running

Those who enter races regularly: 1 minute of walking for every 4-6 minutes of running

Experienced competitive marathoners: 1 minute of walking for every 6-8 minutes of running

significant number are limping along with injuries or significant fatigue developed during the training program.

MOST MARATHONERS DON'T ACHIEVE THEIR GOAL BECAUSE THEY HAVE OVERTRAINED!

Mistakes which produce injury:

- too many miles per week

- not enough days off from running each week

- running long runs on successive weekends

- running the long runs too fast

- running too fast on the recovery days during the week

By working too hard and not providing sufficient quality or quantity of recovery, fatigue builds up and slows well-conditioned runners down in the marathon itself.

allows the prime running muscles to recover and rebuild.

Once the instructor mentioned "type A running personality," the questions seemed to shift toward time goals and other competitive issues. Suzi turned to Laura and said that they could leave now. As they headed out the door, Tom waved to Suzi and said in a business tone, "Eight o'clock...I promise."

This reminded Laura to ask a question she had been saving to ask for two days: "What happened when Tom came over to 'consult about responsibility' the other night?"

Suzi: "I had a light supper prepared for us and waited....and waited. He finally called at 10:30 saying that he had pulled an 'all-nighter' the night before, had sat down on the couch to watch the 7 o'clock news and fell asleep. He begged to reschedule for tonight."

Laura: "Did you....and do you believe him?"

"I guess...."Suzi said with a somewhat bored look on her face. "I guess his actions say something, but I'm not sure what it is."

Laura: "What did you say about the word 'guess' in the vocabulary?"

Suzi: "You're right. Yes, I believe him and I approach this as strictly business."

Laura: "It seems to me more than that. I have those vibes."

Suzi: "I think I know Tom well enough to not expect anything other than friendship."

Laura: "Maybe this is just a marathon relationship. Like they were saying in the clinic tonight, it starts slowly, takes a long time to get anywhere but lasts."

Suzi: "Don't get my hopes up."

53

The Earlier You Take the Walk Breaks, The More They Help You

You've got to start the walk breaks before significant fatigue sets in, at least in the first mile. If you wait until you feel the need for taking them, it's too late. They will give you little help. Even waiting until the two-mile mark to take the first one will reduce their potential effectiveness.

The Discount Rule: The earlier and the more often you walk, the bigger the *fatigue discount*.

To put it in shopping terms: You're getting a discount from the pounding on legs and feet when you take walk breaks on long runs. If you walk often enough, start the breaks early enough, and keep the pace slow enough, a 10-mile run only leaves six to seven miles of fatigue and pounding and a 20-miler leaves your legs feeling like you've covered only 13 to 15 miles.

HOW FAST SHOULD THE WALK BREAK BE?

A slow walk is fine. If you have a type A running personality and want to walk fast, make sure that you don't lengthen your walking stride too much. Monitor the tightness of your hamstring and the tendons behind the knee. If you feel tension there, walk slowly with bent knees to keep that area relaxed. Again, a slow walk is fine.

RACE WALKING?

Some "type A" runners with time goals have learned the technique of race walking. In the marathon and on long runs, this technique will allow many runners to go faster during the walk break than the running portions. Because a race walk uses different muscle groups than those used in running, this is an appropriate shifting of muscle use and

Innovations which can reduce residual fatigue

■ *Walk breaks on all long runs*

The long ones are only designed to build endurance. Walk breaks don't reduce the training effect of the long run at all: you receive the same endurance from a long one at 14 minutes per mile as from a long one run at seven minutes per mile.

■ *By running two minutes per mile slower....*

...you'll speed up recovery. Slow the pace of your long runs to account for heat, humidity, hills (other 'H' words) and other factors. The overall concept is to cover the distance at least two minutes per mile slower than you could run that distance on that day (if you were running it as fast as you could go). For those who don't know what they could run, guess conservatively and then run slower than that. If you run three minutes per mile slower than you could run, you'll recover even faster.

■ *When in doubt, take an extra day of rest*

If you've just done a long one, a speed session, a race, or a combination of runs which may have left you more tired than normal, take an extra day off from running (or at least run extremely slowly).

■ *Monitor your overtraining signs*

When your pulse rate before getting out of bed is five percent above normal, take an extra easy day. If it's 10 percent higher, take the day off from running.

■ *Be sensitive to your weak links*

Pay attention to any possible irritation at the sites where *you* tend to get injured (knees, I-T band, plantar fascia, etc.). Take an extra day or two off at the first sign of inflammation, loss of function, or any of the signs which might be an early warning sign of injury.

■ *Remember to take advantage of your "discounts!"*

The earlier and more often you take walk breaks, the more you'll reduce fatigue. If you wait until you start to feel tired to take the walk breaks, they won't help you.

On a 20 mile run, for example....

If you walk one minute every five minutes from the beginning you'll incur only 12 to 13 miles of pounding.

If you walk one minute every 10 minutes from the beginning, you'll incur 14 to 15 miles of pounding.

If you walk one minute every five minutes starting at mile five to seven, you'll incur 15 to 17 miles of pounding.

If you walk one minute every 10 minutes starting at mile five to seven, you'll incur 17 to 19 miles of pounding.

FRAMING THE MARATHON EXPERIENCE

As the clinic got into issues of time improvement and competition, most of the "goal: to finish" crowd left. The remaining 50 or so were divided into two groups: 1) competitors aiming at the Boston Marathon and 2) those who had enjoyed their "to finish" experience and wanted to improve time a little bit. Jeff Galloway was fielding questions which were primarily asked by group one.

"I've tried to run a marathon slowly, and I became more sore than I was after a fast one."

If you're getting sore or feeling more effort when going slowly, then you're running inefficiently. By shortening your stride and keeping the feet low to the ground, you incur very little exertion. In this very efficient running mode, your main running muscles are mostly resting.

I've talked to several fast runners who seem to be running correctly, yet still became sore after a marathon. After a few more questions, however, I learned that they went into the marathon with a long run of only 19, 16, or, in one case, 12 miles. Whenever you ask your body to go that much further than you have gone in the recent past, you can predict that there will be some muscle retribution afterward.

To reduce the chance of soreness under any long run mileage increase, don't run with the same form every step of the way. By taking walking breaks early and often you'll accomplish this.

"Why should I waste a marathon by running slowly?... I don't understand how you can run a slow marathon. You have to train for six months and I want to make the most of this once, or twice, a year, challenge."

I understand where you're coming from. For my first 60 marathons, I was the competitor. When the gun fired, the force of my being was directed at reaching the finish line as I would in any race: with nothing left. While I ran some fast times including a 2:16, I did not enjoy these experiences. When I placed well, such as a win at Honolulu and fifth

Framing the Marathon

This exercise is designed to expand the ways you can enjoy your 26.2 mile trip. The longer ahead of time you start the framing process, the more ways you'll find to appreciate the marathon itself. In each case, eliminate the time-oriented rewards.

If you haven't already done so, you should start a "Mind Power" notebook. This will be your mental guidebook which will help you fine-tune your mental training. As you discover patterns of rehearsals which inspire you, write them down. As you collect positive experiences, write them down. This helps you to catalog a more formidable experience "resource library" and gives more magic to the words and phrases you attach to specific experiences.

In the section on mental rehearsal, you'll begin with an outline. As you fill this in with specific advance experiences, you are molding the way you'll feel in the marathon. You can significantly carve out enjoyment, in advance, which will influence the race itself. By 'framing,' I mean setting up a process which will open you up to a wide variety of experiences during the marathon and enhance your enjoyment and growth.

1. Write down what you will look for and seek out as you run the marathon:

- getting to know some of the folks around you

- picking up on the energy of the spectators along the way

- getting a feel for the personality of the city

- looking for places along the course where you'd like to return

- other items which are meaningful to you

2. Write down how you'd like to feel as you run your relaxed marathon:

- enjoying the confidence of running within yourself

- appreciating the glow bestowed by exertion

- feeling the support of the spectators

- gaining strength from the others around you...you're moving through the challenge together

and seventh place finishes at Boston, the afterglow was compromised by weeks of healing: soreness, tiredness, blisters and ego (which always told me, even when I ran well, that I could have run faster).

But during my past 40+ marathons, I've learned that you can 'frame your marathon' to enjoy it in many ways. Framing means arranging your expectations so that mind and body work together to appreciate many components of the marathon experience: getting to know the people around you, gaining a sense of the personality of the city you're running through, enjoying the act of exertion itself, etc. There are many positive thoughts, emotions and happenings which can be savored and enjoyed by those who are staying within themselves as they cruise the course. Time goals cut you off from most of this.

You are the captain of your ship as you sail through the marathon. Only you should decide what is important about that marathon. About 85 percent of today's marathoners appreciate and enjoy the act of finishing the marathon and take so much more home than the finisher's medal and official time.

- bouyed up by the sense of meaningful purpose of completing the marathon
- other feelings

3. Write down how you will feel after the marathon

- having enough left to talk to people and enjoy the refreshment area
- enjoying a great shower
- walking around with a friend or two, with no major aches, pains or fatigue
- enjoying the meal you've earned and sharing the experience with others
- feeling a little tired but having plenty of energy since you've stayed within yourself
- feeling a great sense of accomplishment
- continuing to enjoy the sense of achievement while recovering quickly afterward

4. Be Creative!

- imagining you're writing a detective novel and seeking clues and venues for your story

- planning how you would paint the interesting areas you're running through if you had a canvas
- training yourself to snap a mental photo of specific scenes...with details
- designating people along the way as characters in your novel: what are they up to?

■ Write these down into the margins of your outline.

■ Go over them every week (every day or so, if possible).

■ Add other items in each area as you go through the program.

■ The experience becomes more alive and fun....with each rehearsal.

■ This leads to the same pattern in the marathon.

■ Use this evolving 'story line' as you move from marathon to marathon.

[For more on this process, see the chapter on The Marathon Mind.]

57

"None of them are left in this room. You scared them off when you started talking about speed," quipped a runner with a 3:20 marathon goal.

Galloway: "But that's one of the primary reasons those of us who are left, the 'type A running personalities,' need to address this issue. If you don't cultivate more rewards from the marathon than the time, you'll burn out on participating in this classic race and maybe on running itself."

THE "MARATHON A MONTH" CLUB

The marathon leader explained how a growing number of folks in the training groups had started a collection of marathon experiences. Informally calling themselves the "Marathon a Month" Club, they run one long run every three to five weeks in a different city by entering marathons. Members have to have gone through the Galloway Marathon Program, and....

◆ must run each marathon at least two minutes per mile slower than they could run it on that day,

Jeff Galloway's Experience

From a 2:38 marathon to a 5:10 marathon in one year....and happier!

A few years ago, I trained to run a marathon faster than 2:40. In spite of my eight to nine minutes per mile pace on daily runs, I believed that my 45+ year old legs could average six minutes per mile (if I could add some regular speedplay to my program). A session of mile repeats every other week (building up to 13, running each at 5:40) seemed to be doing the job. My longest run, three weeks before the race, was 29 miles (at 8:30 pace). Despite pushing the pace too fast in the middle of my target race, the Houston-Tenneco Marathon, I achieved my goal, with two seconds to spare!

Several months later, I was asked to help someone run his first marathon. He guessed his performance potential to be just over four hours, but stomach problems pushed us over the five-hour barrier for the first time in my marathon life.

The 5:10 marathon was a much better experience than the faster one. I received the same satisfaction from finishing the slow one as I did from finishing the fast one. An even bigger benefit was revealed during the recovery.

Three days after my five-hour marathon, I was running smoothly, easily and as fast as I wanted to run. There were no aches or pains and no lingering problems. Quickly and easily resuming my normal running program, I enjoyed the glow of satisfaction from having re-established marathon endurance.

Four weeks after my 2:38 marathon, the pride of time goal achievement had worn off, yet my running muscles were still stiff. For several weeks, I continued to feel regular bouts of lingering tiredness. During those many weeks, I longed for the day when I'd feel smooth and fluid again.

I've articulated a pattern from analyzing many other slow and fast marathons, which have been run by me and thousands of the folks with whom I work. The slower you go, particularly in the beginning, the faster you'll recover from the marathon. I believe very strongly that the satisfaction is identical whether you register a personal best, a personal worst, or anything in between. Finishing a marathon bestows great personal achievement and accomplishment. Period!

Certainly there is significant meaning in training for and realizing a time goal in the marathon. I recommend, however, that this be reserved for very few occasions (once every 12-24 months).

When you enjoy a marathon and recover quickly afterward, you'll reinforce all of the positive behaviors and internal connections you've developed in the training. I believe that one should have at least three very slow and enjoyable marathons for every fast one—to keep the balance.

I'm not denying that our egos are important sometimes and that some runners need to feed them with an occasional accomplishment. Don't give up the pursuit of a time goal if this is what you want. Just realize that focusing too exclusively on speed and time has led to burnout for many runners.

I want you to enjoy running for the rest of your life. So....take it easy!

♦ must write down at least 10 positive
  aspects of the trip,

♦ must have one funny or interesting story
  about the trip or the marathon (true or
  made up), and

♦ must share stories and other feedback in
  the group run the following week.

Those who want to run a faster time can
use the last marathon in the series to do
this. Many start a marathon program by
focusing only on the time goal. By the end
of their schedule, leading to the time goal
marathon, they have enjoyed the group and
the "fun concept" so much that they often
abandon the time goal and enjoy another
one with their friends. "I'm not going to let
the clock interfere with my fun!" said one
club member.

59

A Faster Marathon

*A*s the talk turned exclusively to faster times, the remaining "fun marathoners" left. The rest of the group was ready to get faster, and it couldn't come fast enough. Several indicated that they were only a few frustrating seconds away from their goal. Most of the questions, however, continued to come from the competitive veterans (ages 22-69) who were locked into issues of personal performance.

Tom took notes for two reasons: 1) to relay significant information to Chris and 2) to possibly expand his marathon team-building program in the future. Tom was already using the Galloway program on a license agreement. In future years, a speed challenge might give the competitive folks a chance to express themselves in a positive way.

TO RUN FASTER....YOU MUST RUN FASTER

You can't run all of your runs slowly if you want to run fast in the marathon. But you can't go too fast either. By running the speed play too fast, for example, you will prepare your muscles to go out too fast in the marathon and pay dearly for that later. The best type of speed is that which simulates the marathon experience. This will encourage the exact type of endurance/speed adaptations necessary to go faster on race day.

Strength and coordination are developed simultaneously with the other improvements generated by speed sessions.

The cardiovascular system adapts

* The heart pumps more blood into the exercising muscles.

* Waste products are withdrawn more quickly from those muscles.

Your oxygen processing system becomes more efficient:

* Oxygen is absorbed more efficiently from the air.

* Oxygen delivery to the muscles allows you to burn fat longer.

Adaptations occur inside the muscles due to the challenges of speedplay:

* Fat-burning makes you more efficient.

* You also become more efficient when burning glycogen.

* Waste product removal gets more effective.

* Individual muscle cells work at a higher capacity for a longer period.

* Muscle cells learn to work together, in systems.

You develop the mental strength to go further:

♦ You develop instant and continuous mind-body feedback.

♦ You learn how to dig deeper and push through doubt.

♦ You learn the difference between real problems and the lazy messages of your left brain.

[For more information on the changes in muscles, see Galloways Book On Running, pp. 38-43.]

But every time you run fast, you increase the chance of injury, you stress and fatigue the main running muscles, and you increase the chance that you'll not recover before the marathon itself. To do your best in the marathon, all of your components should be ready for top performance, working together, and trained to make further adaptations under stress. The stress of speed play is necessary for you to run faster, but you need to monitor fatigue to avoid injury or overtraining.

RECOVERY! RECOVERY! RECOVERY!

THE theme of a time-goal program is *recovery*. If you build enough rest into your program before you need it, your body will be continuously recovering, rebuilding and adapting for the performance demands of your goal. By preventing extra fatigue and taking extra rest even at the first hint of slower recovery, you can maintain a steady performance increase without taking a week or more off due to injury or overtraining.

Recovery Enhancers

■ Enough days off from running each week

■ Long runs which are slow enough— with walk breaks

■ Walking the rest interval between mile repeats

■ Starting out every run very slowly (at least three minutes per mile slower than you could run the distance you plan to run). You can speed up later in the run if everything is okay....*just start very slowly.*

■ Making sure that you are recovered enough from the weekend sessions before you do any tempo running, accelerations, etc. during the maintenance runs on weekdays.

61

MONITORING OVERSTRESS

Keep a log book next to your bed and write down your pulse rate before you get out of bed each morning. Do this before you've had a chance to think about anything stressful, like getting up, work, etc.

Why? When your exercising muscles are over-fatigued, they don't have the resiliency to help move the blood through the system in the smoothest way. The heart must work harder and registers this with a higher heart rate.

When to take a day off: After several weeks of listing your heart rate, you'll be able to tell what your lower baseline levels are. When you see a five percent increase over your low baseline, you should take an easy day. When the heart rate is 10 percent above baseline, just take the day off from running.

How many days per week?

Almost every marathoner, including most of those training for the Olympic Trials could benefit from two days off from running per week. Age will determine, and ultimately dictate, how many more days off you will need.

- Those in their 30's can get by with two days off per week.

- In your 40's....better take three days off from running per week.

- If you're over 50, it's best to shift to every other day.

If you've been running six or seven days per week, I'd start by cutting back by one day per week. As the long runs reach 15 miles and beyond, cut one more day out of the schedule. You can actually increase mileage to running days by adding an additional run (if recovery is proceeding well). Alternative exercise can be done on non-running days, but take it very easy the day before:

- your long one,

- races and

- your speedplay day.

Example: The late Dr. George Sheehan improved by reducing from six days to three days.

As he approached the age of 60, Dr. Sheehan's marathon times slowed down. For years, he had been running five miles a day, six days a week. Admitting that his competitive days appeared to be over, the running cardiologist cut back to three days a week, while increasing his daily mileage to 10 miles. In other words, weekly mileage held steady at 30 miles per week, while he gained three extra rest days.

After about three years of this schedule, at age 62, George ran the fastest marathon of his life: 3:01. He gained more training effect from one 10-miler than he did from two successive 5-milers. Even more significant was the recovery he received by taking a day off between runs.

Remember that heart rate is also affected by stress, elation and other emotions and thoughts. Try not to think about anything before taking your pulse.

MILEAGE HELPS—BUT AT GREAT RISK

By adding mileage to your program, you'll improve overall conditioning and improve the chance that you can achieve your time goal. But higher mileage dramatically increases injury risk: it is *the* leading cause of injury by a wide margin.

There are some ways to increase total mileage and reduce the chance of injury:

- By increasing mileage very gradually

- By adding a short additional run to a running day

- By starting and finishing your running days with a mile each of very slow running

(at least three minutes per mile slower than current 10K pace)

Be aware of all the early warning signs of injury or over-fatigue and back off at the first indication of trouble.

AS WE GET OLDER

Since it is possible to continue to improve times at any age, many runners over 45 are elated when they run personal records or high age-group performances...and forget that they're over 45. The exuberance of achievement will push marathon improvers at any age into over-fatigue before they know it; the older the runner, the longer he or she has to pay for the excessive training.

Unfortunately, there are few early warning signs of overtraining in a marathon program. Most of those who get into trouble are increasing gradually enough; they just don't have enough recovery time built into their program. The progressive build-up pushes the muscles beyond their limits so gradually that the effects are usually masked by internally produced stress hormones. Once the resource reserve has been used up, older runners must endure a long recovery period.

PAST THE AGE OF 45:

- Fatigue comes on more quickly but is usually masked by stress hormones.

- It's easier to push into overtraining without warning signs.

- The worse the overtraining, the longer the recovery:

Fatigue takes twice as long to recover from (compared to the below age 35 group).

Over-fatigue takes five to six times longer to recover from (compared to younger groups).

THE FATIGUE-PRODUCERS:

- too many days of running per week

- too many miles per week

- too many races

- speed sessions

- the very long, long runs

The volume of miles which most time-goal marathoners put into their program is enough to produce overtraining among the over-45-year olds. It's so easy to push just a bit too hard on races, speed sessions, or any of the other components, but the recovery from stepping over the line is significant.

REDUCING INJURIES FOR 45+ MARATHONERS

- Add an extra day off from running (to a minimum of three running days per week).

- Slow down long run to a pace of three minutes per mile slower than you could run that day.

- Add walk breaks to long runs, from the beginning.

- Walk for two to three minutes (minimum) during the rest interval in speed sessions.

- Carefully monitor resting heart rate.

63

LONG RUNS CAN IMPROVE MARATHON SPEED

By increasing beyond 26 miles, you'll build reserve endurance which will boost performance in many ways:

- You'll push your "wall" past 26 miles.

- You'll have the strength and stamina to maintain a hard pace during the last three to six miles when most competitive folks slow down.

- With reserve endurance, you can often get away with a few small pacing mistakes.

YOU MUST RUN SLOWLY OR YOU'LL LOSE THE BENEFITS:

- You get the same benefit from a long slow one as you do from a long fast one. You'll just recover faster from a long slow one.

- Going beyond 20 miles in the long one helps marathon stamina dramatically but you must run slowly. By pacing these long ones at least two minutes per mile slower than you could run that distance on that day *and* taking walking breaks, you'll get the job done!

- Running slower will help you recover faster and therefore keep the legs ready to do speed sessions on the following weekend.

- Liberal walk breaks will also speed recovery from the long ones. Remember that these one-minute walks must be taken early and often to give your legs the relief needed.

* Make sure the maintenance runs during the week are done slowly enough.

Sometimes a slight bit of fatigue will appear on the second or third day after a long one or a speed session. Take it very easy if that happens.

ACCELERATION-GLIDERS

To improve running form and efficiency, accelerations can help you greatly. When your form improves, a speed increase will occur naturally.

BENEFITS OF ACCELERATION-GLIDERS

- They warm up the legs before speed sessions, hills or races.

- By focusing on these gliders, you teach yourself efficient marathon running form.

- They help you develop the capacity to glide or "coast" for segments of 50 to 200 meters, resting the major running muscles so that they will perform better later.

ACCELERATION-GLIDERS MUST BE DONE

♦ regularly—at least twice a week

♦ with no sprinting—no major effort used

♦ low to the ground to minimize effort

♦ using quick turnover of the feet and legs

HOW TO DO THE ACCELERATION-GLIDERS:

1. It helps to have a slight downhill to get momentum going, using the last 20 to 30 meters of the downhill as momentum to get right into gliding at an increased pace.

2. Keep the legs and body relaxed throughout, but particularly at the beginning.

3. If no downhill is available, pick up your leg rhythm by shortening stride length and gradually increasing the turnover of your feet and legs. (Turnover is simply the number of steps you take per minute.)

4. When you feel comfortable at the faster rhythm, let the stride lengthen out naturally, but don't let it get too long. (Avoid any feeling of tension or over-stretch in the back of your legs.)

5. You're now up to speed so just glide....keeping feet low to the ground, using very little effort.

6. Let this gliding continue for 50 to 200 meters.

7. Rest by jogging between accelerations. You may also take walking breaks as needed.

YOUR ACCELERATION-GLIDER PROGRAM:

1. Read the section in this book on marathon form. During the gliders you want to practice using this very efficient technique, which will allow you to do so more naturally in the marathon itself.

2. Warm up before each session with one to two miles of easy running (with walking breaks if you wish).

3. Keep the legs relaxed throughout the warm-up, the gliders themselves, and afterward.

4. Ease into the gliders, using downhills as noted above to get you started on each. In this case, the downhills act as the accelerations. If you don't have a down-hill available, accelerate by shortening the stride, picking up the turnover rate of the legs, and then gradually lengthening out the stride as it feels natural. The "gliding" will follow.

5. Work on the marathon form mentioned in the form chapter later in the book. Keep your feet low to the ground, body upright but relaxed, and maintain a smooth, quick turnover while using little effort.

6. Start with three to five gliders and increase by one or two each session to a maximum of 10 or 12.

7. Two of these sessions per week will help to mechanically reinforce form improvements, which will help you in the marathon itself.

8. You can use these as a warm-up before hills, speed sessions or races. You may also do them during your recovery/maintenance runs each week.

65

HILLS BUILD STRENGTH

*E*veryone can benefit from doing some hill accelerations. Hill training provides a gentle and effective transition between very slow running and the faster speed play needed by veteran marathoners for faster performance. If you're just starting to run, you shouldn't jump into hill play. But those who've been running regularly for six months or more can benefit from the strength increase which only hill training can give. You don't have to have a time goal to benefit from play on the hills.

HILLS: THE BEST STRENGTH TRAINING FOR RUNNING

Hills provide resistance to the main running groups, primarily the calf muscles; the regular but gentle uphill stress encourages these muscles to develop strength in the act of running. Weight training, in contrast, builds static strength in only one range of motion at a time. Since weight work can strengthen some leg groups more than others (and knock your running motion off balance), it is not recommended for runners. Hill training strengthens as it coordinates the dynamic action of running and can bestow all the running power you need.

When runners of all ability levels run hill sessions regularly, they develop the lower leg strength to support body weight farther forward on their feet. As the foot rolls forward in the running motion, greater

support strength will allow the ankle to be loaded like a strong spring. The result is a more dynamic lift-off of the foot as the ankle releases its mechanical energy. Due to

the incredible efficiency of the ankle, more work is done with less energy expended by the muscles. Such conservation of muscle resources allows one to run further or faster or a combination of both.

IF YOU'RE DOING HILL TRAIN-ING FOR THE FIRST TIME...

Beginning hill runners should be conservative. It's too easy to run too fast in the first few sessions without realizing it. DON'T PUSH THE EFFORT! Run at a comfortable and non-fast pace on each incline during the first few hill sessions. The grade of the hill will be enough of a challenge to bestow a training effect. After three hill play sessions, you may run the hills a little faster.

HILL TRAINING RULES:

- Never run all out!

- Never go to the point that you're huffing and puffing and can't talk.

- Don't run so hard that you feel significant tension or extreme exertion in any of the muscles or tendons in the back of your legs. If this happens, slow down immediately and shorten your stride. (The lengthening of the running stride out of its efficient range can cause injury, extra fatigue and long recovery.)

BENEFITS OF HILL TRAINING:

- Strength from hill training helps runners shift his or her weight farther forward on the foot and gain a more efficient "lift off" with each step.

- It strengthens a set of muscles which are used as back-ups for the main running muscles.

- It helps the cardiovascular system adapt to faster running without going into oxygen debt.

MARATHON HILL TRAINING:

- Take a very slow one to two-mile warm-up and warm-down.

- Pick a hill that is 200 to 800 meters long.

- The grade of the hill should be very gentle.

- Run up; walk down.

- Run with a smooth, continuous effort over the top of the hill.

- Never sprint or run all out. Just maintain an increased turnover rate over the top.

- Start with two or three hills, and increase by one or two hills per week until you can run 8-12 hills.

- Don't feel like you have to increase the number each session. Back off if tired or sore.

HILL TRAINING FORM:

- Maintain upright body posture.

- Feet should stay low to the ground.

- Keep your stride short at first; pick up the rhythm until you feel comfortable.

- Keep your rhythm going quickly and smoothly over the top of the hill.

- When the incline increases, shorten your stride to maintain turnover rate.

The length of the hill segments is longer in a marathon program than in a 10K or 5K training routine. These longer inclines develop *endurance muscle strength* as opposed to *explosive muscle strength*. Due to the distance increase, each should be run slower than you'd run hills of shorter length.

As in the other elements of training, it's important for hill sessions to be done regularly, in order to produce the adaptations desired from the legs and muscles and to improve overall running efficiency. Since hills will prepare the running muscles for a higher level of performance, the greater the number of weekly sessions, the more you will benefit from the added strength and running efficiency when you shift to speed

play. When speed sessions begin, hill
training is terminated.

REMEMBER TO PUT THE **PLAY** IN HILL-PLAY

By picking an interesting hill, you can
improve your motivation and fun. You may
vary the cadence or turnover of your legs in
segments of the hill. When you have a hill
play group, there is always the potential for
more fun. (Just be sure that you aren't
running faster than you should.)

SPEED PLAY

THE RIGHT TO HAVE FUN

Let me introduce you to a new type of speed session....one which offers the invigoration of going fast and the satisfaction of knowing you're getting better. You'll be able to joke with friends or yourself throughout the session and provide games which keep the experience interesting.

Starting now, we have abolished the old, archaic speed work and replaced it with a clean, upbeat and uplifting speed play. You're going to like it so much that you'll finish each session wanting to do more. And because you don't do more than assigned, you'll look forward to the next session.

Set up your speed session in an interesting area. You can also change the venue if variety helps make it more interesting. Bring music, a clock (if possible), and banners which are funny, inspirational or instill pride. Some runners bring along a few posters with uplifting graphics.

Many runners like to read something before the speed session. Humorous, entertaining, informative....any reading will offer the chance that the left brain will be preoccupied so that it won't bother you with negative messages and excuses.

Running with a group will improve morale, increase and maintain motivation, and make the session more fun. The require-ments of the group are as follows:

- You can start together,

- But don't run the pace of someone who is faster than you.

- When in doubt, take more rest between repetitions, even if the rest of the group is not.

DO THINGS THAT ENSURE FUN

- Require each member to bring to each session 1) a joke, 2) a controversial viewpoint, and 3) some spicy news.

- Set up games in which runners of all abilities can run the same repetition, with the winner being the one closer to his or her assigned pace.

- Alternate the jokes, etc. so that there is a continuous flow of entertainment.

- Use the walking between repetitions for other fun activities.

WHERE

A track is not necessary. Road segments, a park, well-packed trails or other safe venues are just as good. Wherever you run, make sure that the mile is accurately measured. During the first few sessions, a track can help by giving regular timed feedback, usually every quarter mile. This helps to set the internal pace clocks more quickly. Also important is the ability to hear music as you make the loops of the oval. When choosing a road segment, avoid downhills that are too steep or give you too much advantage. Likewise, avoid uphills which are too steep and will force you to either slow down or overwork to maintain pace.

SPEED AND ENDURANCE....
SIMULTANEOUSLY

Running faster in the marathon requires that you develop a special type of speed-endurance. This means that the actual pace of the speed segments is only slightly faster than marathon goal pace. You're developing the capacity to maintain a moderate pace over a long distance. Compared with speed sessions for shorter distance racing goals, those for the marathon emphasize building endurance by

70

- running longer repetitions (usually mile repeats)

- increasing the number of repetitions: up to 8, 10 or 12 mile repeats (Faster marathons require more repetitions.)

LEARNING HOW TO PACE
YOURSELF

You'll gain a sense of pace at the same time you're developing the capacity to run mile after mile in the time you need. It's actually detrimental to run the mile repeats faster than your schedule prescribes (20 seconds faster than goal pace). If you exceed this speed limit, even in the beginning of the speed session, it becomes difficult for your internal pace clock to acquire the pace judgement needed in the marathon itself. A fast start will either leave you struggling at the end of the session or produce tired muscles which require a long recovery.

RECOVERY, RECOVERY, RECOVERY!

Finally, the need for recovery cannot be overemphasized. Because the long runs and the speed sessions are long and fatiguing, everything possible should be done to speed up this important process.

- Strict adherence to the pace of the speed repetitions to avoid going too fast

- Lots of walking as rest between each mile repeat—when in doubt, walk some more

- Enough easy days (and easy running) between the weekend sessions

HOW OFTEN?

To encourage the adaptations and improvements in form, rhythm, etc., speed sessions must be done regularly, that is, on most of the non-long weekends starting about 16 weeks before the marathon (see the schedules for specific frequency). By adding some other innovations to your program, such as tempo or pace runs during the week, you'll maintain and extend the faster running form and performance benefits gained from mile repeat sessions into all of your runs.

PICKING YOUR GOAL

The most important part of the speed development process is the very first step: picking a goal which is realistic for you. It's okay if your goal is slower than you are capable of currently running. This is a strategy which has led to many personal records. By setting yourself up for a performance that has some challenge but is realistic, you will take pressure off, stay in your right brain longer, and often achieve at a much higher level.

If your goal is too far ahead of your ability level, then you set yourself up for disappointment and fatigue. By overestimating your capacity, you'll force yourself to run the speed sessions too fast. You just won't recover between speed days and long runs.

Time-tested, realistic goal prediction:

1. Run at least three 5K races on non-long-run weekends.

2. Take two or three of your fastest ones and average them.

3. Chart your equivalent performance on a "predicting race performance chart."

[That chart can be located in the back of Galloway's Book On Running.]

You'll be fine-tuning your racing form and technique after you've run two or three 5K events. If the courses were hilly or the weather conditions were adverse, you may conservatively estimate the time you honestly believe you could run under better conditions. The prediction table in GBR gives equivalent performances for race distances, including the marathon, which have been very accurate.

What a great reality check! If your 5K performances don't predict the time you'd like, swallow your pride and select a less ambitious time goal. This means that you'll be slowing down the pace of the mile repeats and the early pace in the marathon.

Always be conservative in choosing your goal. If the 5K performances predict a 4:30 marathon, shoot for 4:40 or 4:45. It's always better to finish the marathon knowing that you could have run faster: you've already started the momentum and motivation to do it.

WARM-UP

Whatever speed play format you choose, get the blood flowing through the muscles in a gentle warm-up. This introduction to exercise allows the tendons, ligaments and muscles to warm up together and begin working as a team. A good warm-up will decrease the chance of injury and increase the intuitive cooperation of components within the muscles.

◆ Walk for 5-10 minutes.

◆ Jog VERY slowly for 5-10 minutes.

◆ Jog another 5-10 minutes at a comfortable pace.

◆ Do 4-8 acceleration-GLIDERS.

◆ Walk for 5 minutes.

STRETCHING

If you can't resist doing a gentle stretching routine before running, be very careful. Research has shown that stretching before running doesn't help you for that run, and it may increase your chance of injury. It's easy to overstretch a muscle that hasn't been engaged in much activity. This will leave the muscles tighter than before and more open to injury.

Don't make the most detrimental stretching mistake of trying to "loosen up" a tight muscle by stretching the heck out of it. A slow walk followed by very slow running and walking for 10 to 15 minutes will allow the muscles to relax and warm up better than any stretch routine. Tight muscles tell you that you need to ease off on them until they feel loose.

On these days some runners require three to five miles of super easy walk-running to warm up. As we age, we need more slow

71

warm-up distance at the beginning of every run. When it comes to the warm-up, slower is always better.

The best time for stretching is probably just before bedtime. If you must stretch before running, do so very gently. Above all, never push into a tense or tight muscle but maintain a relaxed extension.

[For more stretching information and specific stretches, see GBR, pp. 158-169.]

REPEAT MILE INTERVALS

The most popular form of marathon speed play is that of "interval training," used by world-class athletes for most of the 20th century. In this format, measured segments (repetitions) are run at a pace that is slightly faster than marathon goal pace, followed by a rest interval. This process is repeated many times. Shorter distance goal races, such as the 5K and 10K, use shorter repetitions of 400 to 800 meters. The longer repetitions, such as mile repeats, have been overwhelmingly the most successful distance in the Galloway program. Thousands have used mile repeats to improve their marathon times.

While 800-meter repetitions can give a significant training effect for the marathon, the mile distance helps to mold together the components of marathon form and exertion at one time.

LONGER REPETITIONS, SUCH AS THE MILE:

- force your legs and feet to find more efficient ways of running, by eliminating or significantly reducing extraneous motions and getting the most efficient "lift-off" from each step

- develop better pace judgment, teaching you not to start races (and speed play) too fast

- help the internal systems to work together and become more efficient: muscles, pacing, intuitive connections, and instinctive efficiency adjustments

- fine-tune the components of performance, such as energy sources to the muscle, waste removal, hidden resources to keep going, etc.

- develop the mental strength to continue running at a good pace even after fatigue sets in

- teach you when to keep going and when to stop to avoid damage

PACE OF REPEAT MILES

Each mile should be run about 20 seconds faster than you want to run in the race itself, followed by a walk of at least 400 meters. If you feel much more comfortable with shorter distance repetitions, go ahead with 800-meter or 1200-meter reps. Your pace on the shorter reps can be increased to an average of 25 to 30 seconds per mile faster than marathon goal pace. It's still better to do repeat miles or to alternate between miles and reps of shorter distance.

ADJUST FOR HEAT, HUMIDITY, ETC.

Even during the extreme heat of summer, you can continue doing speed sessions, but be careful. If you notice yourself or anyone in your group having symptoms of heat disease, stop the session and get medical attention immediately.

The best time of the day to do speed sessions on warm days is very early in the

72

morning, before the sun rises. Be advised, however, that when the temperature is above 65 degrees, you *must* run slower (and may also cut the distance of the reps to 800 or 1200 meters). Instead of 20 seconds faster per mile than goal pace, make adjustments as follows:

When the temperature is 65 degrees, run mile repeats 18 seconds per mile faster.

When the temperature is 70 degrees, run mile repeats 15 seconds per mile faster.

When the temperature is 75 degrees, run mile repeats 12 seconds per mile faster.

When the temperature is 80 degrees, run mile repeats 9 seconds per mile faster.

When the temperature is 82 degrees, run mile repeats 5 seconds per mile faster.

When the temperature is above 85 degrees, don't do the session; wait for a cooler time.

* Note: when you feel that there is any possibility of heat disease or a cardiovascular problem, abandon the exercise, cool off and get help.

WALK BETWEEN EACH MILE REPEAT

It is better to walk between the repetitions to minimize fatigue and recovery. Most runners should walk 400 to 600 meters between each of the repeat miles. Walk more if you feel the need. The extra walking will not reduce the training effect of the speed session. You receive the same conditioning from speed play of 8 x 1 mile with a 800-meter walk as you do from 8 x 1 mile with a 400-meter walk. If you have a heart rate monitor, keep walking until the heart rate goes below 70 percent of your maximum heart rate.

HOW MANY MILE REPEATS?

If you haven't done any speed play before, start with only one or two mile repeats. Veterans can begin with four to five repeats, and others can pick a starting number somewhere in between. On each session, increase the number of repetitions by one or two until you reach the upper limit for your respective goal:

Time Goal	# of Mile Repeats
4:01 and slower	6 x 1 mile
3:30-4 hours	8 x 1 mile
3:15-3:29	10 x 1 mile
3:00-3:14	12 x 1 mile
Below 3 hours	13 x 1 mile

73

PRACTICE *GLIDING* DURING EACH MILE

As you alternate between the prime running motion and your gliding motion, you'll save the muscles which do most of the work. The reduced demands of the gliding motion allow the main running muscles to regain a small amount of resiliency even as you are moving at a significant speed. By gliding early and often in speed sessions and in the marathon itself, you'll feel stronger at the end and will recover faster from each speed session. Most importantly, you'll develop the teamwork between muscles which will bestow great performance benefit in the marathon itself.

The gliders should be a natural part of your running, but be sure to start them within the first 500 meters of each mile rep. A glider of 50 to 100 meters, done about every 400 to 600 meters, is often enough to help you integrate gliding into your racing routine at the same time that it helps you fine-tune your running technique. Be sure to go back and re-read the section on acceleration-GLIDERS to reinforce the concept.

FARTLEK

Literally meaning "speed play," this free-form method of speed development can accomplish all of the objectives of interval training and add a mental strengthening component to your training. Used as a substitute for interval training or other speed play, fartlek is usually performed on non-long-run weekends instead of mile repeats.

+ The "speed" part of fartlek should equal the total distance equal to the number of mile repeats you would have done on the track, according to the time goal schedule you are following.

+ Make sure that you're resting the legs by walking between the speed segments.

+ By shifting back and forth between use of muscle groups, you'll develop greater performance capacity. For example, instead of running the same pace throughout a fartlek session, you can alternate between pace running, accelerations, gliding and speed-effort.

EXAMPLE:

The speed segments should be at least 3/4 mile long but give better marathon conditioning if they are one mile or longer (1600 to 3000 meters). Let's say that you choose a segment that is 1.2 miles long (about 2000 meters).

1. Start the segment at marathon pace.

2. Several times during the first .6 mile (1000 meters), put in some acceleration-gliders which would vary between 100 and 200 meters, each time going back to marathon pace. In other words, start at marathon pace, accelerate for 50 meters and glide for 50 to 100 meters, returning to marathon pace. Repeat this process two or three times.

3. From about .8 mile to 1.1 mile, shift into "speed effort" and pick up the pace to about 25 to 30 seconds per mile faster than marathon goal pace, and then glide during the last .1 mile.

4. Walk for three to five minutes between each fartlek session.

5. Four of these fartlek segments were done in place of a 6 x 1 mile marathon speed session.

6. The three other segments varied between 1.3 and 1.8 miles (2200-3000 meters).

FARTLEK RUNNING MODES:

+ marathon pace—running smooth and natural so that you feel comfortable at that pace

+ accelerations—picking up the turnover for a short distance, not spending much effort

+ gliders—relaxed and quick turnover motion which follows an acceleration with practically no effort expended

+ speed effort—picking up the turnover for a longer distance, running faster than goal pace. You'll spend some effort doing this, but try to stay smooth and comfortable for the duration of the pick-up.

MENTAL STRENGTH

The mental tenacity you receive from fartlek training is enhanced by not setting specific limits on where you'll end each segment, each acceleration, each glider, etc. By going beyond artificial barriers, you'll learn to intuitively coordinate the performance demands of the running body with available resources. In so doing, you reduce the chance of negative messages from the left brain when things get tough in speed sessions and in the race itself. You'll still get those "pings" from the left side, but they just won't bother you as much.

Fartlek desensitizes you to the discomfort and uncertainty of pushing, gliding and pacing beyond your current limits. As in other training components, fartlek must be done regularly to force the systems to work together, to coax out adaptations from the exercising muscle cells, and to develop the intuitive capacity to become more efficient in every way. By pushing through mental and physical barriers at the same time, you'll find yourself continuing to run when tired or uncertain. Fartlek develops a sense of focus and resource coordination not found in other forms of training.

[For more on fartlek, see Galloway's Book On Running and Return of the Tribes.]

TEMPO TRAINING—AT MARATHON GOAL PACE

During the week, time goal marathoners can run parts of the easier runs at marathon pace. As long as the legs, feet and cardio-vascular system have all recovered from the weekend's long or speed sessions, this race-pace running gives you a chance to lock into the exact cadence "clock" you need for your goal.

After a warmup, which includes a few

acceleration-gliders, run one to two miles at marathon pace. Your goal is to make marathon pace seem "normal." If the paces and effort levels of hill training and speed sessions are adjusted to your current ability (and you've recovered from the long or speed runs on the weekend), you should feel "at home" with marathon pace after a few repetitions.

Ease into each of these "marathon goal miles." As you get up to speed, you want to feel smooth and efficient at the pace you've chosen for the marathon. Even doing one or two of these every other day can help further your "pace education."

A walk of 400 to 800 meters between these "paced miles" (or a jog slow jog of 800 meters or more) should leave you completely recovered. It's important to remember that this is not supposed to be a stressful speed session: no significant effort required to do each mile and no significant fatigue afterward. If you're working hard to maintain your marathon pace in these sessions, jog for the rest of the session. This either means that you're just not ready for the chosen pace or you haven't recovered from the runs of the previous week.

TROUBLESHOOTING SPEED SESSION PROBLEMS

Q: *I can't finish a speed session*—my legs just can't keep going at the pace needed. What's wrong?

A: If you're having trouble maintaining pace on the mile repeats, there are several possibilities:

1. Your goal is too ambitious for your current fitness level—adjust to slower repetitions.

75

2. You went out too fast in the first part of the speed session—slow down in the beginning.

3. Fatigue from other sessions is still there—you need more rest days or easier rest days.

4. You need more rest between mile repeats—double the walking between each mile.

Q: *I feel great on the repeat mile sessions* and have no trouble running them 40 seconds per mile faster than my goal pace, *but my legs don't 'have it' in the marathon itself.* Won't running the mile repeats faster help me run faster in the marathon?

A: No! You're actually hurting yourself by running the mile repeats faster than your assigned time (20 seconds faster than goal pace). The 20-second pace increase will develop the performance capacity and the pace judgement which has a proven record of marathon success. The effort required to go faster than this can keep you tired for many days and compromise the other quality sessions in your program. Stick with the schedule for your best chance of success.

Q: *Between the mile repetitions, I've been jogging instead of walking* because I've heard that I'll get in better shape. Is this true?

A: No. By doing more walking between the hard repetitions, you won't lose any of the conditioning of that speed session. The extra rest during each repetition or speed segment will help the legs start recovering from that speed session while you're doing it. Walking between mile repeats performs the same function as walking breaks during the long run, keeping the running muscles from getting overextended. If you've been running at the pace that you *should have* on the mile repeats, liberal walking breaks in mile repeat sessions will allow you to recover within a day or two in most cases.

[For more on the practical aspects of speed play, see the "Mile Repeats" chapter.]

76

THE BLOOD SUGAR
EFFECT

"You don't look like you want to talk about anything....but especially responsibility," Suzi said as she greeted Tom at the door and walked him into her kitchen.

Tom laughed at Suzi's honesty: "I feel a bit worn out, but the speed clinic revived me....I guess."

Suzi: "You need a blood sugar boost. I stocked up on chocolate PowerBars and the strongest coffee....knowing you were coming over."

It took Tom less than two minutes to finish off the first PowerBar. As he doctored up the dark fluid in the mug which he called "Suzi's Strongest," Tom sat down on the couch and watched a nutrition videotape Suzi was currently playing on her recorder.

As Tom settled into the cozy couch, he leaned against Suzi, who moved slightly away from him, quickly explaining that she was playing the tape to refresh her memory about how nutrition and exercise work together. Tom listened to the first few minutes of the tape as he sipped the coffee and worked on his second PowerBar and said:

"You're into one of your fat-burning missions, I can see it in your eyes."

TEACHING THE MUSCLES TO BURN FAT

One of the most significant changes which occur as you get into better marathon shape is the adaptation of your exercising muscles to burn both stored sugar and fat. Those who are in poor physical condition will not be able to go very far without running out of energy:

- Untrained muscles are not conditioned to burn fat and must rely on glycogen for fuel.

- Unfortunately, the supply of this fuel is small and runs out quickly.

- Glycogen also produces a great amount of waste product, which slows you down.

By slowing down the exertion level, and mostly walking, beginners are better able to increase their endurance limits and teach the exercising muscles to burn fat. The long walks, and then the long walk-runs, are the most productive venue for this 'teaching' to occur.

THE BLOOD SUGAR CRASH

Have you ever felt hunger, accompanied by...

+ loss of concentration,

+ reduced desire to go on, or

+ a stream of negative messages to slow down, stop or choose another activity?

This is the effect of low blood sugar (LBS). The bad news is that even the most conditioned athletes will suffer this type of 'energy crisis' when covering more than about 15 miles. Beginners hit their blood sugar walls much sooner.

The good news is that you can counterattack. By eating a good, carbohydrate source before running and during the second half of a long run, you'll keep your spirits high and reduce the effect of the left brain messages coming from the blood sugar crisis center.

FUEL CHOICE: FAT OR SUGAR

Fuel for exercise can come from two sources:

+ Body fat (which must be broken down into a form that is usable by the muscle and delivered to the site of exertion)

+ Stored sugar (glycogen) which is readily available in the muscles

For the first 15 minutes of exercise, glycogen is burned as fat is broken down into free fatty acids and triglycerides. If we are trained enough to maintain the speed and the distance covered in that session, the muscle begins a transition into fat-burning. If we are still within our training range, we'll be burning almost exclusively fat after about 45 minutes.

+ training range: exercising at a pace and a distance that is within your current capabilities. Example: Your longest run in the past two weeks is eight miles, which you realistically estimate that you could run in 80 minutes. Your trained range would be 10-minute running pace when running up to eight miles.

If you're running slower than 10-minute pace for a distance less than eight miles, you would be within your training range. Therefore, after the first 15 minutes of exercise, your muscles would shift into fat-burning. After 45 minutes, most of the calories burned would be from fat.

IS THAT WHY I FEEL BAD WHEN I BEGIN EXERCISE?

Yes. Glycogen is an inefficient fuel, producing a significant waste product (mostly lactic acid). As it accumulates and tightens the muscle, you'll find it difficult to exercise. This is one reason why you don't feel good at the beginning of a run.

Here are some other factors which make the first part of exercise uncomfortable:

+ Muscles which are "cold" or at rest don't respond well to exercise until they become irrigated with blood.

+ Tendons and ligaments are also usually tight at the beginning and loosen up after 10 to 15 minutes.

+ Generally, as all of the systems get up to speed and work together, you feel better and run better.

HOW MUCH FAT CAN YOU BURN ON A LONG RUN?

Running burns about 100 calories per mile, with very little increase at a faster pace. When you run within your training range, you'll burn 100 calories of fat. If you increase the pace or the distance so that you're outside of your "range," the 100 calories will come, increasingly, from glycogen. By running significantly slower than your training range, you can go further and increase the total number of fat calories burned.

By slowing down your pace significantly, and inserting walk breaks, you'll be able to increase your distance beyond the training range and burn fat at the same time. Using the example above, if the runner slowed his or her pace to 12 or 13 minutes per mile, he or she would probably be able to run 11 to 12 miles before hitting an endurance wall and shifting back to sugar-burning.

In other words, faster running tires the muscles sooner so that you can't go as far in a session. It's the distance covered when you exercise which can significantly increase the fat burned.

Walk breaks will extend your training range more quickly, with only a slight decrease in fat calories burned per mile. Because you're able to go significantly further when you "walk-break," you're increasing fat-burning significantly. [For more information about how walk breaks influence calories burned per mile, see Return of the Tribes, p. 37.]

FAT IS THE PREFERRED FUEL

While the amount of glycogen is very limited, our supply of body fat is far greater than we could use. No offense intended here, but even a 140-pound man with one percent body fat has over 200 miles of fat fuel on board.

Fat is a clean-burning fuel. It leaves very little waste product from exercise, and this small amount can be easily taken care of by a fit exercising system (as long as you stay within training range).

Untrained muscles will burn glycogen, which is stored in the muscles, the liver and other areas. You want to do regular endurance training to increase fat-burning capacity because:

◆ Glycogen supply is limited;

◆ When glycogen is burned, it produces a high percentage of waste product; and

◆ The waste product builds up in the muscles and reduces their performance.

By doing some endurance exercise at least three days a week, you train the muscle cells to burn fat. To stay in the fat-burning zone, you need to:

◆ Exercise at an exertion level at which you're capable;

◆ Don't go more than a mile or two further than you've gone in the last two weeks; and

◆ Start each session very slowly.

Slow long runs train the muscle cells to become better fat-burners. The gradual increase in distance stimulates thousands of working muscle cells to improve fat-burning capacity over an increasing distance. By running extra slowly, and taking walk breaks, you'll stay within training range and burn fat longer.

79

TEACHING THE MUSCLE CELLS TO BURN MORE FAT....EVEN WHEN SLEEPING AT NIGHT

By increasing more of your runs to 45+ minutes, you'll encourage the muscle cells to burn fat as fuel continuously, not just when you exercise. Endurance-trained fat-burning cells will choose fat as their fuel when you're sitting around at the desk all day....*and even when sleeping at night.* As these thousands of little furnaces become efficient fat gobblers, they can become a major weapon in your personal "battle of the bulge." This extra "fat burning dividend" gives you some control over your body fat accumulation:

◆ Will you hold your weight this year or add five pounds?

◆ Will you take off eight pounds or stay the same?

Exercise regularity is crucial (at least three sessions of 45+ minutes each week) if you want to keep moving these muscle cells into the fat-burning column. The reduction of your "fat blanket" seems to be triggered by consistently engaging in sessions which

◆ elevate body temperature by exercising a great number of muscle cells

◆ maintain this increased temperature for significantly more than 45 minutes

◆ are done very regularly (every two days or at least three times a week)

INTAKE IS THE OTHER SIDE OF FAT REDUCTION

You'll find out later about how to limit fat accumulation by selection of foods and frequency of eating. To reduce the fat blanket and keep it off, both sides of the fat equation must be accounted for.

80

THE ENERGY CRISIS

Suzi moved to turn off the VCR and get on with the evening's discussion, but Tom stopped her. The speaker was moving into an area he had found to be increasingly more significant to him: the infamous "blood sugar letdown" after the age of 40.

Suzi politely listened for a while and leaned over toward Tom, who gave her a few more inches of "couch space." As the PowerSnack and the strong brew took hold, Tom became glued to the screen. He had been having some major concentration letdowns during long runs which he suspected might be related to the lowering of blood sugar.

WHAT IS THE BLOOD SUGAR LEVEL?

The level of sugar in your blood will determine how you feel: how well you will concentrate and how effectively you can deal with negative messages received from the left side of your brain. Most folks wake up with a blood sugar level which is stable and slightly low. Eating snacks which are loaded with sugar will elevate the blood sugar level (BSL) too high. Once BSL reaches a certain level, it triggers a secretion of insulin, lowering the BSL lower than it was originally. You'll feel hungry, sleepy and more lethargic than before.

The best counterattack is a snack providing a modest boost of the BSL and also providing some mechanism which can sustain this increase over a period of time. Certain foods or combinations of nutrients will produce this effect. In each case, it is better to choose low-fat foods (less than 10 percent of the total calories come from fat).

- Choose complex carbohydrates instead of sugar foods (simple carbs): baked potatoes, rice, low-fat breads, low-fat pasta (and their accompanying low-fat sauces and coverings).

- Soluble fiber in snacks like PowerBar will coat the lining of the stomach. This can keep the BSL from rising to the level that will trigger an insulin release, and it will slow down the release of sugars in the food over an extended period of time.

- Carbohydrate in combination with a modest amount of protein will stablize the BSL.

  Example: Two thick pieces of whole-grain bread, coated with mustard or no-fat cream cheese, with a very thin slice of low-fat turkey breast.

Low blood sugar produces a significant stress to your system, which will activate your left brain. Expect to hear a stream of things coming from that logical but negative source, such as "why are you doing this," "slow down and you'll feel better," "stop this exercise and you'll feel great." Relief is often a PowerBar or a bagel away!

MANY OF THE "MIDDLE-AGE CROWD" NOTICE BLOOD SUGAR LETDOWNS

Some look on it as another betrayal of the 35+ body, when they experience hypoglycemia or low blood sugar symptoms for the first time in their lives. Relax, this is a common occurence. More reassurance is the realization that you can do something about it. Older runners who have this LBS condition will need to ensure that they're eating often enough.

EATING CONSTANTLY, ALL DAY LONG

Your BSL is best maintained by eating a modest breakfast and then a series of small snacks all day long. By eating a small or modest amount, before you get hungry, you'll avoid the "starvation reflex" which leads to overeating.

Breakfast gives you a sustained feeling of well-being throughout the morning and reduces the chance of a significant drop in BSL. By eating low-fat snacks (such as pretzels, bagels, PowerBars) at the first sign of a slight hunger or BSL drop, you'll maintain energy, mental concentration and attitude. Without some breakfast, you'll probably get behind in the blood sugar war, staying hungry all day and overeating at some point.

You don't have to eat a big breakfast. By having a modest amount of fuel in the stomach (healthy snacks throughout the day and night), you've got a better chance to maintain a steady BSL, avoid hunger which leads to overeating, and maintain a good energy level.

Sample Breakfasts:

- 1-2 bagel(s), fat-free cream cheese, fruit

- 1-2 bowl(s) of cereal, skim milk, two pieces of toast with light jam

- 1 bowl of oatmeal or other hot cereal, two pieces of toast, juice

- 2 egg-substitute eggs (or 4 egg whites), toast or bagel, juice

- 4-8 ounces of fat-free yogurt, musli cereal, fruit cocktail, juice

THE STARVATION REFLEX

If you want to burn fat and/or maintain a good energy level, it's counterproductive to extend the time between snacks or meals. A blood sugar "debt" is often produced by waiting, causing you to go on an eating frenzy, which further increases fat accumulation:

- The longer you wait, the more you'll stimulate the fat-depositing enzymes

- So...more of your next meal will be deposited as fat on your body.

- The waiting period increases appetite, causing you to overeat later.

WAITING TOO LONG BETWEEN SNACKS WILL LOWER YOUR MOTIVATION

You may not feel like exercising in the afternoon because it's been too long since you've had a snack. As the time increases between significant snacks of food, your BSL drops and so does your motivation, concentration and attitude.

Galloway's Confessions
About Low Blood Sugar

During my first 60 marathons, I thought that low blood sugar was a 'given:' that I was going to crash with it when running more than 20 miles. Even on my best marathons I finished feeling exhausted, unmotivated, unable to concentrate very well, and very hungry but often nauseous. Assuming that a good nap would help revive the spirits, I'd often hit the bed or couch (or a good shade tree) and not eat a significant snack for several hours. Unfortunately, resting or sleeping never restored vitality, and I usually arose with more stiffness and an even lower blood sugar level.

Then I discovered PowerBars. By attacking the blood sugar condition before it got too low, I learned that you can not only feel good during the latter stages of a marathon, but you can also have a good attitude all evening.

There are many foods which will effectively boost the BSL. The 'secret' ingredient is soluble fiber which coats the stomach lining. This slows the absorption of sugars so that 1) the level doesn't get high enough to trigger an insulin reaction, and 2) you'll receive a steady stream of energy for an extended time.

The formula which has worked successfully for most of the Galloway program marathoners surveyed is as follows: the equivalent of a whole PowerBar about one hour before the marathon (with at least eight ounces of water) and then pieces (with water) of a second PowerBar starting just before the halfway point. You want to continue to eat these pieces until the end (with water) to maintain a stable and significant BSL.

During my past 40+ marathons, I've followed this formula. Yes, I've had several 26-mile jaunts when my legs crashed and I had to shuffle in. But thanks to the PowerBars, my spirits soared, and I felt great all evening.

83

INCREASING THE LONG RUN WILL HELP YOU MANAGE THE BLOOD SUGAR LEVEL (BSL)

By gradually increasing the length of your long run (with walking breaks), you'll push back the threshold of this blood sugar crash. As the muscles become better fat-burners, they make many adaptations which increase the efficiency of each use of glycogen. This reduces the quantity of glycogen needed for any use: long run, daily activity, etc. This means that there is more glycogen available to you later to maintain BSL at a higher level for a greater time and distance. It is most important that you run the long ones at least two minutes slower than you could run that same distance on that day.

As you extend your endurance barriers, you'll go further before experiencing the discomfort of LBS. Your energy system becomes increasingly "stingy" with the glycogen you have and delivers a better quality of fuel at the same time.

Long runs also stimulate the exercising muscles to store more glycogen. By the time you have increased your long one to 20 miles and more, you not only use less glycogen per mile, you'll have a greater deposit in your bank.

The significant improvement in the storage, shifting of supplies, and consumption of glycogen is a prime example of how the human organism is designed to improve when faced with a series of challenges. On each long run as you push further than you've gone before, you stress the limits of glycogen resources. This stimulates the systems to improve in every way to deliver better quality and quantity on your next long one. Further efficiencies in the use of glycogen are realized as you repeat this challenge in a series of long runs.

COUNTERATTACKING LOW BLOOD SUGAR (LBS) LEVEL ON LONG RUNS

84

Even if your BSL is ideal at the beginning of a run, it is certain to be dramatically reduced as you push your limits beyond 15 miles (and many runners experience the "crash" before this). Almost everyone will suffer low blood sugar at the end of these runs if he or she does not eat quality carbohydrate snacks before the start and during the second half of the long one.

BLOOD SUGAR BOOSTERS

Even the most conditioned marathoner will suffer a blood sugar crisis when he or she goes more than about 15 miles. The only way to win this battle and boost the BSL is to counterattack. Whether you use PowerBars or other foods, here are the principles which have led to blood sugar success:

1. Choose a food that is low in fat (less than 10 percent of the total calories of the food in fat) but which contains significant soluble fiber.

2. Most runners need 200 to 250 calories about an hour before the long run to keep the blood sugar level sustained until the halfway point (of a run beyond 15 miles).

3. If the food is a solid, like PowerBar, be sure to drink at least four ounces of water for every 100 calories of the food.

4. Cut the solid food up into small pieces for easier consumption during the second half of the long run.

5. Drink water with each piece.

6. Test your eating routine during long runs to find the right time sequence, quantity, etc. for you.

CHOOSING AND TESTING ENERGY FOOD

There are many foods advertised as sports energizers. As is found in all commercial products, some brands make inflated claims. First, determine what you need from the snack. Next, evaluate the possible products, with the help of knowledgeable running friends, sports nutritionists, or trustworthy running store staff.

Next, try several of these in long and short runs and choose one or two to fine-tune for the marathon itself. Use your chosen foods on as many runs as possible before using them in the marathon.

You and your digestive tract can learn to like just about anything. Don't give up on a food because it doesn't taste good at first or doesn't seem to work for you the first time. Take small amounts of the food with water at first. Over time, you can increase the amount of the food as your systems learn to digest and use it.

ENERGY-BOOSTING CHOICES

♦ High carbohydrate foods with soluble fiber (PowerBar and related products)

Supplying a moderate boost of energy, these products usually deliver a good BSL for an extended period. Be sure to check the label of the product you choose to ensure that it is low in fat (fat calories are less than 10 percent total calories). Eat a portion about one hour before the run and pieces of the product throughout the second half of the run—always with water.

♦ High carbohydrate "goos"

These thick-but-sweet products have the consistency of paste. They usually deliver a stronger BSL boost at first, which wears off after several minutes. Read and follow the directions on the package, and try them out in training runs extensively. Because they are somewhat liquid, they get into the blood stream quicker than the "bar" products, but it is still wise to take water with each packet, if available. Once you start taking these, you must continue consuming them until the end of the run to avoid blood sugar letdown.

♦ Fluids with sugar (mostly electrolyte beverages)

While these can be an excellent fluid replacement before and after training runs, the electrolyte beverages tend to send the BSL into a rollercoaster ride when taken in the marathon itself. Without a substance such as soluble fiber to slow down the absorption of the sugar (and maintain the level), you can easily encourage an insulin reaction by drinking them regularly. If you are desperate and feel the need to drink some of these products, dilute them with water.

♦ Concentrated carbohydrate fuels

There are several fluids on the market which offer a great amount of carbohydrate in a small bottle. Similar to syrup, these fluids take a while to digest and require fluid from your body to do so. As they will tend to dehydrate you, they are not recommended for drinking either the day before, the morning before, or during the marathon itself (or during comparable times in training runs). Their concentration will often cause fat accumulation:

the fluid goes so quickly through your digestive system that you're hungry before you've had a chance to burn off the significant number of calories.

♦ Hard Candies, etc.

One of the most reliable "boosters" is the inexpensive, little hard candies. Each one of these supplies so few total calories that insulin response is unlikely. If you start eating one about every mile during the second half of the marathon, you will gain some BSL boost.

It's always better to drink water at every stop when taking these candies. In addition, a pre-marathon snack of quality carbohydrate is recommended to maintain BSL until the halfway, hard candy boosters. As they have no soluble fiber, keep taking them. Unlike the "bar" products, sugar candies don't provide a longlasting boost.

Look at the fat content of any exercise snack—and energy bars specifically. It is recommended that you choose bars in which the fat calories comprise less than 10 percent of the total calories. The more fat, the longer it takes for them to be digested, and the more likely it will be that the food will give you a lethargic reaction instead of an energetic one.

85

Suzi was beginning to fade and leaned a weary head on the couch in Tom's direction to show it. Tom was assimilating the ideas from the videotape, was definitely 'revved up' by caffeine and PowerBar and seemed to ignore her fatigue behaviors. He turned off the VCR tape, which was shifting to another speaker.

Tom: "That's a good presentation...I've never seen it."

Suzi (mumbling): "Your ex-sweetie was the speaker....and you haven't watched it?"

Tom: "Yea, you know, she called the other day mentioning that she'd taped this segment for a Galloway program videotape. I nearly fell out of the chair when she said that she's joining the marathon program. She used to put me down about its being so....*extreme*."

86 Suzi (waking a bit): "What did she want?"

Tom: "It was strange for her focused mind....she just wanted to talk."

Suzi (standing up): "This sounds like she's making another run at you."

Tom stood up and looked at Suzi, sensing a type of energy he hadn't noticed before, which attracted him. Without thinking, he put his arms around her. She resisted and wiggled away.

Tom: "I don't know why...but you're....very interesting."

Suzi: "You came over to talk about responsibility...."

Tom: "You *would* get back to business."

Suzi: "Maybe I feel too much ....'responsibility.' I know it gets in the way of things...."

Tom: "And that's possibly one reason why you've got my interest...."

They both agreed that the morning would be a better time for talking over Suzi's role in Tom's corporate project. Suzi offered her couch for the night, and Tom accepted. After giving him a blanket and pillow, Suzi retired. As she turned off the light in her room, Tom noticed that her door wasn't quite closed.

THE INSPIRATION OF THE MARATHON
.....AND THE GROUP

*L*aura had a sly smile on her face as she spotted Suzi standing in front of the Sandy Springs Phidippides store. "Okay, Suzi, what happened last night?"

Suzi was just starting to say "Well, he...." when a car drove up and Sam got out of the car. The driver's window lowered, revealing Bonnie:

"Hey, y'all, this is a drive-by jogger drop. You know I would have been out here, getting sweaty and all that, but the turnip truck is due in our neighborhood any minute, and I don't want Elvira down the street to get the pick of the pile."

Laura told Suzi and Sam how well Bonnie was doing in Fitness 101: that she was already covering three miles with the lead group.

Bonnie: "No big deal....just a bunch of us walking and jabbering. I can jabber with the rest of 'em."

Just as the marathon program director asked everyone to gather around, the smile came off Laura's face, and she whispered to Suzi that she was too nervous, that this didn't seem right. Sam overheard her concern and whispered that he felt the same way. Suzi told them that this was only a case of "pre-game jitters." Captain Suzi put them "under orders" to listen to the speaker and then talk it over. Afterwards, each could decide to join a group for the easy run or go home. The sly smile came back on Laura's face, and the director started explaining the reasons for dividing into pace groups.

MT. EVEREST....BUT IN YOUR BACK YARD

Most of us know that we should be doing more exercise, but we don't. Unfortunately, the left side of our brain needs specifics and drives us into challenges that can be quantified. Well-meaning runners get caught up in the quest for faster times, more races, and age group prizes in themselves. Burnout is often the result when a competitor doesn't get beyond the physical rewards.

In contrast, most of those who complete a group support marathon training program win no age awards and often don't remember their finishing time. Each is initially

87

engaged by the significant challenge, the anticipated bragging rights, and the widespread respect given to marathon finishers by the general population.

"If I can finish that marathon, I will have shown myself—and the world—that I've still got it. No, that I'm better than ever!"

For many of the same reasons, middle-aged searchers have trekked up Mt. Everest. The marathon can be your mountain, and your daily and weekly runs part of the journey to the top. I've seen how marathon training bestows a glow of inner satisfaction very similar to that of standing on a peak in the Himilayas. But it does so much more than that: it leaves one with lifestyle behaviors which can lead to positive changes in many areas of life. A series of wonderful inner rewards open up as you find a lot more fortitude inside than you may have imagined was there.

BONDING WITH OTHERS...
AND SELF

You will soon choose a pace group based upon your current ability level. Together, your "team" of fitness equals will share the challenges, the struggles, and the exhilarations. As a unit, no one will go through a tough day without being bolstered by the others. All will experience the uplifting successes of each. As you give support to others, you'll receive more in return.

Most of you will cross the marathon finish line six months from now with a sense of satisfaction which cannot be described. While we've always had the potential for developing more self discipline, focus, and a capacity for pushing through adversity, the marathon scares us...in a positive way. The touch of uncertainty energizes our inner resources, opening up a steady stream of motivation and attitude enhancement.

Many lifelong friendships are molded here. You'll receive help on some outings and give support on others. You'll learn more about the others in your group than you may want to know. And you'll give strength to others without realizing it. Everyone becomes a real person here, and everyone improves in often unnoticed dimensions.

AN ELITE GROUP

Less than one tenth of one per cent of the population is capable of finishing a marathon. With the help of group energy and support and the gradual progression, you don't realize that you're moving up to this level. As you push through the struggle and share this with your "team," each member earns respect from one another. Most significantly, you'll enhance the inner network of respect for yourself.

FUN

Your primary mission is to have some fun during each run. I'm not saying that every step is wonderful or every hill bestows joy. But as you exchange jokes and stories and let the chemistry of your personalities create a unique group identity, the fun will emerge. At first, you may have to search for it and use your imagination. Soon you'll enjoy a continuous stream of very short but very significant moments of gutteral humor which bring the marathon experience to life.

Try to bring with you each week 1) a joke, 2) an interesting story or news item, and 3) a bit of gossip (just scan the quality publications as you go through the supermarket checkout line). Giving funny awards, meeting for pancakes or bagels afterward, and spontaneous horseplay....all promote the atmosphere which reinforces these positive lifestyle habits.

88

THIS IS *YOUR* PROGRAM

Everyone freely offers a special spark of their unique energy to bring fun and exercise together. The more you put into it, the more you'll get out of it. You'll want to give support when your teammates are having a bad day, and you'll feel surrounded by it when you're in need. You'll make a few phone calls to keep the group together. And each group is expected to supply the water for the large group in turn. As you work together to do all of these, the bonding increases. The effect one receives from this group bonding is far greater than the sum of individual experiences.

GROUP LEADER (GL)

Your leader is a volunteer and needs your help. He or she will be spending extra time to coordinate some of the activities, keep you together and provide some inspiration. Each of you will be pitching in a little to ensure that things go smoothly. The GL's main task is to hold you back so that you'll recover faster and the group can stay together. Above all, don't argue when asked to slow down and stay together....even if it's a bad hair day or your blood sugar is low.

THERE WILL BE SOME ADJUSTING DURING THE FIRST FEW WEEKS

During the first few weeks the groups will be a bit fluid, and some of you will want to move up or down. Please take the advice of your group leader if he or she suggests that another group's pace would be more comfortable for you. The first group priority is that everyone feel comfortable so that the "team" can stay together. Some team members will be faster than others and must take the responsibility to slow down.

Running slower doesn't take any of the conditioning away from the run: you get the same endurance based on the distance, *not the speed*. Running at a slower speed will enhance recovery....so, slow down. If you have questions whether you're in the right group, just ask your GL. The best time to change groups is during the first three weeks, but it's also fine to change after that.

BE SURE TO USE YOUR LOGBOOK

As you fill in the pages of your running log, you'll be writing your "Autobiography of the Marathoner." The anticipation of making an entry in the book can motivate you to get out the door on a tough day. Analysis of your "book" can tell you if you're overtraining or the day when a "problem" became a *problem*.

The more data you record, the better you can analyze the early warning signs and possibly back off before a serious injury develops. Note any irregular feelings, aches, pains, heartrate, etc. You can also make brief notes about feelings, positive experiences, etc.

THE VICTORY CELEBRATION

Count on getting together for a great evening....about 10 to 18 days after the winding down of "marathon season." This will be an exuberant evening of rewards and war stories (some of them being true). Over 99 percent of those who go through the program are victorious in completing the marathon—even those of you who are doing little or no running now.

During your group runs, you'll enjoy the stories which individuals tell about themselves, their bosses, etc. There will be a number of humorous happenings which occur on these outings. Whether you use your logbook or other notes, keep track so that the recounting of your year can be full of fun with the flavor of the "moments" along the way.

GROUP RULES

1. Help your group leader by sharing the load.

2. You should be able to talk continuously: No significant huffing and puffing!

3. Take walk breaks early and often. When in doubt, run slower and take more walk breaks.

4. If you're feeling tired, tell the GL so that the pace can be reduced.

5. When you're feeling great, slow down and stay with the group—don't pull them ahead.

6. Your safety is your responsibility. Don't assume that others are looking out for you.

7. Your health is your responsibility. Get checked out by a doctor who knows about endurance exercise; confer with him or her when needed. Get help before medical problems occur.

8. Wear your official shirt on every long one.

9. Drink water all the time (until you hear sloshing in your stomach).

10. Don't add to the schedule.

11. Make it fun...and everything else can come.

After questions, the Program Director (PD) had each group leader take a specific position around the room. Groups were set up, based upon fitness level. Before the groups took off, the PD had one more word of wisdom:

"There will be a reward for the group with the best nickname. By the way, you're not allowed to identify your group by specific pace. During the first few weeks we want the groups to develop a sense of bonding based upon the personality of their group and a general common fitness level. We don't want any group to lock into any desired pace because that will vary from week to week depending upon weather, group togetherness, etc."

"We've got a treat for you when you return. Rita Brown will introduce you to world of marathon rehearsal. She'll take you through a mental tour of your goal so that you can start your mental training program. Be sure to take it easy so that you'll have as good a mental training session as you will a physical one."

Crazy Jim had arrived late and slipped into Suzi's group, as inconspicuously as possible for one clad in a brand new lime green, black, and international orange warm-up. In one sentence he told Suzi that 1) he'd discovered a great discount sports store, 2) he hadn't run during the past week, 3) he was going to let her be his pace guide on this run because of his lapse in conditioning, and 4) he would move up on future runs with those who shared his more advanced athletic ability.

Three minutes into the run, Jim saw a lawyer chum two groups ahead and took off to talk with him.

90

THE POWER OF REHEARSAL

A s Suzi headed down the final straightaway back to the store, Laura was saying how confident she felt about exercise. "I can't believe how insecure I felt

before the start of this run and how great I feel now." There were two women and two men jogging and walking nearby who agreed and were so pleased to be finishing three miles for the first time in their lives....with no aches or pains.

All were looking forward to the mental rehearsal session when they returned to the store. "The woman who's presenting this has worked with groups of all kinds, including NASA's astronauts. She's particularly involved in marathon rehearsals and has run 25 marathons herself."

Just before they reached the driveway to

Phidippides, they caught Crazy Jim who was limping. Back at the store, Jim shocked everyone as he took off his shoe. There were at least five broken and bloody blisters. The store manager asked Jim where he'd gotten that shoe, that it was a relic. The company had made a manufacturing mistake with a few models and had off-loaded them at discount stores. Jim almost looked embarassed as he admitted that *that* was where he had gotten them. "But I got them at half price." To his credit, Jim started talking with the manager about a shoe that would work for his foot...in the running motion.

REHEARSAL RITA BEGINS

We're going to take a mental tour of the marathon. By doing this over and over again, you'll develop a confidence in finishing which is similar to that of veteran marathoners. Even more significant, you'll be gradually adding realistic details and situations to positively overcome the physical and mental challenge experiences of the marathon. This mental *conditioning* will make you tougher and will build the specific confidence needed to confront the same problems in the 26-miler itself. Your long runs help you to 'desensitize' to most or all of the possible items which *could* go wrong. You can then anticipate and find solutions or inner strength to get the job done.

PRINCIPLES OF MENTAL REHEARSAL

◆ Break down the experience into a series of small events:

1. None of which is challenging in itself.

2. Each of which leads directly and automatically to the next.

◆ Desensitize yourself to the uncomfortable parts:

1. By mentally experiencing them, they aren't as bad when you *run* into them.

2. The more you rehearse problems, the more solutions you may find for them.

3. When you mentally "tough it out" in rehearsal, over and over, it's easier to "gut it out" in the marathon itself.

◆ Rehearse every possible "problem" you could have in the marathon itself:

1. When in doubt, rehearse it—it's better to be prepared for anything.

2. Rehearse each to be worse than you expect it to be in the marathon.

   - Problems which are less intense than rehearsed are less likely to engage the negative left side of the brain.

◆ Rehearse often!

1. Rehearse parts of the marathon every day.

2. Concentrate on those aspects which make you the most apprehensive.

3. Go through each segment, dealing with each problem and getting through it.

4. Mentally, you can find several solutions to the same problem.

5. At least once a week, do at least a quick mental rehearsal of the marathon, as we are doing now.

THE MENTAL MARATHON....
STEP BY STEP

First, let's talk through the night before. You've had a full day of walking around the expo,

◆ drinking four to six ounces of water each hour,

◆ snacking on PowerBars and other low-fat (low-salt) snacks all day and all evening, and

◆ sharing good experiences with friends and with other marathoners from around the country.

Now that it's bedtime...what's going through your mind?

"I'm not going to sleep a wink."

"It's going to be rough tomorrow."

"What have I gotten myself into?"

Yes, all of these are legitimate questions which will come....and pass through. These negative thoughts will come from your left brain, which is programmed to respond to stress. The more you frame the marathon as a stressful experience, the more negative messages you'll receive. But it's just as easy to frame it as a positively challenging journey.

When the Left Brain Bothers You.....

*Diffuse the stress by saying that you're **not** going to push yourself:*

- Its going to be a walk
- You have all the time in the world to finish
- This is your day to smell the roses

Focus on the positive effect of your marathon experience:

- How you feel more invigorated
- The training has improved your attitude
- Your focus is better
- You're positive because you're doing something very positive for yourself

Gain a vision of yourself crossing the finish line:

- Sure you're tired but satisfied
- The sense of accomplishment is unlike anything you've ever experienced
- You've found new sources of strength inside
- The medal around your neck symbolizes all of this—bestows a wonderful glow

Walk around or jog around:

- The forward motion creates positive momentum

- Your body is designed for forward motion and responds positively when you move
- Natural endorphins relax you and settle you down
- This gets the right brain connected to the body, allowing you to bypass the left brain

Tell a joke:

- Laughing helps to engage the right brain
- It bestows a gutteral confidence
- Collect a few funny thoughts and jokes which you can call up with a key word
- Even if you tell it to yourself, learn how to laugh with yourself

Have a number of positive success stories:

- The best ones are the many little successes you've had in marathon training
- You can also draw from the success stories of others
- Trade stories with the runners around you
- Positive behavioral experiences build a positive attitude and inspire positive behavior

93

THE BATTLE: LEFT BRAIN VS RIGHT BRAIN

- An inner-brain conflict will occur every time you put yourself to the challenge.

- The left side has a million logical reasons why you can't do something.

- The right side won't try to argue; it will just try to get the job done using its unlimited supply of creative, spontaneous and imaginative ways of steering you in the direction of that which you are capable.

- In most cases, it's easy to get out of left brain control by relaxing, taking the pressure off yourself, and engaging in a right brain activity, such as laughing, story-telling, or low-level physical activity (walking, for example).

Okay, now, how about some positive thoughts about the marathon?

"Knowing it's over."

"Having my psychiatrist tell me that I'm okay—even if I want to do a marathon."

"The satisfaction of finishing with the medal around my neck."

On the first two, your left brain is still in control. Now the medal....the medal around the neck...That's the bottom line! Let's start there—you're wearing *your* medal! Sure, there are aches and pains, but overpowering it all is the feeling of accomplishment and personal satisfaction. This is a significant achievement which you did with your own resources. You had to pull from the various sources of your inner strengths and you did. No one can ever take this achievement away.

This glow will color every other part of the experience. When you start to feel unequal to the task, you'll come back to this very powerful inner feeling which you receive from finishing.

94

THE NIGHT BEFORE

Yes, you're nervous, but it's normal to feel this way. You've got everything laid out for the morning according to your checklist [see the Resources]. You may be so nervous that you won't sleep at all. That's also okay because you don't need to sleep the night before a marathon. The crucial nights are the two before the last one. Sleep deprivation may be a good thing when it's limited to the night before the marathon. Many marathoners, including some world-class performers, have run their best times after a sleepless night. The important concept is that lack of sleep is not going to bother you. In other words, it's not the lack of sleep, it's the worrying about not sleeping the night before which will engage the left brain and produce negative messages.

So you're resting, thinking about all of the things that are about to happen to you. You may decide to read or you may just lie there resting. If it's an out of town marathon, be sure to bring a magazine, book or something which can keep your interest in those hours of darkness. Positive, interesting concepts or stories are best, but anything that has worked in the past is fine. I bring along the newspapers which pile up on my doorstep between trips.

WAKE-UP CALL

You're motivated to get going and begin a water-drinking routine: four to six ounces every half hour. As you collect the items on your checklist (see Resources), you develop a vision of the positive, successful feeling you're going to have with the medal around your neck. When the negative side of your brain, the left side, starts to send negative messages, think of the medal around your neck and move into some productive activity.

THE LINE UP

Hopefully, you'll be connecting with friends as you go to the start. It helps to know, in advance, about the area of the start, how you'll get there, the problems, etc. In New York City, for example, you must board a bus quite early and sit under a tent for several hours. At the Marine Corps Marathon, you will be walking or taking the Metro to the start, in all probability, and it's a fairly long walk.

You're joking with friends or folks as you walk to your starting position and wait for the gun. You've spent a little time preparing for this with some interesting stories and jokes, which you will be sharing. As you're laughing, you realize that the left brain is kept under control and can't unload many negative thoughts.

Trying to overwhelm the left brain with distracting left-brain activity: *it doesn't work*

Some folks try to counter the negative left brain activity with logical challenges. For example, to counter the message "This marathon is going to hurt," some will mentally work on a math problem or construct some business situation or analytical exercise.

While this may distract your left brain for a while, it keeps you under its control. It is only a matter of time until a major or continuous stress wave will overwhelm this temporary distraction. When your stream of mental messages is hooked to the left hemisphere, you'll tend to get increasingly more persistent messages of a negative nature.

The greatest drawback of this approach is that you lose the intuitive capacity to reach toward that which you are capable. By shifting into the right side, you have the opportunity to search for hidden strengths and find spontaneous motivation, inspiration and even entertainment which you didn't know were there.

Jeff Galloway has several sentences which I've started using. The themes carry throughout the marathon and go like this: "I feel relaxed and ready to glide. I've got plenty of power." When you receive even the hint of a left brain message, squelch it with a positive behavorial thought and take a few jogging steps—reinforcing those thoughts.

I love this lesson more than my other sessions because I got hooked on marathons three years ago, when I was literally 'running away' from stress. Unlike other stress avoidance methods I've used, this one really worked as I've used it to shift from an unhappy homemaker and secretary to a single mom, professional counselor and runner.

Probably the greatest benefit you'll receive from rehearsal is the opportunity to mold your experience in advance so that you know how you'll react to a series of possibilities. Each long run teaches you a few more problems, unrehearsed situations and rough edges which must be refined and molded into the next rehearsal: it gets better and better in addressing your own needs and anxieties.

By including more and more challenges into your rehearsal, you'll leave few unexpected situations which could jolt you into the left brain. Be sure to be creative as you're being realistic. For example, you can anticipate having interesting conversations with people from all over the U.S. (or the world). The more positive and realistic your rehearsals, the more receptive you'll be to meaningful occurrences in the marathon itself.

95

THE START

You begin to get uneasy when the announcer calls everyone to the start. But as you share energy with the people around you, tell jokes, or mentally revisit some very successful experiences, you're feeling comfortable and secure. The gun fires and you gently move with the people around you. You're all in this together, moving forward towards a positive goal. It's a mass migration in which you're destined to triumph!

At times, you'll be tempted to go faster to express a few hidden, competitive urges (which you may not know you have). But you hold back. Realizing that there is plenty of time and distance to run the pace you wish, the first few congested miles don't bother you as you continue to go with the flow. Several times you find yourself feeling good and starting to run faster than you know you're ready to run so you return to a realistic pace (or better, a conservative one).

You're tempted to not take the first few walking breaks, pushed forward by your left brain ego. But at each place for a walk break, you walk. As people go by, and you're tempted to cut the break short, you resist the temptation. Soon you're into the flow of the breaks—mentally segmenting the distance.

If the left brain tries to insert a stress message about how far you have left to the finish, you immediately focus on your next walk break, saying out loud 'just ____ more minutes' (fill in the number of minutes you'll run before walking).

Many of you will be walking a minute every mile. After a few miles you'll make it a game to focus on a few individuals who are running at your desired pace. You follow them with your eyes as they get ahead on walk breaks, and you playfully catch up with them by the end of each running segment. By the 15-mile point, you'll have to choose another set of people because your original group has dropped off the pace by running continuously.

CHALLENGES

It is better to know the course you will be running (see the specific course descriptions in the race flyers). But if you're unsure of exactly which course you'll be running, you can rehearse a generic marathon. It's even better to over-rehearse the challenges; if you're prepared for a more difficult experience, then a less demanding one won't engage the left brain as much.

Hills present a variety of challenges. In the early stages, you may have a tendency to run a bit too hard going up so you hold yourself back. When you reach a difficult uphill, a slight shortening of the stride will relax the legs again and keep you moving with strength. When hills get difficult later on, you continue to shorten the stride, even as short as tiny 'baby steps,' if needed. This allows you to keep moving and get the job done. It's always better to rehearse hills that are longer, steeper and more frequent than those actually on the course. If you over-rehearse the difficulty of the last six miles of the marathon, you'll be in a better position to enjoy the end of the marathon itself.

The most significant challenges will come during the last six miles when the left brain is going to be activitated by a variety of stresses: fatigue, blisters, aches, fatigue, low blood sugar, dehydration, *fatigue*. Your greatest enemy at any point in the marathon is not the stresses or even the negative left brain messages which are generated by them: It's the internal doubt which your left brain promotes and upon which it feeds. By focusing on magic words and phrases which feature your past successes (See section on "Magic Marathon Words" in this book and "Mind Power" in Return of the Tribes), you'll have a great tendency to ignore the alarmist negativism and earn your success.

GUTTING IT OUT

Most of the problems, insecurities, and resulting negative messages can be managed and overcome by digging down a little deeper into your reservoir of intestinal fortitude. This source of strength comes directly from your spirit, which has the capacity to continuously generate positive momentum. By rehearsing yourself through these low points, you not only become stronger but also you develop the intuitive paths which can connect you to these

96

Discriminating Between a Real Problem and a Left Brain Trick

The left brain tries to protect you by sending a stream of negative messages designed to hold you back, to slow you down, and to stop you. The more stress you're under, the more negative messages you'll receive. In the beginning, most are the result of psychological stress... anticipations and fantasy stress. Towards the end, the left side is activated by real experiences: fatigue, more physical stress and internal discomfort. Mental rehearsal can desensitize you to these negative messages and reduce their effect upon you. That's why it's beneficial to rehearse every possible problem you could have, over and over again.

But the real problems must be confronted: injury, heat disease, respiratory infection, etc. You must continuously evaluate an injury, for example, and decide whether running a marathon will cause you to stop running afterward, for many weeks or months of healing. It's always better to take some extra time off at the first sign of an injury, get the repair process started, and do another marathon later...if that is the only option.

Your instincts are usually pretty good when it comes to heat disease and respiratory infection. These are serious health problems and should be avoided at all costs. If there is any chance that you have a virus, etc., which has gone into your lungs, do not run. When you feel any of the signs of heat disease (clammy skin, hot and cold flashes, loss of concentration, etc.), stop and get help. Be sure to read the section in the Resources on this subject.

While you can 'gut it out' through uncertainty and physical discomfort, it's never a good idea to try to 'bluff your way through' heat disease or respiratory infection. Always be more conservative and delay your marathon if needed.

Also, be aware that your left brain has another personality—it can push you beyond your limits. You 'type A' runners are particularly at risk, as are those with time goals. When you've set yourself up for a performance which is too ambitious for that day, the left brain can sometimes take you out too fast in the beginning.

Your instincts are usually the best. One of the great strengths of running is that it teaches you to use and listen to the intuitive, gut messages, for they are almost always correct. Just as you shouldn't let the left side hold you back at the end, when you're intuitively capable, don't let it call you a 'wimp' because you're holding back due to internal problems.

97

resources in the future: for fitness, work, personal challenges, and other areas of life.

ON TO THE FINISH

And so we end where we began. The positive flow of energy toward the finish line is your destiny, pulling you past the challenges, through the doubts, and out of the depths of uncertainty itself. You've done this yourself, and you've developed a lot more than physical capabilities along the way. That medal symbolizes a significant internal journey which has unlocked treasures that will continue to enrich you.

IN ONE YEAR...

*S*uzi and Sam were struggling with choices as they made their way through the cafeteria line at Georgia International University. After putting back about 10 items and picking up three more, Suzi settled upon a Greek salad and mini loaf of French bread. Sam just kept accumulating vegetables as he progressed through the line and then mentioned to Suzi that he ate too much bread when he was in Greece and needed to lose some weight.

Suzi started to tell Sam that it wasn't the bread that caused him to gain weight, but the feta cheese and the olive oil; but after Sam's next statement, she realized that he was joking with her.

Sam: "You mean that my momma wasn't right when she told me that dipping my food in oil let it slide through without my body getting the calories?"

Suzi: "It may slide through, but your body (not your mind) will be expanded by the experience."

Sam and Suzi talked about how their lives had changed in a year. Now that he was managing his own research institute, Sam reported, he'd discovered that the added responsibilities had taken away all of his "free time" at work, that he had to quickly move from one aspect of the business to the next...and regretted being so "businesslike." He also missed the chance to talk to his staff about what they were doing in other than work activities.

Suzi: "But a business has to stay in business. Your first obligation to yourself, your company, the NSF, and other funding groups is to make it work. You are your company. If

you don't make it happen, your employees don't have a job."

Sam explained that he had always been the originator of the research. Before separation from the university, a staff person stayed in touch with the NSF, kept the financial data on track, and managed the staff. On top of that, Sam now had to spend chunks of time traveling, doing public relations, and projecting the institute ahead one, three and five years.

Sam: "The marathon program has already helped. By going into this expanded, endurance world every week with my group,

I feel that my 'sense of direction' has been restored. When I dropped out of exercise last fall in Greece, I felt my mental focus slip a little bit, every couple of weeks. What is most gratifying is that in only four weeks of renewed exercise, I feel the return of those benefits which took me three months to receive when getting ready for the Peachtree 10K.

"It's also helped me mentally to envision my group members as the messenger organization ....the focus of my research. The ancient coaches debated whether messengers should stay active all year or not. The number of messengers needed during the winter months was much less and so half of them returned to their home towns, stopped exercise, got fat, and did little or no productive work. The other half continued to run and put the continued energy into other enterprises which often led to their real career path. While I know from my research that humans were born to run and that we directly enhance all positive aspects of our existence when we exercise regularly, I'm only starting to feel 'at home' with it as I go beyond an hour on most of my marathon outings.

"But I wanted to thank you for encouraging Bonnie," Sam continued. "More than anyone, your comments in that group support session at the bagel shop really helped her. I also believe that her involvement is helping us to work out problems in our marriage."

Suzi was most surprised that Sam was talking about his problems with her. She interpreted this as a sign of improved self-confidence which he was receiving from his group and the exercise itself. Sam explained that he and Bonnie had increasingly taken each other for granted and had not confronted the individual changes which happen so gradually over two decades. To bring the problem into focus, Bonnie

resented the Peachtree training program Sam had joined last spring with Tom and Suzi. At the same time that Bonnie was trying to find some self-respect in home and kid-managing, she saw Sam gaining confidence and growing. Of course, the other stresses in his career changes increased her anxiety and negativism.

"Have any of the issues become clearer?" asked Suzi.

Sam: "It didn't seem so at the time, but the very fact that she was lashing at me for being 'different' was getting some emotion out in the open—for the first time in years. As she criticized and I responded, we started to re-establish an honest and direct communication which two young people began over two decades ago. We're still on different clouds...but we're talking."

Suzi: "How did she get interested in Fitness 101?"

99

Sam: "I knew better than to suggest it. A few of the statements you made in that bagel session hit home. Then she saw that the others in the class were about her age, about her weight, about her fitness level (zero)."

"Keep talking with Bonnie, Sam."

Suzi had to go, but she wanted to see some of Sam's research and his new office. So they did.

THE MARATHON SHUFFLE

s they walked back to his office, Sam explained to Suzi that he was currently translating from ancient Greek manuscripts found at the site of a training school for ancient messengers—recently discovered just East of Athens in Vouliagmeni, Greece. When Suzi looked over the first 10 pages in English, she was impressed that the ancients had organized their ideas into a textbook.

Suzi: "Look, here's a section on running form!"

Sam said that the Greek messengers were taught to stay low to the ground, to shuffle. "The teaching environment was very similar to the seminars during our marathon program: sessions were mostly outside and included a short lesson of concepts, brief practice, questions and answers, and more practice."

With some prodding, Sam explained the concepts in the text. "These people were superb athletes, often covering 30 miles between breakfast and lunch to deliver a message. After a few vegetables, maybe even a Greek salad, they returned with the reply before nightfall. They had to be efficient. Messengers were trained to run upright, keeping their heads directly in a line with the shoulders, the hips and feet. Above all, messengers learned to keep their feet close to the ground.

"The instructor in this text tells messengers to run as if they were sliding over the surface. The feet are to be so sensitive to the terrain that messengers could tell when they

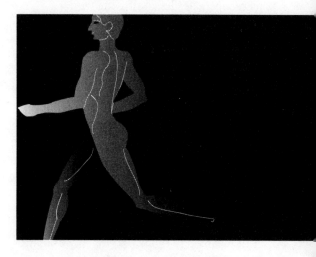

struck a pebble, what size it was....and often from what type of rock it came. They were to barely touch the ground so that no dust would be seen rising as they went down the path."

"Speed wasn't an issue. Whenever it was mentioned, the text said that a faster journey came from efficiency of movement and not upward bouncing nor leg quickness for short distance. Runners were especially cautioned not to reach out when they stepped. I suppose this refers to what we call "overstriding.""

HIGH PERFORMANCE SHUFFLING

*"D*ad, I really like it in Colorado, and I've been able to do okay with jobs.... but the winter is starting to seem like forever."

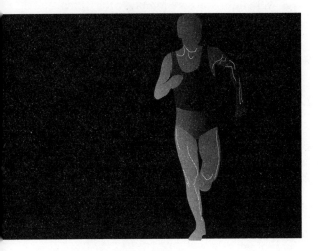

Tom sensed (as only a father can) that Chris wanted to ask for money to travel home. But father's intuition also told him that Chris needed to maintain his 21 year-old, male, independent pride. So he shifted gears and asked Chris how he had done in the Olympic marathon trials earlier in the day. Chris had told Tom during the weeks leading up to the race that he was only running for experience and had no chance to do well.

"Actually, Dad, I was calling to ask if you could send me some money so that I could come home during Easter."

But Chris had a great commentary on the race. Knowing that he didn't have a chance to qualify, followed his father's advice for the first time in a marathon and went out conservatively from the beginning. Having run a 28-miler under the effects of Colorado's high altitude, Chris knew that he had a great shot at the top 10 and moved up from 100th at the mile, to 50th at the five-mile, and 19th at the 15-mile. At that point, the front runners who had gone out too fast were struggling, and Chris had one in sight about every 300 to 400 meters. It was a game through 22 miles, when he moved into tenth place. He made the decision to see how well he could do and picked up the pace to pass one after another. As he reached the final stretch leading to the finish line in downtown Charlotte, Chris was in seventh place but had two other runners in sight. Tired at this point, he decided to coast in—until he realized that the fifth place runner was a rival of his father's, the infamous Dylan.

Chris didn't think about what he should do, he intuitively computed the distance to the finish, the lead which Dylan held, and the resources he had inside him. At first he didn't even notice that he had passed an old childhood running friend, Tim Kennedy, who encouraged him as he moved into sixth. With just enough distance left to pass his father's adversary, Chris quietly but strongly zipped by and claimed fifth place.

Chris: "I turned around in the chute and said 'my father Tom Burke knows you.' "

Tom: "What did he do besides groan?"

Chris: "Yes, he groaned and it was probably the most dreadful groan I've ever heard."

Then, reverting to some parent-child role, Chris asked, "Do you want me to repeat, uh, profanity?"

Tom: "No."

Chris: "Then he didn't say anything."

Chris reconfirmed his good feelings about Colorado living, since accompanying his mother there on an August vacation. "There are so many things for us to do, you know, people in their 20's," Chris added. He looked up a running friend who had a spare couch. While working as a waiter, he let his running slide for a month, until a new waitress was hired—who happened to be a national class runner. As he struggled to get back in shape by running with her, they became good friends.

"She was close to the American 5K record and needed someone to run speed with. It was only my male ego that kept me close to her on the first few workouts...."

"You mean *playouts.*"

"No, Dad, I meant WORKouts! She didn't take any prisoners when she dragged me to the track."

Tom ran up a big phone bill that afternoon as Chris told how this friend, Melissa, had already left for Southern California to train for the Olympic Trials in the 5K. That was another reason for the call.

"Dad, maybe you can help her out. She was training for the Home Depot Half Marathon in San Francisco....but kept losing her normal fluid motion at the end of long runs and in the race itself."

When Tom asked for specifics, he discovered that Melissa was running her long ones almost as fast as she could run....and at high altitude. From the symptoms of her feet and legs, Tom suspected that this was only aggravating a form problem.

"Chris, do you remember last spring about the time you came to Atlanta, I was having trouble after long runs. When Galloway told me that loss of form at the end of long runs was due to overstriding early in the runs, I didn't want to believe him. I felt too good and was running easily until I got up to 15 miles—then I wobbled in and felt weak. My legs were tight and sore for days afterward. But after a few videotape sessions, I had to agree. When I consciously cut my stride back (and my pace), from the beginning of the run, I started feeling better and better at the end of the long ones—and recovered twice as fast! Recently, I've done a couple of 23-milers, and it's taken only taken two days or so to recover. When you're overstriding *and* running too fast from the beginning of a long one, you increase the damage significantly. The two-minute rule applies to everyone running beyond 15 miles (pace of long ones should be at least two minutes per mile slower than you could run that pace on that day)."

Suzi slowed the walking pace as she noticed that Laura was huffing and puffing between words. They were making a significant grade change on the southernmost part of the Chastain Park fitness trail. With Suzi's encouragement, Laura took a deep breath and finished her train of thought.

"I guess I feel like I've been beaten down every time I've tried to establish a relationship, and I'm ready to go into hiding...do you know of any good convents around here?"

Suzi started to order her, again, to take the word "guess" out of her vocabulary and then changed the conversation by asking how Laura was feeling. The latter said that she felt her legs were wobbling, and there was a slight ache behind her right knee. The psychologist explained that she had pains in the same areas during her first few months of the program. Through a video form clinic, Suzi discovered that she was overstriding—especially when tired.

Laura: "I thought that when you're going along with someone stronger, or more fit, and your legs get tired, that you were supposed to keep up by reaching farther forward on each step."

Suzi: "For a while, it works...and then every things goes, at once."

Overstride: Puts You Outside Your Mechanical Efficiency

Even a slight overstride of an inch or so will push your running motion beyond its most efficient alignment and aggravate the mechanical action of legs, knees and joints. At first, the main driving muscles have enough resiliency to give you a false sense of smoothness, enhanced by the action of the muscles running strong. But this extra burden brings on fatigue more quickly.

Once the calf and the hamstring muscles are fatigued, the joints, tendons and ligaments take extra abuse, and running form becomes inefficient and rough. The longer the distance of the run, the more muscle resiliency will be retained by a shortening of the stride length early in the run (and staying lower to the ground).

103

Chris: "But even if you're right, how can I get her to listen? You know, women can be very hard-headed sometimes."

Tom: "I don't know anything at all about how to deal with hard-headed women. If you find something that works, please tell me, Chris."

Tom got the fax number of the restaurant where Chris was working and promised to send a diagram and a form analysis of the '95 Boston Marathon race between Uta Pippig and Elena Meyer. After talking about the contrast of styles between a tiny pixie stride and a powerful athletic motion, Chris noted that his friend Melissa was more like Meyer, with a tendency to overstride.

Tom felt badly that his business start-up and the clinic in Greece had preoccupied him,

Efficiency Wins: The Battle of Running Form in Boston 1995

A classic confrontation occurred in the Boston Marathon between the efficiency of a marathoner and the strength and power of a 5K/10K runner. From the starting gun, Uta Pippig looked to be cutting her classic marathoner stride too short. Her closest competitor, Elena Meyer, appeared to be playing her cards right by going out slowly, forcing Uta to shoulder all of the pressure of pacesetting.

By the mid-point, Uta had built a modest lead and was running so smoothly that her quick turnover gave the appearance of weakness. With a tiny stride and no knee lift, she appeared to be jogging. This signaled to several experienced observers that it just wasn't her day. Elena, however, sensed this, and began her drive to overtake the leader. The South African's strong, athletic leg motion led many experts to say that it was only a matter of time before she would pull even with the German.

At 15, 17 and 19 miles, it continued to appear that Meyer's long and powerful stride must be taking big chunks out of Pippig's lead. The TV commentators noted how wimpy the German's turn-over appeared. But to the surprise of all, a time check showed that Pippig's lead was *increasing* slightly.

By 22 miles, Meyer had dropped out with muscle cramps and Pippig had picked up her pace. But when the camera showed the leader, she still looked like a jogger. That short and wimpy stride with no knee lift resulted in a 2:26 marathon—one of the fastest woman's times of the year.

How to Run a Marathon Efficiently

Marathon form is most efficient when you don't feel any noticeable effort, when running is almost automatic.

- Feet should stay low to the ground—no noticeable knee lift.

- Upright posture—Your body should be balanced with head over shoulders, over hips, so that no muscle power is needed to keep the body in position.

- Stay light on your feet. Those who want to improve times should increase turnover rate instead of stride length. (Turnover is the number of times your feet touch each minute.)

- The feet do not spring dramatically off the ground; they gently "lift off" in a reflex action as the body rolls forward.

- During most runs, concentrate on eliminating discomfort and noticeable effort in the exercising muscles. Strive to feel relaxed, comfortable and smooth.

and he hadn't stayed in touch with Chris. Certainly, he was proud of his son and told him so. But he really wanted to see Chris and looked forward to running with him again. The sending of the plane ticket also got *his* competitive juices flowing. Intuitively, Tom felt that this could be the missing ingredient, the spark which would bring his hill play and speed program into focus. He had four weeks to fine-tune fitness in order to challenge his son in a *play-out*....and maybe even a WORKout.

TROUBLESHOOTING FORM PROBLEMS

Quads too tired, sore or weak

When the main running muscles get tired, your stride length shortens as you slow down. The best strategy in this situation is to shorten the stride a little more and allow for a slight slowdown. Many runners, however, will try to maintain the same pace by using other muscles. The quadriceps on the front of your leg above the knee can allow this (for a while) by lifting the leg and maintaining a longer stride length. But the quads are not designed to do this and will fatigue easily. Afterward, you can usually count on two to four days of soreness, at least.

Sometimes quad soreness is directly related to running more downhill than you are used to running. Even when using a short stride while running downhill, some effort is required of the quadricep muscles—especially on long downhills. Many runners aggravate this by overstriding as they go down. Yes, it is tempting, and it is easy to extend the lower leg out in front of the body too much to pick up speed. To keep the legs and body under control, the quads must then be used as brakes. Not only is this an inefficient use of muscle power, but your quads will complain for several days afterward, especially after a long run. The recommended technique is to maintain a short stride and let gravity move you down with little effort.

Light exercise every day (such as walking on flat terrain) will speed up the recovery of sore quads. It is not a good idea to massage them, stretch them or exercise them too hard while they are sore.

Discomfort, pain, or weakness behind the knee

Another sign of overstriding is pain or increased discomfort behind the knee. When you reach out further than you should with the lower leg, you're out of the knee's efficient range of motion. The full impact of your body's weight must be supported by the knee and through a mechanical range in which it is weakened. This is a hinge joint and was designed only to support body weight in the act of moving forward, with the foot directly underneath.

When your main running muscles become tired, they cannot give the knee any protection from this repeated abuse. As the tendons behind the knee become more stretched out during the run, the knee is forced to assume body weight in a straight or "locked out" position. Downhill running and faster running tend to bring on this problem.

Always try to maintain some bend in each knee when running. A shorter stride length will reduce the chance of this overstride problem. Do not try to stretch the tendons behind the knee at any time. Light massage with a chunk of ice can help. (Get a doctor's permission before using anti-inflammatory drugs.)

Running Form very "wobbly" at the end of long runs

Most runners feel great at the beginning of long runs. It's natural to be tired at the end, but when the legs aren't supporting you well, you've overdone it in the beginning. The greatest downside of this condition is that you can easily aggravate your "weak links": those areas where you tend to experience injury.

This condition is totally preventable. Start the long ones a lot slower—at a pace that is

105

at least two minutes slower per mile than you could run that distance on that day. It is also wise to take one-minute walk breaks every three to eight minutes (from the beginning!).

Shoulder and neck muscles tired and tight

If you're leaning forward as you run, you'll have a tendency to compensate by holding the head back, which uses the muscles of the shoulder and neck more and produces fatigue more rapidly. When the body is held upright, the head, neck and shoulders are in alignment and require little or no muscle power to keep them in position.

Those who hold their arms too far out from the body will also overextend the muscles of the shoulder and neck. The ideal arm motion is minimal, with the arms held in a relaxed position next to the body. When the lower arm goes through a small range of motion alongside the shorts and the upper part of the arm hardly moves, there is little fatigue in the arms, shoulders or neck muscles.

Lower Back very tight and over-fatigued

Another sign of too much forward lean is a tired and tight lower back. By maintaining an upright body posture, you'll avoid the tendency to overstress the back. If you think that your back muscles are weaker than they should be, talk to a physical therapist (etc.) about some strength exercises to compensate. One that has worked well for me is the back curl. Do not try this or any strength exercise, however, until you've been given clearance by a strength expert.

Hamstrings tired or sore

You're lifting the foot behind you too far and/or extending stride too long. The longer stride is particularly a problem at the end of the long run as it overextends muscles like the hamstring, which are already tight and tired. Try to keep stride short, especially at the end of the run. Your back leg motion should have the lower part of the leg parallel to the horizontal—at its highest elevation.

Knee pain

When the main driving muscles get tired, they can no longer control your "safe" range of motion, and the resulting wobble can leave you in pain, sore or injured. A slower early pace, and walk breaks, will help the legs stay fresh.

Sore Feet and lower legs

You're pushing off the ground too hard and probably too high. Stay closer to the ground, lightly touching it, and maintain a short stride.

Lower Back tired and sore

You're leaning forward as you run. Straighten up and shorten stride.

STRETCHING WARNING: Even if your legs are tight after running, don't stretch at that time. A gentle period of massage and stretching before bed will give you the benefits without as much risk of over-stretching. Never try to "stretch out" a tight leg muscle during a run—except for the I-T Band.

HILL PLAY

After five straight days of rain, the weather on the day of the first hill play session was perfect. Since most folks were looking for a chance to get outdoors and exert themselves, it wasn't surprising to see a record turnout. At first, the instructors were challenged to organize everyone into manageable groups. Suzi and Laura initially lined up in the same group, along with too many others who self-described themselves as "beginners." As the organizers subdivided, Suzi volunteered to be an "advanced beginner" since she had run the Peachtree 10K the previous summer.

Tom was fired up. He couldn't wait to take on the challenge of the most difficult hill in the park. After talking with the instructor, however, he realized that a more conservative approach would reduce the chance of injury, while producing the same level of performance after four sessions.

For someone who had been running less than a year, Sam had made great progress on hills. "I find that the struggle against the incline energizes something inside me. I feel more 'alive' as I gear up to meet the challenge."

The instructor knew Tom and asked his opinion on several items, especially during the first lesson on hill running form. After a brief demonstration, the groups were organized for the hill repetitions.

HILLPLAY SESSIONS

WHEN?

On non-long-run weekends, before marathon speed play begins

WARM-UP AND WARM-DOWN

A good walk of five minutes gets the blood flowing and the tendons and muscles warmed up. Start running very slowly, and jog for at least .5 mile before doing any hills. The warm-down should reverse the warm-up. Runners and competitors could add four to eight acceleration-gliders just before the hills and could increase the warm-up and warm-down to at least one mile.

HOW STEEP

The incline of the hill can increase to the maximums listed: one to two percent for both beginner groups, three to four percent for runners, and five to six percent for competitors. The grade is measured from horizontal being zero percent and perpendicular being 100 percent.

Hill Form

The resistance of the hill will strengthen the lower legs through repetition. Bouncing, high push-offs and long striding are counter-productive to marathon hill form. Many runners aren't reminded about their form imperfections on the flat, but the extra effort required going up will aggravate form flaws. Your goal is to find the way of running which is easier, lighter on your feet, and which requires less effort. By increasing leg and foot turnover, you can often run faster while you run easier.

Run relaxed: Don't contract the muscles or strain to keep the right alignment.

Posture upright: Head is over shoulders, over hips, and all are lined up over the feet as they assume the weight of your body. Your alignment should be perpendicular to the horizontal and not the incline of the hill. In this way, you're most efficiently distributing the weight of your body as it interacts with gravity.

Short stride: Keep shortening the stride until you feel a slight relaxing of the hamstring muscles (back of thigh). If your stride is too short, you'll feel that you're slowing down due to choppy steps and loss of fluid motion. Too long a stride is noted by tightness in the hamstring and/or the quadriceps muscle (front of thigh) and significantly more effort required for only a small increase in speed.

Feet low to ground: The less you have to lift your feet, the more effort you'll conserve.

Quick turnover: Those who want to improve speed and strength can gradually increase the cadence or turnover of your legs and feet.

As the hill gets tougher: Keep reducing stride length, while trying to maintain or increase turnover of the legs and feet. Remember, stay light on your feet and keep feet low to the ground.

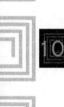

108

HILLPLAY ORGANIZATION

The instructor got Tom to help in setting up the groups. They started by almost reciting the definitions listed below. When groups were too small or too large, they worked with the groups on either side to make the size more even while producing groups composed of folks of similar fitness level. Finally, four groups were formed, which equally divided up the crowd.

DEFINITIONS

Beginners have been running for less than three months, and have never done any kind of speed play.

Advanced beginners have been running for more than three months but have never done speed play.

Runners have been running for more than six months and have done some speed play.

Competitors have been running for years and have done regular periods of speed play.

BEGINNER HILL PLAY

Grade: (one to two percent) so easy that you barely feel the incline

Distance of hill segment: 50-60 meters long (about half of a city block)

Pace: about the same speed as your easy running on flat land (no huffing or puffing)

Recovery: walk slowly down the hill, and walk at the bottom for as long as needed

How many hills? Repeat the hill, as before: two to three hills on the first session, with an additional hill each week until you reach a comfortable number (maximum 8-10 hills).

ADVANCED BEGINNER HILL PLAY

Grade: (one to two percent) easy, so that you barely feel the incline

Distance of hill segment: 50-80 meters long

Pace: a little faster than the speed of your easy running on the flat, but no sprinting

Recovery: walk slowly down the hill and walk for threre to five minutes at the bottom (more if needed)

How many hills? Repeat the hill, as before, starting with two to three hills, and building to eight to 10 hills,

RUNNER HILL PLAY

Grade: (three to four percent) easy for the runner, but greater than that for the beginner

Distance of hill segment: 150-300 meters

Pace: no faster than 10K race pace, and usually slower

Recovery: walk slowly down the hill and walk for three to five minutes at the bottom

How many hills? repeat the hill, as before, starting with two to four and building to 8-10 hills

[Note: The distance range is longer in hill play for marathons than that for shorter distance events. Make sure that you keep stride length short to maintain turnover without tension in leg muscles. Avoid overexertion, and avoid extending your lower leg too far in front of you.]

COMPETITOR HILL PLAY

Grade: (five to six percent) pick a grade which will allow you to maintain a steady speed and turnover over the top. If that means less of a grade, that's fine.

Distance of hill segment: 300-600 meters

Pace: about 10K race pace, adjust to maintain smoothness, relaxed leg muscles, and turnover

Recovery: jog and walk down the hill, walk for two to three minutes at the bottom

How many hills? Repeat the hill as before, starting with three to four and building to eight to 10 hills.

[Note: The distance range is longer in hill play for marathons than that for shorter distance events. Make sure that you keep stride length short to maintain turnover without tension in leg muscles to avoid overexertion and to avoid extending your lower leg too far in front of you.]

NO COMPETITION!

Competing is not allowed during hill sessions. (Legs in varying stages of conditioning, which are not warmed up as they should be, can be pushed to injury when individuals try to stay with someone who is feeling good and in better condition than he/ she is.)

PUTTING THE "PLAY" INTO THE HILL

The instructor showed how to *innovate* with spontaneous, but non-stressful games. Weaving in and out of group members, cutting corners, and playing tag were just a few of the suggestions. Tom mentioned how he made a game of changing pace in the

109

middle of hills, alternating between quick turnover, 10K pace, and gliding. The instructor showed Runners and Competitors a road course he called "the rollercoaster." Most had fun as they glided down the hill and used the momentum to help push them up the next hill. This was particularly beneficial for those who were running their marathons on hilly courses.

LONGER HILLS FOR THE SPEED DEMONS

While the hill play leader got the beginning groups started, Tom volunteered to organize the "runners" and the "competitors" into separate groups. Since he had gone through the Galloway Program instruction training, Tom could explain the differences between marathon hill play and hill sessions for shorter distances.

- Run longer hills
  - Run hills which are 30-50% shorter

- Run the hills with no strong push off
  - Run smoothly, but hard

- Maintain a quick, smooth cadence
  - Run up with more strength

- Feel that stride length is a bit short
  - Maintain a stride which feels normal

When the instructor returned, Tom had generated a sharing session in which about half of the veteran marathoners were asking questions and the other half, having used the technique, were giving very helpful suggestions and answers.

Q- "Won't these longer hills keep you tired?"

A- "Not if you run them with the short stride indicated above. Through practice, you'd be amazed how fast you can turn your legs over when going uphill. By not overextending the hamstring or calf muscles, your legs feel reasonably fresh, even at the end of the session."

Q- "Just how short is this *short stride*?"

A- "On my first two hills, I cut the stride too short. It felt choppy and I couldn't be fluid with my running motion. When I extended it a little more, I was smooth again. While I know that I'm holding my forward leg back from going to full extension, I got used to it. After three hill sessions, I was running faster with this shorter stride than I had been running before with a longer stride."

Q- "How do you pick up the turnover?"

A- "Don't expect it to happen all at once. First, ensure that the hamstrings are loose and ready to respond to a quick turnover.

- The difference between the shortened stride and a stride which feels like it is giving full extension may be only an inch or so.

- You only need a slight stride shortening to relax the main running muscles.

- Relaxed muscles are more resilient, can respond quicker, and return to do it again quicker. This means quicker turnover."

110

Jeff Galloway:

Short uphill stride helped me run my fastest marathon....at age 35

The 1980 Houston-Tenneco course had several significant rolling sections, and this worried me. I had strained my hamstring eight weeks before the race and had to lay off from fast running. As the time closed in on the marathon date, I discovered that the only speed sessions I could do were hill repeats with a shortened stride. While the injury was not fully healed, I picked up the turnover and jokingly told myself that I was the fastest "short strider" in the U.S.! The hill's resistance gave me the quality of speed play needed to run a high-performance marathon. The stride reduction released the tension on the hamstring and allowed it to continue healing. Not only did I recover while doing quality work, I passed about two dozen competitors while going up hills in the race itself. They were huffing and puffing, and I was zooming by at my normal respiration rate. I ran strong to the finish in a lifetime best of 2:16.

151

It's Too Cold!!!!

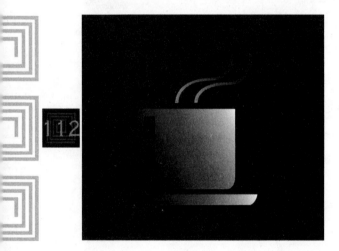

*A*s Suzi drove home from work, she knew it was her day to run, but thoughts of delay raced through her mind. The trees in Piedmont Park were doing a significant

wave as they responded to the force of a Canadian blast from the Northwest. As she walked up the steps to her house, she heard the phone and raced inside. It was Laura.

"Yes, Laura, it's very cold and you don't have to go outside if you don't want to....I don't mean to sound like a judgmental parent....I'm just getting home, it's dark outside and I don't feel like exercising either....Okay, here are some pick-ups that have helped me when I need to get out the door on a cold day:

Cold Weather Warm-Ups

1. Tell yourself that you're not going outside, but that you'll feel better when you get on some comfortable, warm winter clothing just to walk around the house.

2. Start preparing a hot beverage: coffee, tea, hot apple juice, etc. Play some inspirational music on the radio, CD, tape, etc.

3. Put on several layers of clothing—depending on the weather.

4. Drink your hot beverage, and eat a PowerBar or other low-fat energy snack.

5. Cover up your head and ears and walk around the house to the tune of your music. You're starting to feel good and you're warming up. If you have a piece of exercise equipment, get on it for five to 10 minutes and then walk for a while.

6. When you get warm enough, go outside for just a minute or so. Walk around this short amount of time and go back indoors. Be sure to tell yourself that it's not *that* cold outside.

7. Alternate inside walking with other exercises (equipment, dancing to music, video, etc.). Run in place if you wish.

8. When you've warmed up enough, go outside for a few more minutes, walking and running this time. Make circles around your block so that you can get inside whenever you need to. Don't ever let yourself get too cold.

9. On some days you'll find your layering adequate and the weather such that you can do your normal run or walk. On other days, continue to alternate indoor and outdoor activities until you feel that you've had enough exercise.

"Yea, I have a sheet from the Galloway Program about dressing for cold weather... where shall I fax it?....Oh, you're still at work.

"While I'm looking for it, I've got to tell you that I wasn't going to exercise myself until you called. As I've been going through these steps with you, I'm getting motivated....my tea is almost ready."

Dressing for cold weather success (and survival)

1. Wear a series of thin layers. Close to your skin, you'll want something warm. Polypro is one of a series of winter fibers which keep the warmth close to the skin but allow extra heat and perspiration to escape.

2. Cover up all extremities with extra layering: hands, ears, toes.

3. Men, wear an extra layer or two as underwear.

4. In extreme cold (when temperature or wind chill is below 10 degrees Fahrenheit, -11 Centigrade), do not expose any skin, if possible. Even when there is minimal exposure, put Vaseline or other cold weather insulation/protection on any area which may incidentally be hit by the wind (eyelids, etc.).

5. Start your run/walk going into the wind. This allows you to come back with the wind.

6. If you start to get very warm, remove a layer (long sleeve T-shirt, etc.) and tie it around you or put into a fanny pack in case you need it later.

Note: Don't let yourself sweat because it is likely to freeze and leave you very cold. Remove a layer.

More Cold Boosters

- Think of Ivan in Winnipeg who, this afternoon, will be running on a river frozen 12 feet thick when the high temperature is minus 30 degrees.

- Think how good you will feel when you've finished and have "conquered" the elements.

- You don't have to be held hostage by the weather. Learning how to deal with the cold gives you significant confidence and independence during the winter months.

- Think of the Finnish exercisers, and others in the Artic, who will see little or no daylight during most or all of the winter months.

"I know what you're thinking, Laura. No, I've asked around and have heard of NO case of a runner or walker suffering lung damage due to breathing cold air. The air you breathe doesn't go directly into the lungs, it has several buffer zones where it is warmed up."

"You're right, sometimes it's sad to have all of the excuses blown away....but it opens up a whole new world out there....for those of us who are tough!"

"I think it's easier for Suzi the Ohioan to say that than for a little southern gal from Ft. Walton Beach, Florida."

Clothing Thermometer

What to wear as it gets colder (In Fahrenheit)

60 degrees +	Tank top or singlet and shorts
50-59 degrees	T-shirt and shorts
40-49 degrees	Long sleeve T, shorts or tights or wind pants, socks or mittens or gloves
30-39 degrees	Long sleeve T and T-shirt, tights and shorts, socks or mittens or gloves and hat over ears
20-29 degrees	Polypro top or thick long sleeve T, another T-shirt layer, tights and shorts mittens or gloves, and hat over ears
10-19 degrees	Polypro top and thick long sleeve T, tights and shorts, wind suit (top and pants), thick mittens, thick hat over ears.
0-9 degrees	Two polypro tops, thick tights and shorts (and thick underwear or supporter for men), goretex or similar thickness warm-up, gloves and thick mittens, ski mask and hat over ears, and Vaseline covering any exposed skin.
minus 15 to minus 1	Two thick polypro tops, tights and thick polypro tights and thick underwear (and supporter for men), thick warm-up, gloves, thick (arctic) ski mask and thick hat over ears, Vaseline covering any exposed skin, thicker socks on feet and other measures for feet, as needed.
minus 20 and below	Add layers as needed. Stay in touch with the outdoor and ski shops for the warmest clothing which is thin. Watch your feet. There are some socks which heat up...and other innovations.

Note: These are only recommendations; use the combination of layers which works best for you.

114

WHY WASTE THE
MARATHON ON THOSE
UNDER 40!

As Suzi was paying for her pair of Phidippides socks, she noticed that there was something special about the crowd in the store. Then it hit her. Almost all of the

folks were over 50—but in good health and vitality. Having seen a continual stream of those of similar age who were not upbeat and had no vitality, Suzi liked what she felt: a sense of dedication to fitness as a lifestyle. When a speaker gathered the crowd together, Suzi listened.

"HOW MANY OF YOU ARE PLANNING YOUR FIRST MARATHON?"

Over half of the crowd raised their hands. While several asked questions, some wanted

to reflect upon their lives:

"Sure, I could have gotten into shape before, but I was young. What is youth anyway but a time to be irresponsible about fitness and other things?"

"Now that I'm retired, I find that marathon training gives my life a 'fiber' which energizes me and gives structure to my eating and other important retirement activities."

"One of the fondest memories of my grandparents is the strange things that they did...many of which I now find myself doing. It's sort of my mission to do something weird that my grandchildren can talk about...some lifestyle project that will help them some day."

The speaker, who was over 65, explained that the marathon was experiencing its greatest boom in history—propelled by two large demographic groups: those over 45, and women. Suzi had worked with many groups of the over-50 crowd and suddenly realized that this gathering had a higher percentage of women (about 40 percent) than in any other group working toward an active and challenging project.

She was about to leave the store when the speaker started describing his transition from a world-class runner to an aging runner. "I go slower now—that's the main difference. But I enjoy my running now more than ever." Suzi's trip to the coffee shop would be delayed by 45 minutes.

VITALITY AND ATTITUDE

"Age is not a factor. Sure my muscles don't feel as good as they did even 10 years ago—but that doesn't matter, as long as I check my ego at the door as I leave the house. It was a wonderful revelation that slowing down allows you to feel great—just about every day. I'll also describe two other factors which speed recovery and make the exercise fun: running every other day and walk-breaks.

"The quality of my life has been based upon two factors: vitality and attitude. Running maintains both at the highest possible level. For most marathoners over 50, attitude is often maintained at a lifetime best level.

"I believe that we become more introspective as we age. Running provides a positive outlet for this continuous inward journey and more time to oneself to organize the brain and get things on track.

"For runners over 50, fatigue is related to the number of running days per week and only indirectly the number of miles per week. For example, many runners have improved by taking an extra day or two off per week, while maintaining the same weekly mileage.

"Our recovery rate slows down each year. By taking more days off from running, we speed up the rebuilding process. At the same time, a higher level of performance can often be achieved by increasing the number of miles run on a running day. Speed and endurance sessions which are specifically designed for the marathon, for example, have allowed many runners to improve as they have pushed up to the next age group."

116

How Many Days Off Per Week?

40 year-old marathoners need three days off from running.

Over 50 year-old marathoners should shift to every other day running.

Over 60 folks should run three days per week and monitor for fatigue.

The over-70 crowd can maintain a significant level of performance by running three days a week and taking walk breaks on every run.

ALTERNATIVE EXERCISE

On non-running days, an alternative exercise will boost performance without pounding. The exertions which produce the most direct improvement are water running and cross-country ski machine exercise. Walking, rowing and bicycle sessions are great for recovery and bestow some indirect benefits. Swimming and weight training help to balance the muscle development of the body but don't help to improve your running. Stair machines, high impact aerobics and leg strength exercises are not recommended and can slow down the recovery process.

As the clinic wound down, Suzi finally left for her coffee. Behind her, as they left the store, a growing chant was heard: "Long live the Panthers." As the group left the store and ran swiftly by her, Suzi noticed on their back the logo of the "Gray Running Panthers."

Suzi hoped to be like them when she grew up.

Performance Tips for the Over-50 Crowd: getting better as you get older

Run twice a day on the running days:

Usually the first run is very slow.

Accelerations or hills can be done on the second one—but be careful.

Accelerations maintain a high leg turnover:

Marathoners in their 50's can do accelerations on each of the afternoon runs.

Marathoners in their 60's can do accelerations twice a week on the afternoon runs.

Marathoners in their 70's can do accelerations once a week on an afternoon run.

Remember that accelerations are merely increased turnover drills and not sprints.

If your legs are tired or too tight, don't do the accelerations.

Long Run Pace: Three minutes per mile slower than you *could* run that distance on that day.

Yes, this is a minute slower than younger runners would go, but it will give you the same endurance, based upon the mileage covered. Remember to account for heat, humidity, hills, and other factors as you set your pace. I start my long runs about four minutes per mile slower than I could race the distance, and I not only feel great at the end of the run, but in two or three days, I'm almost always recovered, even from a 26-miler. I know, I can see the looks on some of your competitive faces. Yes, it will take a longer time to cover these long runs, but this just gives you more time to brag about your grandchildren. In our marathon training groups, grandparents have a priceless opportunity: a captive audience for several hours!

Increase the length of the long run beyond 26 miles:

The purpose of the long one is to build endurance only. The slower you go, the quicker you'll recover. By having at least one long run beyond 26 miles, you can boost your endurance limit, which will allow you to maintain a hard marathon pace for a longer time in the marathon itself. When you go the extra distance, it is crucial to take the walk breaks and adhere to the pacing guidelines. For maximum performance, the longest run should be 28 to 29 miles. Again, you must go extra slowly on these extra long ones.

Take walk breaks every mile, from the beginning, to reduce fatigue:

Put one to two-minute walk breaks every three to six minutes of running from the beginning. This will reduce fatigue while you increase endurance through the long one.

Walk breaks do not reduce the endurance value of the run.

Walk Break Schedule for experienced conditioned marathoners:

50-59 year olds—Walk one minute every five to eight minutes.

60-69 year olds—Walk one to two minutes every four to six minutes.

70-75 year olds—Walk two minutes every three to six minutes.

76 and over—Walk two to three minutes every three to five minutes.

Alternate long runs with other weekend runs:

Until the long one reaches 18, you may run it every other weekend. After that point, run long every third weekend. When the long run reaches 26 miles, you have the option of taking four weeks between. On non-long-run weekends, you may run a slow one of half the distance of the long one or race a 5K—but no longer than a 5K.

Accelerations:

Keep your feet low to the ground—stride short. While staying light on your feet, pick up the rhythm after about 100 to 150 meters, glide by reducing the effort while maintaining the turnover.

117

AGE MAGNIFIES THE DAMAGE

Even young athletes will suffer from the following mistakes. Because recovery rate slows down each year, the negative effects of "stepping over the line" are more dramatic and longlasting in those of us who are.... challenged by age.

Junk miles

Running a few miles on a day when you could be resting keeps the muscles from fully recovering. You're better off not running at all on an easy day and adding those miles to a running day—either as part of an extra warm-up or warm-down or as a separate run.

Starting too fast

Whether on a slow training run or in a race, a pace that is too fast in the beginning will cause a slowdown at the end and/or damage to the muscles, requiring a longer recovery time. It is always better to start out at a slower pace than you think you can maintain. Practically all personal best (over 50) performances are accomplished by running a negative split: the second half faster than the first.

Overstride

When runners of all ages err with the length of their running stride, they tend to overstride. The negative consequences are greater for those over 50 in terms of tendon and muscle damage and the recovery time required for healing. Runners are most likely to overstride when tired at the end of long runs, races or speed sessions. To avoid this problem, work on a lighter step with a shorter stride. The primary sensation is a lowering of tension in the hamstring muscle.

Overstretching

When there is tension in the running muscles, many runners mistakenly try to "stretch it out." Massage is a better treatment mode in this situation. But there's hope. When you feel that you've overdone it, don't stretch the area for an extended period of time, talk to a therapist about massage, and ask your doctor if anti-inflammatory medication is okay.

As in the other situations mentioned above, the damage takes longer to heal when you're past the age of 50. The best strategy is, as always, prevention.

Overexertion in speed or hill sessions

Young or old, every runner pushes too far when doing higher performance sessions.

Again, it is the older runners who have to pay dearly with a longer "down" time when this happens. Be particularly careful when doing faster running than in the recent past.

When increasing the number of speed or hill repetitions, do so very gradually. By taking more rest between repetitions, you'll reduce the chance of overuse injury and speed up the recovery time after each session. When doing a repeat mile session, for example, 40 year-old marathoners should take at least a 400 meter walk between miles. Fifty year-olds need at least an 800 meter walk between, 60 year-olds at least a five-minute walk interval, and those over-70 folks: five to 10 minutes of walking.

HEART RATE MONITORS IN A MARATHON PROGRAM

Note: Before using a heart rate monitor, you must be tested for maximum heart rate. The tables or formulas based on age are only averages and should not be used to determine whether you're overtraining or not. Testing should be done under the supervision of a trained professional. You don't need to go through a Maximum Oxygen Uptake test; the Max Heart Rate test is sufficient and not as involved.

- If your estimate of max heart rate is too low, you'll not receive maximum benefit from using the heart monitor on speed sessions. You're wasting one of the primary sources of biofeedback which the heart monitor can give.

- If your max heart rate estimate is too high, you'll overtrain on speed sessions and risk a long recovery time. It's also possible to overtrain on easy days and not recover between the harder sessions.

Suzi had to put the Galloway marathon videotape on pause to get Tom's attention. He apologized for being so focused on the tape, but he had just bought a state-of-the-art heart monitor and wanted to get the maximum benefit from it. She said that she was working on dinner, a new chicken salad recipe and just wanted to know if he would like any wine. He replied in the affirmative.

When Heart Monitors can help

1. To hold you back during a long run—especially at the end
2. To make sure that an easy day is really *easy*
3. To ensure that "form accelerations" are "easy gliders"
4. To help you improve marathon racing form—without overtraining
5. To keep you from having a long recovery after marathon speed sessions
6. To tell you when you have rested enough between mile repeats in a marathon speed session
7. To serve notice when you're overtrained and need to take some extra days off or easy
8. To make sure that you're not increasing tiredness on marathon pace miles (on Wednesday or Friday)

When Heart Monitors don't help

1. At the beginning of long runs (especially if you try to stay close to 70 percent max heart rate).
2. When you don't know your exact maximum heart rate.

HOLDING YOU BACK ON A LONG RUN

Almost everyone is capable of running faster for three to six miles than they can run for 15 or more. If you wear your heart monitor on a long training run and try to stay close to 70 percent of maximum heart rate, you'll almost certainly run too hard at first, which will make the end of the run difficult and increase recovery time.

The reason for this is as follows. At the start of a long run, you can run slower than you could race a 5K or 10K and feel very comfortable for the first few miles. Running close to 70 percent of max heart rate means that you're at 70 percent of your 5K or 10K pace, which is almost certainly too fast for a long run that exceeds 15 miles.

In other words, you can run too fast during the first part of a long run and still register a heart rate of less than 70 percent of maximum heart rate.

Use the two-minute rule, instead of your heart monitor during the first part of the long ones: Run at least two minutes per mile slower than you could run that distance on that day. This means that you must adjust for heat, humidity, hills, etc. If your pace is slower than this, you'll only benefit from a faster recovery, while receiving the same endurance value as a fast run of the same distance.

The heart monitor can help you regulate subconscious increases in effort between pace checks. I recommend staying below 65 percent of max heart rate for the first half of the long run, during which period you'll probably notice an elevated rate on the hills (telling you to slow down). During the second half, the gradual onset of fatigue will cause the heart rate to naturally rise at the same effort level. Adjust pace to keep the rate below 70 percent during the second half.

MAKING SURE THAT AN EASY DAY IS REALLY AN EASY DAY

The easy runs during the week merely maintain the conditioning you gained on the weekend long run (or repeat miles). To ensure that you're running slowly enough, wear your heart monitor, and stay below 65 percent of max. This conservative plan will limit the possibility of going too hard when you need to be recovering.

SHOULD I RUN MARATHON PACE MILES DURING THE WEEK?

If you've recovered from the weekend long or hard runs, it's beneficial for time goal marathoners to run at marathon pace on the Wednesday and Friday easy runs. Here are some heart monitor guidelines for running parts of the easy day runs at goal pace:

1. Run a slow warm-up, ensuring that heart rate is significantly below 70 percent of max heart rate. If there are any signs of tiredness, just run slowly for the rest of the session.

2. After one to two slow miles, do four to eight acceleration-GLIDERS. These will help your running form to become smoother while you become comfortable running at a faster rhythm.

3. As you start the first mile at marathon pace, monitor your heart rate. Ideally, the rate will stay around 70 percent of maximum, but it's okay if it creeps a bit higher. If the rate reaches 75 percent of max, and you're not running faster than goal pace, just run slowly for the rest of

the session. This is a sign that you're still fatigued from earlier sessions.

KEEPING YOUR "FORM ACCELERATIONS" FROM BECOMING SPRINTS

The purpose of gliding fast during some of your easy weekday runs is to work on more efficient form. You want these quicker turnover "glides" of 100 meters or so to be at a faster pace than you would run normally but without a significant increase in effort or heart rate. The heart monitor can give you this check on reality. If the rate rises above 75 percent on an acceleration, shorten stride, keep feet lower to the ground, avoid pushing off hard, and glide fast. This should keep the heart rate from getting out of bounds.

TO HELP YOU IMPROVE MARATHON RACING FORM

Your speed sessions of mile repeats can not only develop the endurance-speed needed for the marathon, but with the help of the heart monitor, you have the biofeedback necessary to improve form at the same time. [See the section in this book on mile repeats.]

Each mile repeat should be run only about 20 seconds faster per mile than your goal marathon pace. By using a heart monitor, you can teach yourself to run more efficiently by finding form innovations which help you run smoother. Let's say that during the first two mile repeats, your heart rate goes up to between 75 and 80 percent of max heart rate. On the remaining mile repeats, you maintain the same pace and try to keep the heart rate from going beyond 75 percent by running more efficiently. [See the chapter on form for suggestions for improvement.]

MONITORS WILL TELL YOU WHEN YOU CAN START ANOTHER MILE REPEAT——AND HELP SPEED RECOVERY.

By keeping your monitor on during the rest interval, you can tell when you have recovered enough to run another one. You should wait until the heart rate has gone below 70 percent and then walk for at least another 100 meters or so. It is better to let the heart rate drop to below 65 percent of max, if possible. This extra rest will improve recovery.

MONITORS TELL YOU WHETHER YOU'VE OVERTRAINED

Pick a time of the day when you're less likely to be influenced by psychological or emotional items which would influence heart rate. For example, many find that the time right after waking is ideal. Each day, put on your monitor at this time and note your heart rate over a five to 10-minute time frame. If you have less time, then shorten this test period. After a few weeks, you'll establish a base line which tells you what your heart rate averages. Over the span of six to12 months, you will learn what the level is when you're rested, when you're training moderately hard, and when you've overtrained.

- When your resting heart rate (taken under the same conditions, day after day) is five percent higher than the low baseline, take an easy day.

- When the rate climbs to 10 percent or more higher than your low baseline, take the day off from running. You may do some non-pounding exercise if desired.

121

"How is Chris taking the rejection from his female friend?" Suzi said as she apologized for slightly burning the chicken, which was already in the salad.

"He is hurt, as only one can be when you're rejected in your first real relationship," Tom replied, sampling the salad and noting that he didn't taste any burn but detected some unusual taste.

Suzi was concerned that Chris didn't have any friends who were around this week and was somewhat depressed. She told Tom to invite Chris over that evening. When Tom delayed, saying that Chris had said very strongly that he wanted to be by himself, Suzi called Chris and told him that they had prepared dinner for him and needed him to come over and help them eat it.

While they were waiting, Suzi told Tom that Chris would need some special re-bonding during the next month and that they should do running and non-running things together. "I need your help," he told Suzi.

"You've got it!"

THE MARATHON
FAT FURNACE

*W*hile training for a marathon isn't a license to eat anything you want, you'll find yourself eating more energy foods. Marathon training has helped thousands to set up an eating plan which bestows a continuous flow of energy, all day long. The long runs can be the inspiration for a continuous feeding system and the furnace which burns it up.

Opportunities for change of diet

- discover foods which give you a steady flow of energy
- eating small amounts of healthy snacks
- continuously "powering up" with a PowerBar or other sport performance food before exercise
- drinking water or other fluids throughout the day

Bonnie and Laura were settling into the Wednesday night special at Phidippides Sports: a seminar on food and exercise. When the instructor asked what they were hoping to learn from the session, Bonnie didn't hesitate to raise her hand.

Q- **"What special exercises can I do to get this "stuff" off of my hips. I've seen those machines on TV. Which of them really work?"**

A- Unfortunately, none of them. There are no exercises or programs which take fat off specific places on your body. Everyone is programmed to deposit the fat in a specific pattern, and we're programmed to take it off in a certain way. It is only exercise which ultimately burns off the "stuff." As you increase the duration of fat-burning exercise, you'll use fat as fuel, and it will gradually start coming off. The most important advantage of exercise is that it gives you a good attitude and the motivation to keep burning.

FAT IS THE RESULT OF AN ENERGY FUEL BACKLOG

Most people become more sedentary every year. Without the steady burnoff of energy calories from food consumed, the excess will just back up and then be processed into fat storage.

THE EXERCISING MUSCLE CELLS BECOME A FURNACE

As they are conditioned to burn fat, the endurance muscles used in long runs are the best furnace for burning these excess energy calories. Many marathoners complain that they only lost one or two pounds over a six-month training program and fail to see the "big picture." These same persons would have gained two to three pounds of fat during the same period due to lifestyle. But even those who don't lose a pound usually lose several inches of "stuff" around the hips or stomach.

The most significant transformation going on inside your exercising muscle cells is a true revolution: they're changing from sugar-burners to fat-burners. Over the next few months, your "marathon muscles" will learn how to burn fat all day long, even when you're sitting all day and while asleep at night.

LONG RUNS GET THE FURNACE FIRED UP

The continuous movement of the body during long, slow runs uses an incredible number of muscle cells in the legs, back, butt, and related areas. By going slowly, this network of working muscles is conditioned to burn fat for longer and longer distances without extreme fatigue. This gentle but prolonged extention of endurance allows the exercising muscles to adapt to efficient fat-burning. In effect, you're creating a furnace which can burn fat during exercise, while sedentary and when sleeping at night.

SHORTER RUNS DURING THE WEEK KEEP THE *FURNACE* IN SHAPE

Muscles need to be used regularly to maintain their efficiency for the activity for which they have been trained. The easier mid-week runs maintain conditioning gained on the long ones.

YOU'RE RE-ENGINEERING YOUR BODY'S ENERGY SYSTEM TO BURN FAT AND BURN UP POTENTIAL FAT

While long runs are training your muscles to be fat-burners, they are helping to "rev-up" your metabolism a bit. A few extra fat calories burned every hour may not seem like much, but multiply that by 24 hours a day and by 365 days a year. This is often the difference between losing three to five pounds or keeping it on the tummy or thighs for another year.

You're engineering your energy supply and delivery system into a dynamic force which can burn up the extra calories from the second bowl of ice cream. Too many carbohydrate calories will lead to fat accumulation unless you burn them off before they go into storage. This gives you the opportunity to lose another three to five pounds of fat this year.

THE DIET AND EXERCISE *TEAM*

By working on both income and outgo, you'll feel better and burn more fat. As you shift to a diet which is lower in fat and eat snacks throughout the day, you cut down on the addition of body fat by not overeating. When you combine this with regular endurance exercise, you develop the capacity to burn off the excess fuel.

YOU MUST STAY ENERGIZED!

Low blood sugar is at the top of the reasons why dieters do not exercise—they don't have the energy or desire. When you restrict calorie intake, particularly by cutting out meals, you won't have a steady supply and adequate quantity of fuel. Your blood sugar level will drop and you will lose motivation.

MENTAL TRAINING PROVIDES THE FRAMEWORK

To make physical changes, you'll benefit from a mental program which sets up the format for both exercise and diet. Rehearse the process of eating low-fat snack foods regularly and feeling the continuous flow of energy throughout the day. This rehearsal also helps you to shift eating behaviors and choose foods that have complex carbohydrates, soluble fiber, etc. By mentally rehearsing this process several times each day, every day, the new system will become part of you. Mental rehearsal can help make a behavioral change permanent.

The Starvation Reflex: a dramatic calorie reduction causes eventual fat rebound.

A fat reduction program which only reduces calorie intake will often cause you to gain more fat later on. Unfortunately, the restricted diet programs seem to work in the short run. Oprah, for example, lost a great deal of weight by dieting. But after resuming a normal eating plan, she gained more back than she lost. Only when she got into an endurance exercise program did she lose it again—and keep it off. By depriving yourself of calories, you negatively impact the two items which can ultimately reduce your fat "blanket" and keep it off: blood sugar level and the fuel needed to do endurance exercise.

1. A reduced calorie diet lowers your blood sugar level, which lowers your desire to get out and exercise.

2. Without sufficient energy sources, you'll hit your energy wall. A restricted calorie diet doesn't give you enough fuel to go very far during your endurance sessions, significantly reducing the fat-burning and the re-engineering mentioned above.

Humans are capable of depriving themselves of food and/or the (decadent) foods they like for an extended period of time but with negative consequences. The psychological cravings which increase with deprivation will cause you to over-consume the items you've been avoiding at some future time.

Rather than totally cut out a decadent food (which you love) from your diet, tell yourself that you'll always have it available. Then, gradually over the next few years cut down on the amount you eat and/or the frequency. [There's a great section on working these dietary changes into a "food vision" in Return of the Tribes, pp. 32-33.] With an overall mental and physical plan, and enough time, you can also develop a taste for healthy complex carbohydrate substitutes and reduce or eliminate the starvation effect.

[For more on the starvation reflex and how to reduce "cravings," see Return of the Tribes, pp. 39-44.]

THE PRINCIPLES OF A FAT-BURNING PROGRAM

- Long runs on the weekends—producing the "furnace" effect

- At least two shorter runs during the week—to keep the furnace in shape

- Optional alternative exercise on non-running days—for added "burning"

MENTAL

- Mental rehearsal: an experiential vision of your changes: six months, a year, five years

- Rehearse your energy diet, how much better you feel

* Rehearse the physical training, interwoven with the diet

THE ENERGY DIET

* Eating small amounts of food constantly

* Low-fat snacks—acquiring a taste

* Lots of fluids—preferably water (cut down on sugar drinks, fruit drinks)

* Eat a little at the first sign of hunger. The hungrier you allow yourself to become, the more you will overeat.

EXERCISE

* Fat-burning is stimulated by increasing body temperature and keeping it up.

* This exertion session to increase body temperature must be done regularly (at least three times a week).

SET POINT

The human organism is lazy and prefers to maintain its current eating patterns and level of exercise (particularly if it is little or none). Take the "set point" concept, for example. Our bodies become used to a certain level of exercise, a given quantity of calories consumed each day, and a set amount of fat. As we get older, our body fat percentage or "set point" is programmed to increase, forming a buffer against prolonged illness to increase the chance of survival in a worst-case situation. In order to shake the body out of this programmed fat increase, you need a complete behavioral program which attacks on all fronts: Exercise is the furnace, low-fat snacking limits the intake, and mental training keeps the program integrated and on track.

126

Readjusting The Set Point

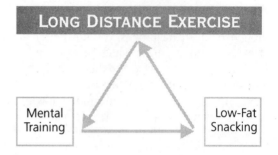

Exercise shakes up the system

A significant change in metabolism is needed to go into battle against fat inertia, but watch out! Not only are most humans able to jump right into too much exercise but each of us is rewarded by the exhilaration of overtraining while we're overextending ourselves. For example:

* We decide on January 1st to fulfill a resolution by running as far as we can.

* Surprising ourselves by how far we are able to go, we push too far beyond our capabilities and are sore for days.

* Unfortunately, the resulting burnout is usually the end of most behavioral change programs.

It is crucial to start with only slightly more exercise than you have been doing in the recent past. This allows for a continuous series of positive experiences as you slowly extend your fat-burning limits.

It takes a while for the system to change. The human organism doesn't always get the message that you're really serious about this regular exercise thing until you do it regularly for an extended period of time (meaning more than three months). Sure, during the first week, you will burn fat and start making some internal changes. But the major "furnace conversions" occur when your muscles and energy systems must make adaptations because the former lazy format is not efficient enough for the demands of exercise. This takes months. Exercise increases metabolism rate, energizing a chain of behaviors which promote the internal changes:

♦ as you burn up calories....

♦ you increase appetite....

♦ eat energy foods....

♦ feel good about yourself....

♦ make more changes....

♦ see the fat start to come off....

♦ which energizes you to continue to exercise....

The mental focusing program reinforces the intuitive rewards, keeping you on track through the months when little change is perceived. Mental reinforcement is as important as the physical form, keeping you focused. Of course this takes some mental energy to stay motivated, and mental training will not instantly counter every negative message you may receive. But if you're mentally on track for your exercise session, it can mean the difference between hanging on to the program or giving up.

The changes made during the first three months are the most significant but are not very noticeable. The internal restructuring from sugar-burning to fat-burning and from a lower metabolism rate to a higher one requires many adaptations, which magnify the amount of fat-burning that occurs later. Mentally reinforce yourself during this period for making these changes. It helps!

"I'm burning it"

"I'm getting more furnance power"

"I'm becoming a lean mean marathon machine"

The regularity of exercise, is crucial, for repetition signals to your organism that you're really serious about changing your metabolism. The regular, sustained increase in body temperature (due to increased calorie burn-off) is the trigger for change.

♦ Elevation of body temperature signals a need for reduction of the fat blanket.

♦ By starting your exercise at a slow rate, you will shift to fat-burning earlier.

♦ By continuing to exercise at a slow rate, you tend to stay in the fat-burning mode.

♦ By exercising as regularly as every other day, you are telling your organism to shift into fat-burning because fat is a more efficient fuel over the long haul.

PROGRAM TO GET THE FAT-BURNING ADAPTATION STARTED:

♦ 30 minutes of exercise

♦ 2 x weekly

♦ and 60 minutes of exercise once a week

PROGRAM TO INCREASE THE FAT-BURNING:

♦ 60 minutes of exercise

♦ 2 x weekly

♦ and 90+ minutes of exercise once a week

PROGRAM TO MAXIMIZE FAT-BURNING:

- 60+ minutes of exercise (every other day)

- 90-180 minutes of exercise on a weekend day

- 60 minutes of non-pounding heat-build-up exercise on most of the non-running days (not on the day before the long one)

NON-POUNDING HEAT-BUILD-UP EXERCISES

You can increase the amount of fat-burning on non-running days by doing the following exercises which raise body temperature. The intensity should be at a low enough level so that you can gradually increase the amount to over 45 minutes and get into *the fat burning zone*.

- Cross-Country Ski machine

- Indoor exercise bicycle

- Rowing machine

- Indoor walking (to the point of sweating)

MENTAL FAT-BURNING

At the same time, a mental training program must be started to keep the change system on track. This occupies or distracts the left brain so that it won't jump ahead of us and expect too much. Be warned that the left side will keep inserting a few negative things, such as "you're not losing weight," etc., etc. You can apply the same format to your rehearsal of fat-burning as you do for the marathon itself. [See the chapter in this book on marathon rehearsal.] The strength of the mental training program can push

through any negative messages and keep you on track.

Suzi noticed a strange look on Bonnie's face after the clinic, a mixture of surprise and revelation, and asked if she got enough out of the clinic.

Bonnie:"It suddenly hit me, about halfway through, that my body can be molded....that there's something I can do about the way I look and feel. Sorry, sisters, that it's taken so long for this country girl to get the message. I think I can learn to like this fat-burning stuff."

128

MILE REPEATS

As the time goal folks gathered at the track, waiting for the mile repeats to begin, a peculiar combination of excitement and apprehension filled the air. Suzi had come over to see how Chris was handling the rejection of his female friend who "didn't want a relationship right now." Laura kidded Suzi, suspecting something less clinical was her motivation for coming out as an observer-knowing Tom would be there. So Suzi counterattacked by recalling Laura's statement about Chris on the way over... something about "being cute."

Since this was the fourth session, the speed groups were fairly well settled and even had nicknames:"The Snail Chasers," "Greyhounds, Dream On," "Type A Drivers," "Left Brain Stompers," "Competitive Marshmallows."

The "captain of speed play" said that he would first talk about the warnings and concepts of speed before they started running. Chris and Tom were late and came walking up to the group just about the time the clinic started.

REMEMBER THE PROBLEMS OF BEING TOO EXUBERANT:

♦ Running the first two to three mile repeats too fast

♦ Going too fast during the first 400 to 800 meters of each mile repeat

♦ Trying to stay up with someone who is faster than you (or is showing off)

♦ Overstriding, especially when you start to get tired

Walk more than you think you need between the mile repeats. This helps your group to stay together and will speed your recovery.

YOU DON'T GAIN ANYTHING FROM RUNNING FASTER THAN ASSIGNED PACE!

By running the mile repeats faster than your schedule says, you actually hurt your chances of achieving your goal.

- Even 15 to 20 seconds per mile too fast on the track can lead to extra tiredness and slow recovery. Such fatigue is cumulative and is often carried into the marathon itself. When you reach the last four to six miles of the marathon, this tiredness will come back to haunt you; your legs will lack the rebound to maintain or increase speed to the finish.

- Your pace clock is messed up when you run too fast on the mile repeats. Running 20 seconds faster than goal pace prepares you to run that pace in the marathon between walk breaks. Your muscles and cardiovascular performance system are gearing up to do exactly what they need to do in the actual marathon. By going faster than this, you train yourself too fast in the marathon itself. This usually leads to an early pace that tires you quickly causing you to slow down at the end of the marathon.

START THE SESSION, AND EACH MILE, SLOWLY

It's always better to go out a little *slower* than you expect to average in the session. This helps the muscles gradually adjust to marathon pace, instead of sending shocks to the system. You're also teaching the energy system to be as efficient as possible.

WALK BETWEEN MILE REPEATS

You can speed up the recovery between each mile repeat and enhance overall recovery from the speed session by extending the walk break between mile repeats. When in doubt, walk an additional 100 to 200 meters. The extra walking can help the pace groups start each mile together. There is no advantage in cutting the rest interval short (unless you're planning to break the world marathon record). You receive the same

benefit from the speed session with lots of walking between miles, as with taking a little walking or jogging between. When you're fully rested between each repeat, you not only recover faster, you're better able to focus on the important aspects of 1) running each mile in the time assigned and 2) running the number of mile repeats listed for that session.

MARATHON RACE FORM

Using your running muscles in the same way will cause them to fatigue quicker. If you regularly change your running form modes, even during a mile repeat, you'll allow the calf and the hamstring to relax. Even a slight relaxation like this, when done regularly during the mile repeat, is often enough to infuse a little leg resiliency. By the end of the speed session, you'll still feel strong, even if you're getting tired, and you'll experience a faster recovery between this exercise and the next long run or race. This process teaches marathon muscles to automatically shift usage during the 26-mile journey itself.

It's crucial to shift early and shift often. You don't have to go more than 50 to 100 meters when gliding, etc., but you must start early and do it regularly on each mile repeat to receive the benefits.

SHIFTING GEARS INTO VARIOUS FORM MODES:

- *Race form*: About 90 percent of your running in the speed sessions and the marathon will be done using this form. This is a very efficient running motion at a pace that is 20 seconds per mile faster than goal marathon pace. There is little effort required when running in this mode, if you're actually in condition to run the pace you are predicting.

- *Gliding*: Every 300 to 600 meters of running at race form, let your feet shift lower to the ground and glide for 50 to 100 meters. You'll feel very little effort when you glide correctly, as you use mostly momentum and mechanical efficiency to move. When gliding correctly, you'll lose only two to three meters every 100 meters. Practice gliding on all of your runs to develop the most efficient motion, using the least effort while moving at the best speed. Practice will teach you how to glide very quickly.

- *Efficient rhythm accelerations (ERA)*: These are very short (10 to 20 yard) leg turnovers. While maintaining race form, pick up the rhythm or cadence of your feet and legs. This will gain back the two to three meters you lost when gliding. Don't lift your knees, don't extend your lower leg out in front of you, and never sprint (run all out). This is meant to be a very short pick-up which shouldn't cause you to "huff and puff." The only change to your running form will be an increase in the rhythm of your legs.

Combining modes: You are the captain of your running ship and may choose the rotation of running form desired. Here's a suggestion of how to arrange the modes during a one-mile repeat: Start with race form for 300 to 600 meters, then glide for 50 to 100 meters, return to race form for 200 to 300 meters, put in an ERA for 10 to 20 meters, then glide, and ERA, shifting back to race form, and gliding in.

FUN INNOVATIONS

The greatest benefit of the shifting process is the opportunity to transform what used to be a *work*out into a *play*out. By finding at least a few ways to divert yourself and/or the members of your speed group, the session becomes an event to look forward to. You're taking an experience which gives significant challenge and satisfaction and combining it with incidents of fun generated by the chemistry of individuals. Here are a few suggestions of how various groups have helped speed become playful:

- *Diversions*: Brief, improv "skits" in which individuals will do something to entertain the others. By planning these, the members of the speed group stay in touch during the week and build a sense of community.

- *Controversy*: It only takes two individuals in a group to have a different viewpoint on an issue for the whole group to have some fun with it.

- *Games*: Even silly children's games like "tag" can lighten up the end of a difficult session. Avoid the temptation to overextend the stride length, etc.

PACE JUDGEMENT

One of the very best lessons to be learned in mile repeats is how to intuitively sense your pace. This will help you conserve resources in the marathon, as well as in other distance races and workouts. Even with the shifting of form modes, you'll learn pace judgement as you increase the number of mile repeats.

Since the others had already warmed up and were ready to start the timed miles, Chris wanted to bypass the warm-up and get on with the "real stuff." Tom suggested strongly that Chris warm up with him but wasn't overbearing. They compromised by deciding to run their first mile repeat with slower groups: Chris joined the "Type A" group, while Tom settled in with the "Marshmallows."

Chris started slowly enough on his mile

warm-up but became impatient at 800 meters. Seeing two other groups ahead, he caught one and almost caught the other one. When he ran back to join Tom and the Marshmallows, who had maintained a mellow nine-minute pace, Tom noted that Chris was still breathing hard.

Chris: "Well, I started with the Type A's.... and had to be true to my group."

Tom: "I'm glad that we still have a sense of humor, before low blood sugar and the left brain gets hold of us."

Chris: "I know just enough about this left brain stuff to suspect that's where that last thought came from."

At the end of the session, Chris was feeling the effects of his quick starts. Tom tried to get him to relax with some gliding, but Chris just couldn't find the right gear. Instead, he wobbled from side to side. This prompted someone in their group to recommend that Chris have his alignment checked. Another said that Chris was designed for performance and just self-destructed when he ran slow. Tom suspected that Chris couldn't do it because it was his father who had recommended it. All of these "jabs" produced others and kept the last part of the session light and humorous. Chris even loosened up and glided a little at the end.

Afterward, Suzi treated the other three to pancakes. As all four talked and joked, Suzi was no longer concerned about Chris. On the way home she told Laura that she could tell that Chris' marathon performance was very important to him and gave him the positive, meaningful involvement he needed to shift away from his personal challenge.

Setting up the group mile repeat session

- Groups are organized according to marathon time goal so that there are at least three to five runners in each one to a maximum of about 15 (with an ideal size of eight to10).

- Timing: It's ideal to have a digital display clock so that each runner can see his or her time each lap. The next best situation is to have a volunteer reading out the time each lap. This job can rotate among the runners who are walking between mile repeats. In each case, the continuous time is read out. Each runner could track his or her pace by noting the time at the start of each mile and subtracting it from the total time at the finish. Example: Amy waited for the clock to click over to exactly 30 minutes as she started her fourth mile repeat. She finished in 40:40, doing the mile exactly in 10:40 (for an 11 minute per mile time goal pace in the marathon).

- Each group starts together, with some "straggling" throughout each mile. Within each group there will usually be three to five different pace goals represented, requiring individuals to be very aware of his or her goal pace from the beginning of each mile.

- Each pace group should have a group leader who helps to infuse fun, holds back those who are going out too fast, and encourages more walking between repeats for those who aren't resting enough.

SLOWING DOWN ON THE LONG ONES

*C*razy Jim had joined a pace group which happened to have three other attorneys. After listening to their law war stories for the first few long runs, the non-legal members of the group first related to Jim and cronies by telling lawyer jokes:

Q- What's the difference between a dead skunk and a dead lawyer....both on the road?

A- In front of the skunk, there are skid marks!

[From Skid Marks...a lawyer's joke book, Shelter Publications]

During a 16-mile run, Jim was feeling great at the beginning and started running too fast. As he moved away from his original group, several non-lawyer members made statements which indicated that there might be an ambulance somewhere ahead. From that time forth, their group was called "The Ambulance Chasers."

As one might predict, the "Chasers" reeled Jim in at the 15-mile mark and told merciless lawyer jokes for the last mile, as they slowed down to accomodate his self-inflicted fatigue. Jim learned a lesson.

Pacing the long ones

- Keep the group together. If someone is huffing and puffing too much, the rest of the group should slow down and stay together.

- It doesn't hurt anyone to slow down on the long run, but it *will* hurt those who try to speed up to stay with the group when they're having a bad day.

- Keep walking on the walk breaks. If you stop moving, the muscles might tighten up and develop muscle cramps.

As the long ones get longer...

- Increase the frequency of walk breaks

- Example:for those who started by running five minutes and walking one-minute

  - When the long one reaches 18 to 20 miles, reduce running to four minutes, with a one-minute walk.

  - When the long one reaches 23 to 26 miles, reduce running to three minutes, with one-minute walks.

- Slow the pace down, especially during the first 10 miles.

133

BY RUNNING SLOWER AT THE BEGINNING OF THE 23 AND 26-MILE RUNS (AND TAKING ENOUGH WALKS)....

- Most runners cover the distance in less time than they would by starting at a faster pace because they don't slow down at the end.

- You'll feel almost completely recovered in two to three days.

- The legs feel fresh when running mile repeats or 5K races on alternate weekends.

THE SIGNS OF RUNNING TOO FAST ON THE LONG ONES:

- Slowing down during the last three to six miles

- Feeling very tired at the end and all evening long

- The long ones take four days or more to recover from

- An increase in nausea and irritation at the end of the run

- Not being able to maintain the pace at the end of the run without struggling

REMEMBER TO EAT!

- By keeping your blood sugar level up, you'll feel better at the end of each long run and have a better attitude all afternoon and evening.

- Practice your eating formula on all long runs and use the formula that works for you.

- The most successful concept found in the Galloway Program:

  - Eat 200 to 300 (low-fat) calories about an hour before the start (one PowerBar).

  - Starting about halfway through the long one, eat 20 to 30 calorie (low-fat) snacks every two miles to the finish (a total of one to two additional PowerBars).

  - Be sure to drink water with each snack.

PACE GROUPS NEED TO HAVE MORE CONTROVERSIAL ARGUMENTS

- As the runs get longer, it helps to have a more involved series of topics.

- Each person in the pace group is required to come with an arguable issue: Politics, gossip, social issues—anything goes.

- Someone should keep a journal, photo history, etc. for the victory celebration.

ALMOST EVERYONE HAS AT LEAST ONE "BAD" LONG ONE

- Group support pulls you through the bad ones.

- By helping others through their tough times, you receive positive internal rewards.

- These tough runs teach you how to deal with tough portions of the marathon itself.

BE SURE TO ADJUST FOR HEAT, HUMIDITY, HILLS, ETC.

- The warmer it is, the slower you must go (2.5 to 3 minutes per mile slower than race pace).

- Be sure to stay hydrated the days before the long ones, during the first part of the long ones, and throughout the run.

JUST _____ MORE MINUTES...

As Jim was gulping down his third glass of water, Suzi and Laura came scampering in. Reading the look on Jim's face, Suzi looked Jim straight in the eyes and said, "Yes, we had a great run today, Jim....and you could too, if you'd just slow down."

Jim admitted that during the last three miles he had been chasing the Ambulance Chasers. He told Laura that she was making him sick because she looked too fresh.

"I didn't realize that I had gone 20 miles until I got back here. From the very beginning I only focused on the next walk break. When things got a little tough I just said to myself: *three more minutes*."

Suzi corrected her: "You said it out loud at least 10 times....and I did too. But we're smiling!"

Laura spontaneously suggested that the group be called "Three Minute Wonders."

And so it was!

YOU'VE BROKEN
THROUGH "THE WALL"

While there are a few more significant challenges to be faced in our program, you've made it through the roughest part of the journey. Over the past two decades, the statistics show very clearly that those who make it through the 17 to 19-mile run will finish the marathon with strength and energy. You've passed through that very significant crack in the wall.

Most (or all) of the challenges and unexpected problems which you'll encounter in the marathon have been faced. Even if you haven't solved each of them, you've developed coping techniques and prevention strategies or at the very least have desensitized yourself to the adversity. As in life, some problems don't have solutions, we just endure them.

Most importantly, you've found new ways to reach down inside yourself, through insecurity and self-doubt to discover that there's reserve strength and support. While this can be as disturbing as it is uplifting, it's the adversity which makes us stronger, more interesting and gutteral. As a result of this experience, we may take with us a little more "fiber" in dealing with other challenges. After each of the long ones, we own a bit more confidence and tend to deal more directly with problems.

The changes have come on so slowly that you haven't noticed, but you're becoming an athlete. Instead of going for the visible awards, you've learned to savor the inner rewards. Nobody but you knows that you got out there on the days when you didn't feel up to it. Very subtle is the satisfaction you receive from continuing five more miles when you didn't feel that you could take one more step. But how do you describe the glow inside on those days when you break through a mountain of left brain negativism and cruise to the finish with strength and confidence?

So you won't bask in the glow of a sportswriter's praise. Your name won't be on CNN for setting a world record, and you won't be bringing home a beautiful silver cup or solid gold medallion. Many of you won't find much, if any, understanding at home or at work. But let me tell you from experience, when you personally frame your marathon effort, it becomes a very significant moment in your life—and it should be. There are very few times when you use all of your resources to touch your potential. You're reaching out to your spirit, and it's answering you with vitality.

Keep reaching!

Jeff

136

WHAT DO YOU DO IF YOU
GET INJURED?

*C*hris woke up at 10:30 a.m. the day after the repeat mile session with a sore Achilles. As he munched on some toast and drank his tea and orange juice, he realized

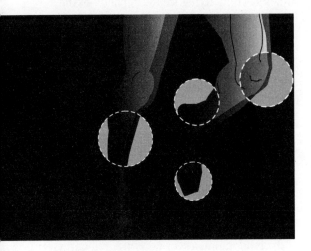

that he probably shouldn't...but he really wanted to run. Since Tom had already left to teach his corporate marathoners and couldn't say no, Chris took off on his favorite eight-mile loop. By the time Tom called in the late afternoon, Chris's Achilles tendon was about twice the size it had been when he had rolled out of bed. After scolding Chris for running on a suspected injury, Tom told him to come over to the "Y" for a water running session and another tongue-lashing.

Injury seeds must have been in the air. While waiting for Chris at the Y's check-in

area, Tom called Suzi and discovered that she was taking a few days off due to an I-T band injury, which she had aggravated over the weekend. The mistake was helping Crazy Jim unload some computers he had found at the Volume Discount store. Laura had moved onto the "injured reserve" list also. Having felt a little tight at the end of her last long run, she tried to "stretch it out" and had strained her hamstring. Tom convinced both to join Chris and him, explaining that he was presenting two short clinics (on injuries and cross-training), with help from one of the best physical therapists in the area.

WEAK LINKS

Everyone has them. Each of us, due to unique biomechanics and structured patterns of motion, tend to aggravate specific areas over and over. When we exercise too many days per week or increase intensity or mileage too rapidly, these sites are usually the first to be aggravated. This can be very positive, giving us an early warning signal to back off before we push into injury. Marathon training is more likely to reveal the weak links than most forms of exercise.

MOST COMMON SITES OF "WEAK LINKS"

1. Knee

2. Foot

3. Achilles Tendon

4. Ankle

BE AWARE OF AREAS WHICH

- get sore first

- are repeatedly sore, painful or inflamed

- take longer to warm up

- have been sites of injury before

- are not functioning in their usual way

As you become more sensitive to these areas, you'll take time off for recovery and treatment at the earliest of warning signs. Quick and early action will cut down on the chance that you'll have to spend weeks or months of recovery later.

IS IT AN INJURY? WHAT ARE THE SIGNS?

- Inflammation: look for swelling around the injury site

- Loss of function: the muscle, foot, tendon, etc. doesn't work the way it should

- Extended pain: which increases or hurts consistently for a week or more

INFLAMMATION:

This is the body's attempt to immobilize an injured area to keep you from damaging the injury further. The excess fluid around the injury notifies you that there is a problem in the weak link. Your range of motion is thereby reduced, which normally limits the extent of further damage to the area. External swelling is usually apparent, such as the swollen area around a sprained ankle.

Internal inflammation is harder to spot. At joints, tendon connections, and in small areas of muscle, it only takes a little bit of inner swelling to reduce the capacity of the muscle and produce pain. Be very sensitive to the possible minor muscle (or tendon) pulls or strains in areas such as behind the knee, at the insertion between hamstring and butt muscle, the adductors, the abductors and the lower back muscles.

Repair and rebuilding of the muscle will be speeded up dramatically as you reduce or eliminate the inflammation around the injury.

LOSS OF FUNCTION:

If the tendon, muscle or other injured part is not doing its job, then several negative forces can be working against you. By ignoring it and continuing to run, you're very likely to injure it further. If you take a day or two off from running at the beginning of an functional injury, you may avoid having to take weeks or months off later due to abusing it.

Running with an injury can produce a new injury by compensation. When the muscle, tendon, etc. doesn't function to capacity, the workload of running shifts to other components which are not designed to handle the stress. In many cases, this produces a series of "compensation" injuries.

138

PAIN, THAT DOESN'T GO AWAY

Temporary aches and pains will come and go throughout a marathon program.

These will usually be gone after a day or so, indicating that you probably don't have an injury. But if you sense an increase in pain or the pain continues for five to seven days, you should treat it as an injury (at least two days off from running, ice and other treatments as necessary). Continued pain, even without loss of function, can be an early sign of internal inflammation.

DON'T TRY TO "STRETCH OUT" A TIGHT MUSCLE!

It's a mistake to push a muscle to its stretch limits when it feels tight or is fatigued. Stretching is actually the third leading cause of injury because well-meaning runners stretch when inflammation gives the sensation of tightness. Muscles which are tight during exercise can benefit from massage, walking and a shortening of the stride length—but not stretching.

The fatigue of long runs and speed sessions will tighten the muscles and reduce strength and range of motion. Stretching fatigued muscles will not improve their performance. It will tear the fatigued fibers, producing injury and increasing recovery time.

Don't be fooled if at first the extra stretching makes the muscles feel good. This is probably due to the endorphins released to kill the pain of the many little "rips" in the muscle or tendon caused by stretching a fatigued muscle.

You're almost certain to overstretch a tired muscle and engage the stretch reflex. This protective mechanism tightens the muscle up in order to protect it. Even while the endorphins are telling you that the muscle is feeling great, you may be tearing them into a serious injury. At the end of long runs or speed sessions, fatigue will loosen the connections, allowing you to easily stretch the muscles into an overextended position.

Moral: Stretching when you're fatigued will usually lead to some kind of stretching injury.

ANTI-INFLAMMATORY MEDICATIONS CAN HELP, BUT ASK YOUR DOCTOR!

Many runners have reported that taking anti-inflammatory medications (ibuprofen, etc.) immediately after a difficult run can significantly reduce the chance of inflammation and injury and speed healing. Be sure to talk to your doctor, even before taking over-the-counter medications because all have some side effects. Taking any medication before or during a run (or the marathon) is not recommended. Whenever taking medications, follow the advice of your doctor and the instructions on the medicine, and discontinue their use at the first sign of potential problems.

139

INJURIES: HOW TO TREAT THEM

- **Get a doctor** who knows running and stay in touch with him or her. Getting a good diagnosis can speed the treatment and get you back on the roads quicker. A good doctor's advice and treatment can speed recovery by several weeks. It can often mean the difference between whether you will get to the starting line of your marathon or the same one next year.

- **Don't stretch** the area until it heals (unless you've injured the I-T band—ask your doctor).

- **Stop activity** that could possibly use the injured site for at least one to two days. In most cases your doctor will tell you that the injury doesn't have to heal completely before you run again, but you must get the healing started and continue a program that doesn't re-injure it. Again, talk to the Doc.

- **Ice!** If the injury site is near the surface of the body, ice massage will usually help. Be sure to use a chunk of ice and rub it directly on the injured area until it is numb (usually about 10 to 12 minutes). This is particularly helpful for all tendon and other foot injuries. Be sure to ice at the first sign of injury, ice as soon as possible after exercise, and keep icing for at least a week after the pain goes away. The regularity of the ice treatment is very important so do it every day! In deeper tendon or muscle injuries ice treatment may not have any effect but should cause no harm.

- **Compression** will help to restrain further inflammation. Wrapping a sprained ankle soon after injury will reduce the inflamation. This is another area where your running-oriented physician should advise you. (You must release compression regularly.)

- **Elevation** can help to reduce inflammation. An injured leg, for example, would be elevated on a pillow or two as you read or watch TV in bed.

- **Massage** can dramatically speed up the healing of muscle injuries. A massage therapist or physical therapist, who is experienced in working with runners, should be able to advise you 1) whether your injury will heal quicker with massage and 2) when it's time to work on it (immediately after injury is not usually a good time).

GETTING BACK TO RUNNING

- If the short (one to two day) layoff from training allowed the healing to start, then easy running on the injured area is usually okay, if it's not causing further injury. Run no more often than every other day and listen to the advice of an experienced doctor who knows running injuries.

- **Choose alternative exercise** which will not aggravate the injured area and ease into it.

- **Continue with your injury treatment** as advised by the doctor. (Ice for at least one week after all symptoms go away.)

- **Gradually ease back** into your normal running routine as the healing takes hold.

[For more information on injuries, see Galloway's Book On Running, pp. 198-227 and Return of the Tribes, pp. 87-88.]

140

Marathon Cross Training (XT)

The XT days

On non-running days, cross-training can give the attitude boost we need while it bestows additional conditioning. The best programs are those which are fun, and therefore draw you back to do them again and again. For this reason, many marathon runners do a variety of exercises in a single XT session to reduce the chance of boredom and burnout.

XT can maintain marathon conditioning while injured

Don't think that "it's over" if you come down with an injury during a marathon program. Over the years, I've met dozens of runners who, while injured, maintained conditioning through significant cross-training and were able to finish the marathon comfortably. During an eight-week injury, one runner ran in the water and came back to do the marathon in a personal best: under three hours!

The best exercises for running

As in any form of conditioning, the best exercises to get in shape as "back-ups" for the running muscles are those which best use the leg muscles in the running way. Water running has produced the best effect for large numbers of marathoners. Cross-

country ski machines have also produced a high level of running conditioning.

The best exercises for fat-burning

Exercises which elevate the body temperature, keep it up, and use lots of muscle cells are best. Cross-country ski machines, rowing machines, and then cycling and other indoor machines can help to increase the fat-burning effect.

Beware of the stair!

Stair machines use many of the muscles used in running. This means that they aren't the best choice for alternative exercise on a rest day from running. But they can simulate hill running, to some extent, if you use them occasionally to replace a running day (or as a second running session on a running day).

Gradually introduce the muscles to XT

+ Ease into each new exercise.

+ For the first few weeks, don't do the same exercise every day.

+ You can, however, do several different exercises which can be alternated.

- To get the best effect for the marathon, it's better to use a slow continuous motion instead of quick, short bursts of high intensity.

EASING INTO NEW EXERCISES

- On the first day go five easy minutes, rest for 20 to 30 minutes, and then go for five more minutes.

- You could start with two to three different exercises, alternating them and gradually increasing the session to one hour.

- During each successive session, increase by three to five minutes on each of the two segments.

- For example:

Session #

1 5min/5min

2 8min/8min

3 12min/12min

4 15min/15min

5 18min/18min

6 22min/22min

- Exercise every day at first, if you wish, building up to two 30-minute sessions.

  - You may then combine the exercise into one continuous session with a frequency of every other day. On the off day, you may do a different exercise routine. For example, look at the schedule at the bottom of this page.

IF INJURED:

- Don't do any exercise which could aggravate the injured area.

- Try to simulate the same intensity and duration of your scheduled running session for that day. For example, if a long run were scheduled, estimate the length of the time you'd be running and spend that time continuously running in the water, on the cross-country ski machine, etc. As you're doing the alternative exercise, try to maintain about the same level of exertion as you would feel when running.

GRADUALLY WORK INTO NEW EXERCISES

- Build up to about the same duration and intensity of exercise you'd be doing if running.

- You can alternate back and forth between many exercises to keep the activity interesting.

- Never push the muscles to the point of tiredness or loss of strength in individual exercises or in the session as a whole.

Mon	Tue	Wed	Thu	Fri	Sat	Sun
H2O run	cycle	H2O run	swim	H2O run	off	long H2O run
strength	swim	strength	X-C ski machine	strength	swim	

IF YOU'RE NOT INJURED BUT ARE JUST ADDING EXTRA FITNESS TO YOUR PROGRAM...

- Choose a variety of exercises for your non-running days.

- You don't need to do any one of the exercises for more than about 10 minutes, if you don't want to. By alternating between activities, you'll tend to avoid boredom.

- Water running and cross-country ski machines are the best for runners.

143

How do you run...
in the water ?

*J*ust as the lecture broke up, Sam walked into the room and asked the group what they were doing at *his* pool. Even Tom didn't know that Sam ran in the water almost every week. They decided to meet at the pool and continue chatting there.

Sam was already into his basic water running motion when Laura and Suzi settled into the pool. Laura said she missed seeing Bonnie since Fitness 101 had been over and asked Sam how she was doing.

"Bonnie and I are celebrating our 20th anniversary this year, and I've never seen this side of her. The Fitness 101 experience was the very first real exercise program in her life! She has continued with her walks, religiously, three days a week. I didn't expect this. Sometimes she's cranky and negative about getting out the door, but she's always in a great mood afterward. You see, this is a change."

When Suzi asked about the change, Sam explained that Bonnie had suffered, increasingly over their 20-year time together, from what Bonnie called "Southern lady crankiness." She would get into a negative mood which would color everything she said, the way she interacted with him and the way she snapped at the kids. "Since 101, when she's in one of those negative squalls, she'll manage it....after she's exercised."

Laura volunteered that she greatly appreciated Bonnie's being direct and open. Sam

said that she had inherited that trait from her grandmother, who would make anyone painfully aware of his or her character flaws. She was always truthful and direct

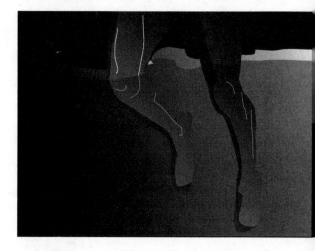

and could be a little too honest. "Bonnie can call a spade a spade. She has a gutteral honesty which has gotten more to the point through the years. But the fitness has softened it. As long as she's doing her walking, she's nicely honest."

Suzi predicted that Bonnie would do the marathon program next year, and everyone was already nominating her for group leader of the year. "She'll keep 'em in line," promised Sam.

When asked about what *she* was doing, Laura replied, "I'm ready to surprise my athletic sister Sarah at the Vancouver

International Marathon. Suzi and I are going to sneak out there under the guise of watching her run it."

Laura: "The greatest benefit I've experienced in this program is a leveling out of temperament. I still have days at work when I feel like I'm just an insignificant robot, overwhelmed and responding to the pressure. But it doesn't get me down any more. I know that when Suzi and I get out on our walk-jog, I'll get the control back."

Laura asked for some direction on how to run in the water. Sam, who had logged the most time in the water, explained two of the formats. At first, Laura tried to "water run" without the flotation belt and frantically moved legs and arms to stay afloat. With the belt, she was relaxed and could focus on the experience of water running itself.

BENEFITS OF WATER RUNNING

- Legs must find the most efficient mechanical path through the water. Extraneous motions of the feet and legs are reduced or eliminated over time.

- The water's resistance strengthens muscles which can serve as back-up strength to the primary running muscles. By alternating off and on, the main running muscles will retain resiliency longer. These smaller "reserve" muscles will also be able to keep you going for a little while if you overuse the main running muscles and need some help to keep going during the last few miles in the marathon.

- You get a great cardiovascular training session without any pounding. Since the prime running muscles are not being used, most injuries can heal.

Water Running Techniques

THE MARATHON MOTION

This is the same running form one would use when running efficiently on land. The body should be upright, not stiff. A slight forward lean is okay, but don't lean too far. The ideal motion is a smooth one, getting quick turnover. Focus on finding the most efficient path through the water. In this way you'll be cutting out mechanical inefficiencies and encouraging an efficient stride on land.

- Knees don't come up very far.

- Lower legs and feet are kicked forward.

- The whole leg is brought behind you, with knee slightly bent.

- Back leg bends to a right angle and then returns forward.

- Arms can be moved through a range of motion similar to that of regular running. Don't exaggerate the arm swing.

CROSS-COUNTRY (X-C) SKI MOTION

This strengthening exercise should be done in short segments of 10 seconds to a minute. By weaving segments into the marathon motion, you'll increase strength in the quadriceps (front of thigh), hamstrings, butt muscles, hip flexors, and lower back.

- The legs are almost completely straight.

- The range of motion is about 20 percent longer than the marathon motion.

- Move the legs like a scissors through the water.

145

Start each segment with a short range of motion, gradually extending it. Over time, you may increase both range of motion and speed, but be careful. Remember that you're building strength and not anaerobic performance. Never extend any motion to the point that you feel at your mechanical limits. And don't work too long in the X-C ski motion so that you're out of breath.

THE SPRINT

For those who have been doing speed play and don't want to risk injury while in a marathon program, the sprint motion can keep the speed components in good form without the risk of pounding or interval training injuries.

- Shorten your marathon motion to about half.

- Keep legs and feet directly underneath you.

- Pick up the turnover of your legs and feet so that you're going through the leg pattern about twice as fast as the marathon motion.

This shouldn't be a true sprint (going all out) because you want to go at a pace that you could continue for one to two minutes. You will be huffing and puffing through the second half of each of these, as they are anaerobic. Start each "sprint segment" by gradually increasing the turnover. The short range of motion directly underneath you will cause your head and shoulders to rise out of the water somewhat. The arm motion should also be a shortened version of the marathon motion to keep up with the legs.

CAUTIONS:

- Make sure that the water running motion is within efficient mechanical range.

- If you're injured, get clearance from your doctor that you're not aggravating the injury.

- Don't overtrain. Just going through an efficient water running motion will bestow benefits. You don't have to push it.

Laura: "I still don't know whether I'm going to hold up in the marathon itself. It is a significant and meaningful challenge, and I'm afraid it's not going to go well."

Suzi: "There's your left brain kicking in again! Put it back on its shelf. It's natural to feel those insecure feelings when you're facing a significant challenge. But you'll do it."

Tom: "I've run 40 marathons, and I still feel those feelings as it gets closer."

Chris: "But you've already done it—you've run the marathon."

For a few seconds, the impact of Chris' statement settled in, and then everyone embraced the truth of it. Yes, they had all run 26 miles and were fully prepared for the challenge on marathon day.

"I haven't thought of this before, but on every other run," noted Laura, "We had to push ourselves two or three miles further than we had ever gone before. We don't have to do that for the marathon itself. We've covered the full distance!"

Tom: "So shall the marathon be our victory lap?"

[For more information on water running, see Return of the Tribes, pp 89-91.]

WHAT IF?

*I*t took longer than expected for Chris' Achilles injury to heal: three weeks. After running easily, every other day for a week, Chris wanted to review the marathon videotape about coming back from injury. So he and Tom invited themselves over to Suzi's for salsa, baked tortilla chips and training advice. Sam arrived shortly afterward to tell of his recent trip to Greece.

HOW DO YOU START BACK WHEN INTERRUPTED BY INJURY, SICKNESS, VACATION, ETC....?

Do you have to start all over if your marathon program is interrupted? Probably not. Most of us are not in a position to quit our job, leave our family and other responsibilities to train for a marathon and must steer our aerobic ship around the obstructions. There are as many ways to rebuild from a layoff as there are problems which cause the interruptions.

INJURIES

- At the first sign of an aggravated "weak link," take an extra day or two off.

- If it's an injury, see a doctor and get treatment immediately: the sooner treated, the sooner healed.

- Start alternative exercise immediately: the sooner started, the more fitness retained.

COMING BACK FROM AN INJURY

- Make sure the healing is continuing as you get back into running.

- Stay in touch with your docror or physical therapist to limit the risk of re-injury.

- Continue to treat the injury as prescribed by the doctor.

    - Ice massage, for example, should be continued every day for two weeks after the disappearance of all symptoms.

SICKNESS

- If Doc allows you to do some low level exercise (30 min, 3 x a week), do it!

- Always avoid the chance of lowering resistance to disease and getting sick again.

- Return to running conservatively after sickness.

TRAINING INTERRUPTIONS OF LESS THAN 14 DAYS DUE TO BUSINESS, TRAVEL, VACATION, ETC.

- You can come back to your normal weekly mileage in two to three weeks.

- But every run must be done slowly: follow the "two-minute rule."

BRING BACK THE LONG RUN

- You may increase the length more rapidly than usual by slowing down and taking more walking breaks.

- The longer your layoff from exercise, the more conservative your "comeback."

STARTING LONG RUN WHEN ON THE "COMEBACK TRAIL"

To designate your long run starting distance after a layoff from exercise, start from your longest run, three weeks before the day you plan to re-start the long ones and:

- take off 20 percent per week if you did no exercise at all,

- take off 10 percent per week if you did 30 minutes of alternative exercise, three times a week, or

- take off five percent per week if you did alternative exercise which simulated marathon schedule.

Chris volunteered himself as an example: Three weeks ago he ran 23 miles. Three days after that, he ran too hard on the mile repeats and injured his Achilles tendon. He did no running for three weeks:

Today his Achilles felt secure enough for a long one. He would have had the following options, in terms of long run distances:

- a 9.2 mile long run, if he had done no exercise at all during the layoff,

- 16 miles if he did 30 minutes of alternative exercise three times a week, or

- 19.5 miles if he did alternative exercise which simulated his marathon schedule.

Chris had either run in the water or exerted himself on the XC ski machine about every other day but for mostly minimal amounts. He decided that 17 miles would be his target for his first restarted long one.

HOW DO YOU PACE THE LONG ONES WHEN YOU START BACK?

- The first two miles should be three to four minutes per mile slower than you could run that distance.

- You could settle into a pace that is three minutes per mile slower or maintain original pace.

* Take walk breaks twice as often:

  - Before injury, Chris was taking a one-minute break every eight minutes of running. When he started his come back, he took a one-minute break every four minutes.

  - Before his trip to Athens (where he didn't run) Sam took a one-minute break every three minutes. When he started back, he walked for two minutes, every two to three minutes of running.

HOW QUICKLY CAN YOU INCREASE THE LENGTH OF THE LONG ONE——AND GET BACK INTO "MARATHON RANGE"?

- Four to five miles per long run: when running more than three minutes per mile slower than you could run

  - and taking walk breaks twice as long

and twice as often as before the interruption

- Three miles per long run: when running two and a half to three minutes per mile slower than you could run

    - and taking walk breaks twice as often as before the interruption

- Two miles per long run: when running two minutes per mile slower than you could run

    - and taking walk breaks as often as before the interruption

As they finished up the chips, Sam explained that he was having some problems with some of the academic advisors of the NSF. They were making it hard for him to build a case for renewing his grant in Greece. There were two problems: Sam was having to do so much of the administrative work that he couldn't devote the time to the political needs of those academic advisors. He needed to talk out the problems directly with them.

The other problem had been resolved by chance in his most recent trip to Greece. There was one era during which the documents of the messenger center were missing. Upon contacting all of the authorities in Greece and in academia, there seemed to be only one person who had researched the area and then vanished. He was a (then) young Bulgarian archeologist who had done extensive research before World War II. Just as the war broke out, he returned to his home and was not heard of again.

Sam: "On the one day last week when I could get out and run, I made a circle of the trails and the three outposts. On the top of the hill where Tom and I found one of these sites was a vigorous old man walking and running and picking up pieces of debris. I

found that the small amount of Greek I knew was barely enough to communicate. He was the missing archeologist. We went back to the hotel, got a translator and talked all night long. I have research options to take me into the next century. Now I can use some administrative help more than ever."

Tom was surprised to see Chris get involved in Sam's story and ask questions about his research. "Chris, do you know anyone who studied small business administration for two years?"

149

MAGIC MARATHON WORDS

*W*ords in themselves are only sounds. By attaching an idea to the word, the power begins. As you extend the associations between key words and specific behaviors you can positively mold your strengths to emerge and your weaknesses to fall back.

This is brainwashing, and it will create a powerful effect when used negatively. But the association of words with a growing set of successful inner responses can unlock the strength you have inside.

As in any program, you must have a continual training program to develop and fine-tune these responses.

- Start by listing the problem areas where you could use some inner strength: relaxation, motivation, continuing under adversity, digging deeper.

- Go back in your memory bank and list beside each problem area, as many specific experiences as possible in which you overcame the problem.

- Attach a key word or phrase to each experience. The more experiences you have "cataloged" under one of these keys, the more powerful their effect.

- Each time you overcome one of these problems again, add a new experience to the category and attach the key word to it.

As you add more experiences, the magic of the words becomes more powerful. You're training your organism to set in motion the same complex set of reactions which

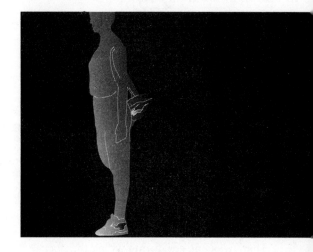

produced the success in the past. Not only does this help to mobilize the elements which can get the job done. Intuitively, you set in motion a search for the many little connections inside which give you a realistic feeling of control and power.

Use these as needed to take off the pressure and bring back the confidence. Add more key words and the accompanying thoughts which make sense to you. Subtract items which don't engage you. You are molding this to fit your needs like a glove.

RELAX

- There's no pressure on me; I'm here to have fun.

- I'm going slow. If it gets tough, I'll just slow down more.

- From the first step, I'm going to relax and enjoy the endorphins.

- I feel comfortable, supported by all of the energy.

- I'm part of a very positive movement.

POWER

- I feel good about myself and what I'm doing.

- This experience gives me control over myself.

- I know what I'm doing when I'm out here.

- This is my heritage; the power of the human migration spirit is with me.

ACHIEVEMENT

- I've developed great self respect through this marathon and the training.

- I created this level of fitness, and I'm very proud of it.

- Each step is giving me benefits.

- This achievement builds upon a long series of successes.

I'M STORING ENERGY

- I've got all day—enjoy!

- Slow down and savor this moment.

- Store this energy away.

WALKING EXTENDS RESOURCES

- The walk breaks push back my wall.

- Every person who passes me is pulling me along.

- This side of the road is my walk break lane; I own it.

- Walk breaks give power.

- Walk breaks are my heritage.

- I only have _____ more minutes (until the next walk break).

- Walk breaks hold back the energy tide so it will surge at the end.

NO PROBLEMS WILL GET TO ME

- I've got all the resources I need.

- Everyone feels discomfort.

- I'm hanging in there.

- I'm working through this.

- The problem is easing; it's going away.

- I can slow down and feel better.

- I can shorten my stride and relax the muscles.

MUSCLES—LISTEN TO ME!

- I'm shortening stride and shuffling.

- Movement pulls out the cramp.

- The muscle is loosening up.

151

I LOVE HILLS!

♦ All the power is there to zoom up this hill, but I'm going to save it.

♦ I'll shorten stride down to "baby steps," if needed.

♦ I'm low to the ground and feeling light on my feet.

♦ My muscles are relaxing; I've got the strength.

♦ The hill is working with me to pull me up.

SHORT (STRIDE) IS BETTER

♦ I'm shortening stride and feeling more power.

♦ Just a little stride-shortening makes the muscles relax.

♦ This shorter stride gives me more control.

♦ Every time I shorten stride, I decrease my chance of injury.

♦ With a shorter stride, I can turn over my legs better.

I'M GETTING THERE!

♦ I'm tired but strong.

♦ I'm feeling better.

♦ I'm tired but proud.

♦ There's plenty of strength left.

♦ The reward is coming.

♦ What wonderful accomplishment!

♦ Less than one tenth of one per cent of the population can do this—I'm doing it!

♦ Tight legs are a sign of accomplishment; I'll shorten my stride and run smooth.

[For more on "magic words" and "mind power," see <u>Return of the Tribes</u>, pp. 141-142 and <u>Galloway's Book on Running</u>, pp. 176-181.]

* And be <u>sure</u> to look at the "Dirty Marathon Tricks" section in the Resources section (back of this book)

152

RUNNING FASTER WITHOUT TRAINING

YOU CAN STILL IMPROVE YOUR PERFORMANCE DURING THE LAST **48** HOURS

While the physical training has been done, you can significantly enhance 1) the way you feel afterward and 2) the quality of your performance by choosing certain behaviors and avoiding others during the final two days. Graduation day is near; don't let your vision get cloudy.

FOCUS

Because of nervousness, the excitement of the expo and the distractions of another city, the marathon, friends, etc., it's easy to lose concentration on a few key items. Be sure to read this section over several times during the last few weeks so that you're more likely to keep the mind and body on track.

YOU'RE IN CONTROL

You need to be in charge of your behaviors during the crucial 48 hours before the marathon. In this way you can control your attitude, your eating, your schedule, etc. This doesn't mean that you should stay by yourself in a hotel room eating salt-free pretzels and PowerBars and drinking water. Being with friends is positive. You have veto power over what goes into your mouth, where you go, and how late you stay out. Being in control of your destiny is the primary step in running faster without training.

BE POSITIVE

Have a list of statements, similar to the ones in the "Magic Marathon Words" section of this book, which you can repeat as necessary. You're going to have negative thoughts slip out from the left brain so we'll work on a way to bypass them and move into the world of the positive:

◆ I have no pressure on myself.

◆ I'm going to enjoy this.

◆ I'll start very slowly.

◆ The people are great.

- Because I started slowly, I'm finishing strong.

- The satisfaction of doing this is un-equaled.

- I've developed a great respect for myself.

Drink!

During the 48 hours before the marathon, drink at least four to six ounces of water every hour you're awake. If you're sweating, drink more. If you prefer to drink juices or electrolyte beverages, then do so. Try to avoid drinking too great a quantity of fluids which are loaded with sugar. Even apple juice and orange juice have a high sugar content so take this into consideration as you watch your blood sugar level. Your best positive attack against dehydration is to drink water continuously while you're awake.

Avoid the dehydrating elements

Alcohol: During the 48-hour period before the marathon, it's best to avoid alcohol completely. Your exercising muscles and kidneys will thank you especially for abstaining the day and night before the race.

Caffeine: For those who dearly love their cup of coffee on race morning....go ahead. But make it just one cup, and drink a glass of water before the coffee and at least one glass of water afterward. Throughout the rest of that 48-hour period before the big event, just say NO.

Salt: This is probably the leading dehydrating agent for most marathoners. Because it's used so widely in the preparation of most restaurant food, you're likely to

consume large amounts of it when you're away from home without realizing it. For this reason:

1. Try to avoid restaurant food during the 24-hour period before the marathon.

2. Eat foods which you know do not contain salt (or are very low in salt).

3. Drink a little more water than normal if you've consumed food which you suspect has some salt in it.

Even one salty meal the night before a marathon will leave you significantly dehydrated for the marathon itself—no matter how much water you drink. So if you go to the pasta-loading party the night before, watch out for the sauce and the garlic bread! (Just nibble on the pasta, and digest the conversation.)

Medications:

Most medications (especially those for colds, flu, etc.) have a dehydrating effect. Be sure to consult with a doctor (who supports and knows the various effects of running) to adjust your medication accordingly.

Eat!

The best eating plan for the 48-hour marathon countdown is the best eating plan for life in general: keep eating low or non-fat snacks continually, all day long. Avoid eating a large solid food meal the afternoon or evening before the marathon.

So if you want to snack on PowerBars all afternoon or have a series of carbohydrate snacks which you know will get through your system quickly, do so. Concentrated forms of sugar (frozen yogurt, syrup, candy) are not recommended.

CHECK OUT THE STAGING AREA

If it is possible, go over the staging area the day before. As a guide, you can't beat someone who has run that marathon before: he or she will know where you'll be arriving, where you can keep warm and relax, and the best way to get to the portion of the road where you'll be lining up. If you get a clear idea of all this ahead of time, you'll feel more in control and will tend to receive fewer left brain messages.

REST

You don't have to sleep, but you must rest. Settle into your home or hotel room and relax in the best way you know. Read, watch TV, listen to music, talk with friends....but relax. Again, take control of your environment and mold for yourself a positive and cozy atmosphere. Don't worry if you don't sleep at all, but lay that head down and store up some energy.

WAKE UP

Set your wake-up call so that you have plenty of time to get moving, gather your gear together, and go through your usual eating and drinking timetable which worked for you during the long runs.

DRINK UNTIL YOU HEAR SLOSHING

From the time you awaken, drink four to six ounces of water every hour until you hear sloshing in your stomach. Whenever the sloshing stops, start the drinking again. It's always better to have water in your stomach, or in your system, than to suffer the devastating effects of severe dehydration and heat disease. During the race itself, drink at every water station—unless you hear the sloshing.

EAT—TO HOLD YOUR BLOOD SUGAR UP FOR THE FIRST HALF

One of the reasons I've advocated eating before all of your long runs is to discover the foods and the pattern of eating which will work best for you in the marathon itself. While about 70 percent of those in our various training groups find that PowerBar digests most quickly and provides the best blood sugar stablizing effect, you should use what has worked best for you in your food countdown before long runs. Eating about 200 to 250 calories of high quality carbohydrate about an hour before a long one has helped many runners to stablize their blood sugar level for the first half of the marathon.

GO SLOWLY IN THE BEGINNING

Almost everyone who performs a personal record in the marathon runs the second half faster than the first. Slow down by 10 to 20 seconds per mile (from your projected marathon pace) during the first three to five miles, and then follow the guidelines in the "Pacing Tips" chapter which follows this one. Many marathoners report that by starting out 15 seconds per mile slower, they have the resiliency to run 20 to 30 seconds per mile faster at the end of the marathon.

TAKE WALK BREAKS

A high percentage of those who didn't achieve the time goal they desired in the marathon by running continuously have been able to significantly improve finishing times by walking for one minute each mile—from the beginning of the marathon. See the section which follows on "Pacing Tips."

EAT DURING THE SECOND HALF OF THE MARATHON

Eating small carbohydrate snacks during the second half of the marathon has helped marathoners improve time goals by boosting the blood sugar level. This maintains mental concentration, sustains a positive mental attitude, and reduces the opportunity for negative left brain messages to creep in. Be sure to re-read the "Energy Crisis" chapter in this book—especially the "blood sugar boosters" section.

HAVE FUN!

By staying within your physical capabilities throughout the first 20 miles, you can enjoy the people, the joking, the sights, and the overall experience...as you are rewarded with the feeling of accomplishment. Be gentle on yourself throughout the marathon and the enjoyment will flow. For sharing purposes, don't forget to bring with you the following: a joke, an interesting story, a controversial issue, and/or some gossip. Of course, bring along anything else like this that doesn't weigh much and will add to the fun.

156

Pacing Tips For the Marathon

***F**or the first three to five miles,* run marathon pace during the running parts and take the walk breaks.

- A one-minute walk break (for the average person) will slow you by 15 to 18 seconds.

- A slightly slower pace will allow the legs to warm up before pushing into race effort.

- Remember to adjust your pace for heat, humidity and hills.

- **Between three and eight miles,** shift to running faster in the running portions, *and* take the walk breaks.

- You will gradually pick up the pace so that by eight miles, you're running at goal pace-when you average the walk breaks and the running segments

- If it's a struggle to pick up the pace, stay at an effort level which is comfortable.

- Don't even think about cutting your walk break short to speed things up.

- **Between eight and 18 miles,** run at marathon goal pace (run faster to compensate for walk breaks)

- Run each mile about 15 to 18 seconds faster than your goal pace, then walk.

- Stay smooth as you ease down to walk, and ease back into running.

- Compute your pace each mile.

- Uphill miles can be slower, and downhill miles can be faster than goal pace.

- **After 18 miles,** you can cut out the walk breaks, if you're feeling strong (and want to).

- An alternative: walk for 30 seconds for several walk breaks before eliminating them.

- If you need the breaks but legs are cramping, shuffle instead of walking.

- **After 23 miles,** you can keep picking up the pace if you feel up to it.

RECOVERY

*C*razy Jim was feeling a bit nervous. He had gone to a two-week seminar on the Internet and had missed the last long run. While many folks at the seminar ran every day, he couldn't talk anyone into going 26 miles during the only free morning most were using for extra sleep. To overcome his obvious anxiety about the NYC Marathon, five days away, he was speaking in cyberspace jargon and getting on everybody's nerves. Tom got the instructor on task by asking a question.

WHY ARE WE TALKING ABOUT RECOVERY NOW—BEFORE THE MARATHON?

By mentally rehearsing the recovery process, you'll automatically shift into that mode after the marathon. Each rehearsal doesn't have to include every segment of the marathon nor does it have to include every brutal detail. But when you mentally focus, right now on what you're going to do from the finish line and beyond, the more automatically you'll do it.

WHAT TO DO BEFORE AND DURING THE MARATHON

- Go out slower than you could run on that day, and either run the second half faster or finish having held back some effort (you know you could have run faster).

- Avoid dehydration at the marathon start by avoiding alcohol, caffeine and salty foods two days before the marathon. In addition, drink four to six ounces of water every awake hour.

- Take every walk break, from the beginning, and pace yourself conservatively, accounting for heat, humidity, hills and other factors.

- Don't overstride when you get tired on hills and at the end of the race.

- Drink at every water stop unless you hear sloshing in your stomach.

- Eat PowerBars or other low-fat, quality carbohydrate snacks during the second half of the marathon (with plenty of water).

AT THE FINISH LINE

- Keep walking to the water, grab two cups and keep walking.

- Walk to the carbohydrate snacks of choice and pick some.

- While walking about a mile, eat and drink.

- If possible, hose your legs with cold water (or pour cold water on them).

THROUGHOUT THE AFTERNOON

- Walk for two to four more miles, very easily—just keep the legs moving.

- Keep drinking non-dehydrating fluids, especially four to eight ounces of water an hour.

- Keep eating low-fat snacks as you wish; you've earned them.

THE NEXT DAY

- Walk (very slowly if necessary) for 30 to 60 minutes.

- Continue to eat and drink as before.

TWO DAYS AFTER: YOUR RETURN-TO-RUNNING DAY

- Walk and run for 30 to 60 minutes.

- At first, you may want to just walk three to five minutes and run one to two minutes. Do as you feel.

- Don't overwhelm the muscles; just gently move them.

- The return to gentle running will speed recovery of muscles.

CONTINUE TO ALTERNATE RUN DAYS WITH WALK DAYS

- Over the next two weeks, continue to walk 30 to 60 minutes followed by a run/walk session of 30 to 60 minutes, gradually increasing the running portions as you feel.

WEEKEND RUNS CAN GRADUALLY INCREASE IN DISTANCE

- Seven days after the marathon, you may run eight to 13 miles, with lots of walk breaks.

- Fourteen days after marathon, you may run as far as 12 to 16 miles, with ample walk breaks.

- Twenty one days after marathon, you may run eight to 12 miles, with ample walk breaks.

- Twenty eight days after marathon, you may run 20 to 26 miles if desired (for those who want to join the "marathon a month" club).

IF YOU WANT TO RUN ANOTHER MARATHON IN THE FUTURE

- By running a 20+ miler every third weekend, you'll maintain that level of endurance.

- Your long ones can be done every three weeks apart.

THE "MARATHON A MONTH" CLUB

- A growing number of marathoners in the Galloway program are self-proclaimed members of this fictitious club.

- In practice, they run an official marathon every four weeks as their monthly long run.

- As long as you're running at least two minutes per mile slower than you could

159

run that distance on that day (and with liberal walk breaks), most can do this quite often, with little chance of injury.

HOW SOON AFTER A MARATHON CAN I REALISTICALLY THINK OF DOING ANOTHER ONE?

- It depends upon how close you ran to your potential in the most recent marathon.

If your pace was...	& your legs felt good in...	you can run the next one...
at least two minutes per mile slower	3-5 days	4 weeks later
at least one minute per mile slower	3-5 days	8 weeks later
at least one minute per mile slower	6+ days	12+ weeks later
at least 30 seconds per mile slower	3-7 days	16+ weeks later
at least 30 seconds per mile slower	8+ days	20+ weeks later
as fast as you could have run	N.A.	26+ weeks later

THE DAY WE BECAME HEROS

s Tom rushed up to Gate C30, the flight attendant at the head of the entrance ramp was giving a final boarding call to all ticketed customers. However, the sound of

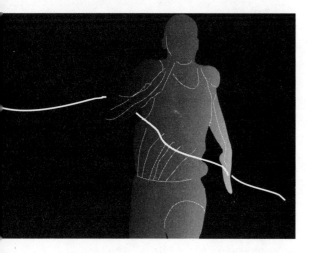

an angry but familiar voice at the check-in counter was overpowering the P.A. announcement.

The 22 year-old ticket agent was standing firm: "I'm sorry, ma'am, but your ticket says 'Suzi,' and your driver's license says 'Susan.' Due to increased airport security, I'm not authorized to let you on this flight."

When Suzi demanded to talk to her supervisor, a 24 year-old named Christian came over and backed up his underling: "You'll have to take this up with your travel agent; we can't let you travel. This is a federal regulation."

Suzi: "At 6:30 a.m. you want me to get in touch with my travel agent!"

Usually calm, Tom was irritated and asked the supervisor: "How many seats do you have left on this plane to New York?"

Supervisor: "Thirty eight"

Tom: "So you're going to delay two paying customers because one has a nickname on her ticket....do you have a senior supervisor around here....someone who's maybe 28 years old?"

161

Luck had it that the concourse supervisor for the discount airline also heard Suzi's melodious tones instead of the final announcement, came over, and straightened out the situation.

As they hurried down the ramp to the plane, Suzi said that she had just used up all of her adrenaline. So much for the last part of the marathon. Tom spotted Sam in the rear of the plane, and they found some seats nearby.

On the way to New York, and in the limo to the city, they all babbled continuously about what they wanted to do first, who they might run into, where to eat. Suzi couldn't stop...she talked about anything that got her mind off the marathon. Tom had never seen her so worked up over anything.

Sam mentioned that he had seen Crazy Jim

at his travel agent's office the day before. He was wearing this very bright U.S.A. jacket that he was obviously very proud of. Sam mentioned that he had brought some flyers by Jim's home/office the week before and had seen Jim wearing the jacket (inside on a warm day) also.

Suzi: "Oh yea, that tacky thing. I'd never hurt his feelings because he traded a computer to get it, but those colors were not quite made for one another."

Sam left to visit a colleague at one of the major museums, while Suzi and Tom went to meet Laura and Chris at the NYC Marathon Expo (PowerBar booth, 2 p.m.). By the time the younger couple arrived, Tom had consumed the equivalent of one chocolate bar and one mocha. "Since you've already had your PowerLunch, come along as a food spectator," Suzi invited.

162 Chris: "Or maybe a referee....if there's some good-tasting food left over."

Chris reported that he felt like "blowing one out." He had a great chance to run well and possibly win some prize money. Laura reported a "Crazy Jim sighting." She had seen Jim wearing a very...distinctive...warm-up jacket. Chris asked Tom if the race tomorrow could count in the father/son cup series. Suzi was starving.

"I'll eat anything: pretzels, chestnuts, even hot dogs...no, not hot dogs."

They walked into the nearest pasta restaurant. After lunch, they went over the bus arrangements made by the Galloway program. Chris and Laura went to meet some competitive friends of Chris. Suzi and Tom just walked down Fifth Avenue, joked and turned in early.

Race Morning: 7:30 a.m.

Crazy Jim was one of the first people to

arrive at the bus stop and greeted almost everyone as they boarded with "Hi, what ya going to run today?" After two street vendors came up and asked him how much he wanted for his jacket, Jim boarded the bus, sitting down near several of his fellow ambulance chasers.

8:00 a.m.

They had closed the door of the bus without Chris and Laura. As the bus pulled out, Tom spotted the couple, running. The missing Indians climbed aboard to a chorus of comments, some of them funny.

9:12 a.m.

The Galloway group disembarked from the bus and found a section of a tent that still had some room. Some played cards, others read the paper, and a few listened to a local news station on a transistor radio. They didn't bring up any of the "adventures" from the night before, saving them for the time together in the marathon.

10: 30 a.m.

Everyone moved outside, shedding extra layers of clothing which were left behind for the homeless. Laura wished Chris good luck, as he moved up to the elite athlete tent. The others lined up with the river of walkers— soon to become runners.

11:00 a.m.

As they moved on to the giant bridge, there were runners as far ahead as they could see. Most of the Galloway groups instinctively moved to one side of the road or the other to be ready for walk breaks.

11:30 a.m.

Chris had to hold himself back; he felt wonderful. But coming over a small hill, he noticed a slight pain on the outside of his heel. Several steps later, he realized that it was a very small pebble which was not affecting the way his foot operated. Should he stop to get it out? He was moving too well and decided to leave it alone since it wasn't bothering him.

12:00 noon

Crazy Jim was feeling better than he had ever felt in his exercising life. While his group could see him because of his jacket, Jim had separated from the ambulance chasers during the first few walk breaks. He told himself at first that he "forgot to take them." But he was beginning to feel that he had made a "physical breakthrough" and just knew that this was *his day*. He could run this one without the walk breaks, he told himself.

12:30 p.m.

Chris had tried to ignore it for a while, but there was a lump on his foot that was increasing in size and in the pain it generated. As he stepped in a pothole while making a sharp turn, he felt a sudden release of pressure....then more pain. The little rock had produced a big blister, which had popped. He was running on a raw foot.

2:00 p.m.

Laura was running with her beginning group and also feeling great. Unfortunately, two of her friends from Fitness 101 were not. She walked with them, encouraged them, and finally went on after both literally pushed her ahead. Laura didn't feel good about leaving them.

3:00 p.m.

Suzi was tired but still had six miles to go. She had used every right brain diversion she knew and their effectiveness was gone. It was time for some "dirty marathon tricks." Then she saw Sam, a speck in the sea of running energy, she sent an imaginary laser

guidance magnetic beam toward him to pull her along. Suzi had gotten too fired up on First Avenue and had spent some valuable resources. Now she needed anything that worked. While imagining the pull of the "beam" on a difficult hill, she walked for a minute and jogged for a minute. While she couldn't see Sam, she used the laser to maintain psychological contact. After 10 minutes of this, she felt better and had made it up the toughest part of the Central Park hills. She expanded her runs to three minutes of running and one to two of walking and sighted Sam again. "The laser was working," she told herself.

4:00 p.m.

Laura had returned to the two friends who were struggling. They were all going through a very rough part of the city that looked "bombed out." The two strugglers had to laugh when Laura said "Yea, though I travel through the valley of the shadow of death...." Laura felt that she was receiving much more from helping them than they were receiving from her.

4:30 p.m.

Suzi and Sam were both wobbling but picking up steam as they approached the finish. Sam had savored the crowd: the spectacle of probably the only day each year that New York City as a whole is supportive and positive. Suzi was feeling the exuberant glow which follows an expansion of your capacity.....beyond what you remotely thought was possible. "This is incredible" was all she could say.

6: 48 p.m.

Suzi and Sam were walking back from their hotel, worried that they had not heard from Chris, Laura, Tom, and even Jim. The chill was settling in as was the dark as they stared at the stragglers coming toward them from the edge of Central Park. Finally, the

163

right "clump" of people appeared. As Suzi and Sam draped hotel blankets and towels on everyone, each tried to speak at the same time.

Chris: "Laura became the tower of strength, pulling two of her Fitness 101 friends through some rough parts".

Laura: "Neither of them should have done this. They had only gone 15 miles in training, but some of their New York friends got them numbers and begged them to come. They were tired, but I got them to do lots of walking early enough. I'm ready to do another one right now!"

Tom: "I didn't come in too far ahead of Laura. During the first mile I ran into one of the top execs at FitLife. He was trying his first marathon also, with a long one of 10 miles. He's always been too competitive and didn't want to take the walk breaks. I had to make an excuse that my bunion was hurting me."

"What bunion?"

Tom: "So we walked for three minutes each mile. By 19 miles he was beginning to appreciate the walking. Throughout the last five miles, he kept saying 'I believe in walk breaks!' This was a big breakthrough....this fellow is quite macho."

Suzi looked at Jim, who was shivering under the blanket she had given him and realized that something was missing. She asked him how he felt.

Jim, in an uncharacteristic low-key tone: "Well, I didn't exactly conquer New York. I didn't take the walk breaks because I felt so good. I just knew it was my day. It wasn't. But I feel good inside. Conquering is no longer an issue."

Tom: "You should feel good inside. Folks, we

were all shuffling so slowly on that long stretch after the finish line, that we couldn't keep warm. The cold wind was brutal. Jim was the only smart one. He just untied his warm jacket from around his waist and put it on. No one was talking but this lady was just ahead: 85 years old....gentle and appreciative...and shivering badly. Jim gave her his jacket.

Jim: "Actually I was tired of someone on every corner in the rough parts of town saying "look at that jacket.""

Everyone celebrated with a baked potato from the corner fast food counter....and then went to bed.

VICTORY CELEBRATION

From the first person who walked through the door, there was a universal feeling of celebration. The members of various pace groups put their assigned covered dish on the serving table and grouped together to tell the "war stories" which hadn't been shared. Since each group had members going to three or more marathons, the sharing was intense, fun and uplifting.

About every two minutes someone asked Suzi what she'd heard from the "Greek Force," and she felt like an answering machine as she pleasantly rattled off..."I haven't heard, but the plane was due an hour ago. Laura is picking them up and bringing them here."

While people were eating, the only two members of the program who didn't make it through their marathon came up for a humorous presentation. Each told what *not* to do in the marathon, with stories about their misguided judgements in eliminating walk breaks early and in adding items to the training schedule.

The director of the program came up next and read a letter he had received along with a box:

In my 20 years of running, my goal has been to finish a marathon. While getting my long run up to 20 miles, I was hit by a drunk driver from behind 11 months ago. The doctor said I'd never run again. He said that I could and should exercise, however, or I would spend most of my remaining days on my back, being fed with a spoon.

I was determined to show that doctor wrong so every day I walked as far as I could. At first it was to the wall in my room. Then I used the hallway, holding myself up on the sides. Then I heard about this walk-run marathon program and determined that this was my ticket to my marathon goal. Everybody except for my grandson thought I was crazy. At first, I ran 30 seconds and walked five minutes. Every other day I got out there, and the running got a little easier. I'll always have a jerkiness from my accident, but I can move now. The run/walk thing has allowed me to move a long way.

Three weeks ago I struggled through the New York Marathon, running for two minutes and walking for three minutes. My grandson was so impressed that he took my picture and put it up on his wall beside the picture of Michael Jordan.

Regardless of how slow I went, and how bad the others felt around me, I always received the most wonderful feeling of human bonding. I was so exhilarated at the end that I didn't realize how cold I was getting. One of the members of your group gave me his warm jacket which I'm sure saved me from a health problem. The only thing I could remember was the "Galloway Marathon" emblem on his shirt. It has taken me the full three weeks to track an address down and send it back to him. I wish I could send more, but as a symbol of my appreciation, enclosed is my favorite dessert: a Big Apple Carbo Cake.

Thanks for getting it to him.

Yetta Davis
Greenville, PA
86 years old, today

A standing ovation for Crazy Jim included a harmonious version of the ambulance chasers' now famous siren as he came up and put on his jacket. For once in his life, Jim couldn't even say one word. He didn't take the jacket off all evening.

Over in the back corner of the room, Bonnie was chanting "Crazy Jim" over and over with the rest of the group. Suzi and Sam were looking out the window every three minutes, afraid that Tom, Chris, and Laura wouldn't arrive before everyone went home.

Sam: "This year's marathon training group was the largest ever, with lots of new people...what do you think is happening here?"

Suzi: "It's part of the responsibility chain which is finally part of our general awareness as a society. We can't morally afford to reward teenage mothers for having illegitimate children....to allow governments to continue to deficit spend....to support businesses which create long-term health expenses for everyone. Each of us must assume responsibility for her or his health and attitude. And each must support others who are positively improving behaviors. Until this generation, it was accepted that such values and behaviors were private and should be left totally to the choice of the individual. As a society, we cannot afford that any more."

Bonnie: "I'm overhearing you guys....you've got to lighten up! Let me tell you, next year when I do this marathon thing....I'm going to be the "lighten up" police. If I catch anyone being too serious, I'll....I'll....get this Crazy Jim fellow to chase you in an ambulance or something worse."

Sam: "Such as....having to wear that jacket of his?"

As the group leaders rewarded their members for the humorous, humane and hero-like behaviors which had occurred during the past six months, Suzi noted what a fine young man Chris was becoming. While certainly affected by the hormonal rollercoaster and instability of life as a "20 something," he had showed her a bit of emotional courage.

Sam: "Chris could have been one of the most promising Greek messengers I'm learning about. They forged the gutteral strength and integrity through honest exertion, just as he is doing. But endurance running at that crucial age of development can enhance the internal strength connections, self discipline and promote a realistically positive attitude—all of which leads a person to his or her potential. In Ancient Greece, some of the best leaders, in a variety of fields, had character-building experiences as young adult messengers.

Just about everyone in the room knew that Tom and Chris were returning from Greece that night, immediately after running the original marathon course of Phidippides, from Marathon to Athens. Most knew that Tom's career project, the "executive marathon team" was being evaluated and might not be renewed. There was also a flurry of friendly wagers over who would win the father-son competition.

As the Program Director was giving his final "thank you's," Suzi passed the word through the crowd that Laura's car had just pulled into the parking lot, and a chant started that got louder and louder: "We want Tom and Chris!"

Tom, looking like he hadn't shaved in a couple of days, gave Suzi a hug and walked to the microphone. Chris and Laura came behind him and stopped near the stage.

Tom: "Were you waiting for us to bring the pizza or something?"

Bonnie yelled, "No, the Greek Salad!"

166

Tom: "I'm proud to award the father-son cup to Chris. Not only did he beat this old man, he ran away from every other person in the field. As this was the 100th anniversary of the very first competitive marathon, it was a very special occasion for the Greek people, who not only honor the champions in their competitions but reward them highly. Instead of a big trophy, Chris was awarded this solid gold olive wreath for outdistancing some of the best European athletes. The Prime Minister was so impressed with Chris' come-from-behind victory that he also awarded him airfare and travel expenses to the original marathon for the rest of his life."

Chris appeared to be a bit embarassed as he took the microphone after a standing ovation and said: "I couldn't help it....my competition hit the wall. Besides, I was the only one in the front pack that had PowerBars."

After a good laugh, someone asked about Tom's business. It was generally felt that Tom was doing missionary work, bringing the marathon lifestyle into a generally hostile corporate world. Most knew that this was a trial and that the results were being carefully analyzed by the number crunchers.

"For the past 12 months, I have had to live, almost daily, with a negative phone call from a young man named Matt Green. He was my worst critic and kept picking holes in the program and my adminstration. But for the past three weeks, I've heard nothing from him. While it was great not to have to cringe every time the phone rang, I didn't know whether he would show up for the marathon or not. His anti-exercise CEO, who was also critical of our program, was looking for any way possible to discredit us and collected meticulous productivity data on everybody in the company.

"As I was trying to stay up with Chris during the first four miles of the race, we did a loop around the tomb of the ancient soldiers at Marathon, doubling back on the crowd. As we passed the crowd leaving the tomb, I saw Green. In his own New York way, he suggested that I talk to him. Due to his tone of voice, I expected the worse. About the only good feeling I had from letting Chris go is that I could breathe without gasping.

"Green started by saying how he hadn't been able to see any way that this marathon program could work and that his CEO had found every flaw, which were many. Overall, he had to admit that there was a slight increase in productivity generally among those who went through the program. For his CEO, however, it all came down to the sales force. None had run before the program started so "the boss" had divided up the individuals into three groups: the marathon group, a control group, and a third group which took a sales dynamics course rated highly by the CEO.

"The marathon group won! When Green analyzed the data, he saw how the psychological profiles showed incredibly strong increases in positive attitude components. Not only were these salesmen more successful, but they worked better with others and were more creative at the end of the six-month marathon training. Green's CEO had promoted him, expanded the marathon program, and was calling Green 'my key man, my marathon man.'"

The warmth of the evening gradually melted into the night as everyone congratulated at least three or four other people in the group. While very tired from the long journey, Chris and Tom enthusiastically accepted the offer from Laura and Suzi to go out for dessert.

"Now, exactly how does this fit into the responsibility chain?" asked Tom.

Suzi: "Let's just say that *I'm* ready for some significant irresponsiblity!"

167

RESOURCES

MARATHON DAY
CHECKLIST

IN GENERAL

- Drink four to six ounces of water every hour.

- Mentally rehearse the marathon, feeling good, overcoming challenges, recovering.

- Eat small carbohydrate snacks constantly.

- Relax with friends or family.

THE NIGHT BEFORE

- Drink four to six ounces of water every hour.

- Eat light carbohydrate snacks like PowerBars.

- Relax, laugh, enjoy the moment.

- Go over the procedure, route, etc. for getting to the start.

- Do a very relaxed mental rehearsal of the marathon, concentrating on the positive.

- Pack your bag.

YOUR MARATHON BAG SHOULD CONTAIN:

- Race number and pins

- Race instructions, map, etc.

- Copy of "Marathon Morning List" (below), and a copy of "Magic Marathon Words"

- Prepare to bring: a controversial issue, at least one interesting story, and at least 1 joke

- Shoes, socks, shirt, shorts, and warm-up suit

- Other clothes if it's cold: tights, polypro top, long sleeve T, gloves, hat, ear covering , etc.

- Water (about 32-64 oz)

- Bandages, Vaseline, etc.

- $20-30 for reserve funds (rapid transit tokens, etc.)

- PowerBars or your chosen carbohydrate source (enough for start, second half, and after)

- Fanny pack or plastic bags, pins

- Some extra "give away" shirts and/or pants as extra layers in case staging area is cold

- Garbage bags as an inexpensive waterproof top and ground cover

"MARATHON MORNING LIST"

- Drink 4-6 oz of water every 30 minutes until you hear "sloshing."

- Eat—according to the schedule which has worked for you in the long runs. (example: one PowerBar with 8 oz water, 1-2 hours before the start)

(example: one PowerBar with 8 oz water, 1-2 hours before the start)

- Bring your bag, car keys, etc.

- Leave at least 30 minutes before you think you'll need to leave...in case of traffic, etc.

- If you have several hours at race site before start, stay warm, get off your feet and relax.

- Sixty minutes before the start, walk around the staging area to mentally rehearse lining up.

- Thirty minutes before the start, walk around for 15 minutes to get the legs moving.

- Jog for 3-5 minutes (very slowly) just before lining up.

- Keep the legs moving, in place if necessary as you stand waiting for the start.

- If going for a time goal, get to the starting area early enough to secure a good place.

- Most of us with the goal "to finish" should line up in the back of the crowd.

- Joke around; enjoy the energy and personalities of the folks nearby.

- Go out slowly. If it's hot, go out even slower!

- Get over to the side of the road and take every walk break, from the beginning.

- Drink at every water station until you hear sloshing in your stomach.

- If you feel warm, pour water over your head at each water stop.

- Each walk break gives you a chance to appreciate and enjoy each mile.

- When tired, shorten stride.

- Don't stretch during the run or immediately afterward.

- You may cut out the walk breaks after mile 18 if you're feeling good.

IMMEDIATELY AFTERWARD:

- Grab water and carbohydrate food(s).

- Walk, eat and drink, for at least a mile.

RECOVERY:

- If possible, immerse your legs in a cold bath, as soon after the finish as possible.

- Walk for 30-60 minutes later in the day.

- Eat carbohydrate snacks continuously for the rest of the day.

- Drink 4-6 oz of water or electrolyte fluid (at least) every hour.

- Walk for 30-60 minutes the next day.

- Run/walk for 30-45 minutes two days after the marathon.

- Continue to alternate: walk 30-60 minutes and run/walk 30-45 minutes.

- Wait at least a week before you 1) schedule your next race and 2) vow never to do another marathon.

DIRTY MARATHON TRICKS

If you've trained according to the schedules in this book and pace yourself realistically in the marathon itself, you will be physically on the express train to the finish. There is, however, a very real mental wall which most marathoners must push through to get within sight of the finish line. By doing your mental training homework, you'll push the wall back closer and closer to the finish.

◆ Mental Rehearsal:

If you've really immersed yourself in regular and effective mental marathon rehearsals for at least 12 weeks leading up to the marathon, you'll cruise through most of the problem areas during the first 18 to 20 miles. An increasingly effective mental rehearsal will keep you on track and off the beam of the negative left brain for most of the marathon. [See the marathon rehearsal section of this book.]

◆ Magic Marathon Words

After the mental rehearsal loses its effectiveness and stress causes the negative messages to increase, it's time for some magic words. By attaching an increasing number of successful experiences to your "magic marathon words," you can flood the brain with positive memories and renew subconscious performance connections which got the job done before. This positive brainwashing will push back the mental wall, usually, to the 23 to 25-mile mark. [See the "Magic Marathon Words" section in this book.]

Just as leg and overall physical fatigue is delayed by regular shifts in running form, mental freshness is maintained by shifts back and forth between the left and right brain. Mental strength is developed through rehearsal and use of your magic words. As you increase the ease of shifting into the right brain, you'll delay even further the point in the marathon where your attitude won't respond.

Dirty tricks are reserved for that aggravating place, late in the marathon, when a growing stream of mental E-Mail bombs from the left brain are invading and attacking your will to go on. Here's a sample:

"It's over. Why don't I just walk to the finish?"

"If I slow down, I'll feel much better."

"Stop now, and I'll feel great."

"Oh, do I feel bad."

"I can't do it today."

Almost everybody gets these messages or worse. You're only in trouble if you listen to them and believe them. Dirty tricks help by distracting the left brain for a few moments so that you can get further down the road. As you find a series of creative images which activate the right brain, you will trigger other imaginative thoughts. These can become visions which will entertain you and may unlock creative solutions to problems, activate motivation, and keep you exercising to capacity all the way to the finish line.

Dirty tricks are merely crazy ideas which can't be grasped by the left brain because they are not logical. Let's go through one of these so that you can see the dynamic aspects of their effects.

Jeff Galloway's Giant Invisible Rubber Band

On all marathons, I carry with me this device, which is mounted to my shorts in the small of my back. When someone passes me in the late stages, my left brain explodes with a stream of negative messages, such as "Look how smooth he/she is running, and how ragged you are." It's easy to listen and give in to those logical messages which are trying to reduce my effort and slow me down.

But instead of believing this source of lazy and distractive ideas, I attack by throwing the giant band over the head of the individual who had the audacity to pass me. For a while, the lead may grow. During the next few hundred yards, I fill in a great number of details, such as imagining how the tension on the rubber band is increasing, cutting off oxygen supply to the brain of the person I "rubber banded." The hope develops that he or she will have to slow down.

At some point I must laugh at myself for believing in such a ridiculous device. But laughing helps to send me into the right side of my brain, and I relax. Limber legs turn over quicker, and I usually catch up with, or pass, the person that passed me.

The giant invisible rubber band worked again!

Even without this marvelous performance enhancement band, we have the capacity inside to run faster. Because we're under maximum marathon stress at this point, the left brain is in control. Dirty tricks allow you to break free for a while.

TWO MAJOR ROLES FOR DIRTY TRICKS

- *Sneak down the road while the left brain is confused*

  The left brain, in all of its logic, doesn't know what to do with "a giant, invisible rubber band." While it is befuddled, you have a window of opportunity for avoiding negative messages and moving toward your goal. The more you get into the vision of the dirty trick, the more time you'll have before the negative side starts spewing its venom again. You may get 100, 200 or 400 meters down the road. But the finish line is only a series of dirty trick segments away.

- *One crazy thought can unlock another*

  Even one imaginative dirty trick can start the creative side of the brain working on other interesting images, visions, and notions which will entertain you and get you closer to the finish. More significant, a series of these "tricks" can unlock inside you the creative process itself, which can mobilize all of your resources in overcoming challenges and getting you to the finish line feeling good.

  The best dirty tricks are the ones that work for you. Only you will respond to the unique chemistry of specific images and crazy concepts. Start concocting these during your right brain runs and remember the ones that work. The more you use them, the more effective they become.

172

Almost any imaginative idea will distract you for a while. To engage the performance components inside, it helps if the "tricks" are related to behaviors which help you in the marathon. Here are a few ideas that have worked for me:

◆ Oxygen molecules

The night before a marathon, I collect several million oxygen molecules in a sandwich bag and pin it on my shorts. During the latter stages of the marathon, when the oxygen doesn't seem to be as abundant, I take off the bag and squeeze it out in front of my mouth or nose. Before squeezing, I exhale completely every third or fourth breath. Just one or two squeezes last about 100 to 200 yards. The best part of this trick is seeing and hearing the reactions from the people around you in the marathon. If you're a real salesperson, you may try to make some money from the severely oxygen deprived folks who went out too fast. Just bring along some extra bags.

◆ Ball Bearing Atoms

This is a high-tech right brain invention which will send you gliding to the finish. As the legs lose their resiliency near the finish, you can shake off of your hair millions of atoms which normally act to help you shiny. As they drop on to your shoes and feet, you'll find that you don't need to stretch out your stride any more. You glide better through the air and stay economically more efficient by staying closer to the ground. When you're losing this effect, shake your hair again. Balding people, like myself, will always appreciate some strategic head shakes from others. A downhill portion of the course will enhance the effect of these virtually invisible ball bearings.

◆ A Giant Hand

The ancient Greeks often imagined that Zeus or another god was helping them in difficult situations. When it becomes tough to go up a hill during those last six miles, call for the giant hand to come in and gently push you up. Most folks find that the hand comes in gently as you get your posture upright. The support increases as you shorten stride, keep feet low to the ground, and let the feet gently lift off when they are directly underneath you.

◆ Your "Inspiration" Shoes

If logistics permit, you might consider changing shoes during the last six miles of the marathon. Both shoes must be broken in, of course. Save your "inspirational" pair for the last part. Just putting them on sends a jolt of invigoration into your feet, up your legs, then through your body and into the right brain. At that point, all types of crazy and innovative things can happen.

◆ The PowerBar Boost

For the marathon journey, you're not bringing just any PowerBar. Pick the ones with the greatest energy potential from your most powerful stash of bars and infuse them with even more energy. Handle the pieces of these bars with care as you don't want to infect everyone around you. As you chew on each piece and drink water you feel the energy move from your mouth to your right brain. Then, instantly it unlocks other pockets of energy which have been hiding until that point.

Have fun with these dirty tricks. Since your only constraint is the imaginative power of your right brain, there are no limits to what you can unleash.

173

HEAT DISEASE ALERT

The most common health problem among endurance exercisers is heat disease. This is a serious condition which has resulted in death in a high percentage of cases, even in highly trained, young athletes.

PREVENTION:

- During hot weather, exercise at the coolest time (usually before sunrise).

- Drink water all day long.

- Avoid caffeine, alcohol and other drugs.

- Wear clothing that is light and loose.

- Eat small, low-fat snacks which you know will not cause you distress (far enough ahead).

- Don't significantly increase duration or intensity.

- Slow down pace even more to adjust for heat, humidity and hills—especially in the beginning.

- Take walk-breaks more often on hot days.

SYMPTOMS:

- Intense heat build-up in the head, significant headache, general overheating of the body

- General confusion and loss of concentration and muscular control

- Over-sweating and then cessation of sweating, clammy skin and excessive breathing

- Extreme tiredness, upset stomach, muscle cramps, vomiting, feeling faint

RISK FACTORS:

- Sleep deprivation

- Infection (viral, bacterial, etc.)

- Dehydration (avoid alcohol and caffeine)

- Severe sunburn, skin irritation

- Unaccustomed to hot weather

- Overweight

- Untrained for specific training session

- Occurrence(s) of heat disease in the past

- Under medications—especially the following: cold medicines, diuretics, medicines for diarrhea, tranquilizers, antihistamines, atropine, and scopolamine

- The following medical conditions:

  High cholesterol, high blood pressure, under extreme stress, asthma, diabetes, epilepsy, drug use (including alcohol), cardiovascular disease, smoking, unfit lifestyle

SEE A PHYSICIAN WHO KNOWS THE BENEFICIAL EFFECTS OF RUNNING AND FITNESS

- Before beginning the program

- If you have any question about any of the above conditions

- If you notice any significant change in body functions, immune response, etc.

TAKE ACTION!

- Watch for heat disease in group members and take action if you think they are in trouble.

- Walk, cool off and get help immediately.

175

BREATHING

By using an efficient breathing technique, you'll not only be capable of a higher level of performance in the marathon but also you'll teach yourself how to acquire a better supply of oxygen and improve almost every aspect of your exercise experience...as well as the way you feel doing the other things you do.

THE CONCEPT OF DEEP BREATHING (ALSO CALLED "BELLY BREATHING")

- You're filling up the lower part of the lungs first.

- Through practice you can quickly inhale and quickly exhale while deep breathing.

- You don't need to fill the upper part of your lungs to capacity.

ELIMINATING SIDE PAINS

The deep-breathing technique can help you reduce or eliminate those irritating side pains which often erupt just when you're getting into your exercise. Such pains seem to be primarily caused by shallow breathing—using the upper part of our lungs in a minimal way. This low energy expenditure method is adequate for our normal sedentary activities and seems to provide sufficient oxygen at the beginning of an exercise session. But it also minimizes the amount of oxygen which you could absorb during exertion and often puts you into debt. If you start your runs with shallow breathing, you'll probably get side pains during some of them. Since side pains are aggravated by

going out faster than you should (even when the pace feels easy), slow down at the beginning of all of your runs if you've been experiencing these discomforts.

DEEP-BREATHING TECHNIQUE

- Quickly exhale as completely as possible every third or fourth breath.

- This almost guarantees a complete intake as you inhale immediately afterward.

- Breathe normally in between the deeper breaths.

- Don't do this deeper breathing more often because you could hyper-ventilate.

- You must start this technique from the beginning of your run to maximize its effect.

Some folks time their exhale to take place as they push off, every second or third step. If this sounds intriguing, try it two ways: 1) breathe out completely as you push off either the right or the left foot or 2) alternate between the left or right foot. To see which method works best, you should attempt one method only during a specific run.

You can practice this breathing method at any time—not just when exercising. Be sure to start each exercise session using this technique. After several weeks or months of regular breathing in this way, it will become your almost automatic breathing method.

For more information on breathing, see Galloway's Book On Running, pp. 152.

STRETCHING

THE GOOD NEWS:

When stretching is done regularly, in the correct way, it will reduce the tightening effect which naturally occurs as we age. Unfortunately, running increases the speed of this tightening. Regular stretching is a positive component of a marathon program when done carefully.

THE BAD NEWS:

Stretching is the third leading cause of injury among runners. While injuries are almost always the result of improper stretching, it is very easy to injure yourself while doing a stretch that seems perfectly safe.

STRETCHING DOES NOT WARM YOU UP FOR A RUN

The best warm-up for running has been the following: 1) walking, 2) very slow jogging and 3) gradually picking up your pace to "normal." Stretching before a run will not warm you up better or sooner, and it won't help you run faster in that run.

THE BEST TIME TO STRETCH:

Pick a time in the afternoon or evening when you're relaxed, when you don't have to rush through the stretch routine, and when your muscles are warmed up from the activities of the day. Most folks find that the period just before getting into bed is the best time for stretching; indeed, stretching helps you relax for an earlier drift into dreamland.

DON'T!

* Stretch when you're in a hurry

* Stretch before running

* Push a muscle into tension or tightness

* Stretch a tight muscle during or immediately after a run

* Stretch immediately after running (wait at least 30 minutes)

DO!

* Take your time when stretching

* Move the muscle gently into a relaxed extension

* Hold it in that position for six to thirty seconds

* Back off gently

* Stretch at least twice a week

The areas of your body which need more stretching due to running: calf muscles, hamstrings, and lower back. Make sure that you choose safe exercises. For more information on stretching, with specific stretches, see Galloway's Book On Running, pp. 159-165, and Stretching, by Bob Anderson.

HOW TO PREDICT YOUR MARATHON PERFORMANCE

By running several 5K races during your marathon training, you can predict how fast you're capable of going in the marathon itself. This was designed by Gerry Purdy and reprinted, in part, from information supplied for Galloway's Book On Running. More extensive charts are offered in Gerry's Computerized Running Training Programs, published by Track & Field News.

1. If you're running your first marathon, use this chart only to see what you could run if you were running to capacity. Then set your goal about two minutes per mile slower than that time. If your first one is slow and enjoyable (and the two are related), you'll continue to enjoy exercise and benefit from it. You'll have the opportunity to run faster in the next marathon... or the one after that.

2. Run several 5K's on non-long-run weekends. Make sure that they are run on certified courses (which have been accurately measured). See what your 5K predicts in the marathon. The more 5K's you run, the better your prediction potential.

3. This prediction is only valid if you have run the 26 to 28 mile-training run (two minutes per mile slower than you could run it) three

weeks before the marathon itself. Those with goals of 3:40 and faster need to have also done the mile repeats as prescribed on the schedules in the front of this book.

4. If the marathon course is hilly or marathon day weather is above 50 degrees F and above 50 percent humidity, your time will not be as fast as it would be under ideal conditions. As the heat and humidity rise, you must adjust your pace to be more conservative from the first mile of the marathon. Be aware of heat disease symptoms and get help at the first sign of these.

5. Don't use your best 5K time to predict your marathon performance. Take an average of your best three times, and then add two to five minutes to the prediction. A conservative pace in the beginning will conserve your resources, allowing you to run faster at the end if you're ready to do so.

6. You may be able to run faster than the table predicts if you haven't done much speed play. To improve your times in the 5K, see Return of the Tribes and Galloway's Book On Running. This usually helps to improve your marathon time also.

5K Time	Marathon	5K Time	Marathon	5K Time	Marathon
34:48	6:01:24	28:15	4:48:17	22:49	3:48:58
34:19	5:56:01	27:54	4:44:36	22:23	3:44:21
33:55	5:51:58	27:35	4:41:00	21:58	3:39:55
33:28	5:46:50	27:16	4:37:30	21:34	3:35:39
32:59	5:41:23	26:58	4:34:05	21:11	3:31:33
32:31	5:36:17	26:39	4:30:45	20:49	3:27:36
32:05	5:31:12	26:22	4:27:29	20:27	3:23:48
31:38	5:26:19	26:04	4:24:19	20:06	3:20:08
31:13	5:21:36	25:47	4:21:13	19:46	3:16:36
30:48	5:17:01	25:31	4:18:11	19:27	3:13:11
30:25	5:12:34	25:14	4:15:13	19:08	3:09:53
30:02	5:08:15	24:58	4:12:20	18:50	3:06:42
29:39	5:04:02	24:27	4:06:44	18:32	3:03:37
29:18	4:59:56	23:58	4:01:23	18:15	3:00:39
28:56	4:55:57	23:29	3:58:15	17:58	2:57:45
28:35	4:52:04	23:15	3:53:46		

FOR A CONTINUED LISTING OF FASTER TIMES SEE GALLOWAY'S BOOK ON RUNNING (APPENDIX)

Marathon Pace Chart

Mile Pace	2 MILE	5 MILE	10 MILE	15 MILE	20 MILE	MARATHON
10:00	20:00	50:00	1:40:00	2:30:00	3:20:00	4:22:00
10:20	20:40	51:40	1:43:20	2:35:00	3:26:40	4:30:44
10:40	21:20	53:20	1:46:40	2:40:00	3:33:20	4:39:28
11:00	22:00	55:00	1:50:00	2:45:00	3:40:00	4:48:32
11:20	22:40	56:40	1:53:20	2:50:00	3:46:40	4:57:16
11:40	23:20	58:20	1:56:40	2:55:00	3:53:20	5:06:00
12:00	24:00	1:00:00	2:00:00	3:00:00	4:00:00	5:14:44
12:20	24:40	1:01:40	2:03:20	3:05:00	4:06:40	5:23:28
12:40	25:20	1:03:20	2:06:40	3:10:00	4:13:20	5:32:12
13:00	26:00	1:05:00	2:10:00	3:15:00	4:20:00	5:40:56
13:20	26:40	1:06:40	2:13:20	3:20:00	4:26:40	5:49:40
13:40:	27:20	1:08:20	2:16:40	3:25:00	4:33:20	5:58:24
14:00	28:00	1:10:00	2:20:00	3:30:00	4:40:00	6:07:08

Note: for paces faster than 10 minutes per mile, see Galloway's Book On Running, pp. 274-275

The Running Newsletter
....with Jeff Galloway

180

What To Look For In A Marathon Training Program

As the marathon has become a lifestyle change project, marathon training groups are springing up all over North America. Because of the group support, training can become fun and your chance of completing the marathon are greatly increased. Because there are a wide range of groups, look for programs which offer the following:

- Running Groups, based upon fitness level

- A leader in each pace group who enforces a slow pace and the walk breaks

- A schedule which gradually increases the long run past "the wall" (@ 23 miles)

- Long runs every other weekend (every third weekend when long one reaches 18 to 20 miles)

- Lots of laughs on every run

- For information on marathon training groups in many North American cities, call 1-800-200-2771.

Athens Marathon – November 1, 1998

Jeff Galloway announced that he will be joining the Apostolos Travel Group as they travel back to the marathoner's mecca: the original run from the seaside village of Marathon to the original Olympic Stadium of the modern games in Athens. This celebration of Phidippides' journey (almost 2500 years ago) and more than one century of organized marathon racing will be offered in a full tour or an extended weekend package. "So much of the experience of Greece depends upon where you stay and how your arrangements are made. Apostolos Travel professionals are Greek and provide cultural and local opportunities which normally wouldn't be available. Their choice of accommodations is superb: a small resort seacost town with scenic trails that Phidippides could have run. Several visits to inspiring ancient sites, most meals and all tour direction are included. This is an entirely different experience than you'd receive if you stayed in downtown Athens." For information, please call 303/755-2888.

Watch for the Galloway Website!

You can stay in touch with training, fat-burning, marathon gatherings, healthy recipes and more by visiting our site on the world wide web. www.jeffgalloway.com

Sign up for this FREE Newsletter. Just call 1-800-200-2771 and leave your name and address for updates, fitness opportunities, trends.

What is a fitness vacation?

A growing number of people each year are choosing to spend some of their vacation time in a positive environment, enjoying hiking, running and just *being* in a beautiful area. This is one of the very few ways to really get away from the stress and become invigorated. It's tough to have to go to places like Lake Tahoe, the Blue Ridge Mountains, and the Oregon Coast, but somebody has to do it!

- Record holders don't attend. These are folks who are getting started or want to do more.

- You can learn techniques directly from the people who developed them.

- In a relaxed environment, lifelong friendships are made.

- Motivation, commitment and mental breakthroughs are covered.

- Your specific questions can be addressed, training program modified, etc.

- This fun time will be remembered for life!

- For more information on the various types of fitness vacations, call 800-200-2771.

Fat-Burning Tip: *"Increase the length of all of your runs to more than 45 minutes."*

Slow your pace down, and add a few more one-minute walk breaks early in the run, if necessary. Once you reach the magic 45-minute barrier, those who are running (and walking) within themselves will be burning mostly body fat as fuel. By continuing to do this regularly and extending the distance and time, you'll help the exercising muscle cells to become fat-burners.

Energizing Tip: *"Eat before you get really hungry."*

If you wait until you're significantly hungry, you'll almost certainly overeat. By eating small snacks at the first sign of hunger, you'll maintain the energy you need for job or school, sustain concentration, and avoid building up extra calories which will be converted into fat. Avoid snacks which have sugar (including fruit and fruit juices) and those with more than 15 percent of the calories in fat.

What about supplements?

Jeff: I don't see any harm in taking minimal doses of the anti-oxidants, and I take 500 mg of vitamin C and 400 iu of vitamin E daily.

One of the few products on the market that has excellent research to back it up is Endurox. This supplement has been shown to speed recovery between exercise sessions and to encourage fat burning. I've noticed that while taking it for the last year and a half, I'm able to run four or five days in a row without getting tired legs – versus fatigue after three days BE (before Endurox).

It's unlikely that taking vitamins will cut out the lulls or doldrums during the day. This is usually due to low blood sugar and can be corrected by regular doses of PowerBars. After six years and about 100 competitive products, I have found that PowerBar delivers the best sustained energy level for exercise and for life in general.

For further information, visit the Endurox website at www.endurox.com

Jeff Galloway's Fitness Vacations

LAKE TAHOE

Imagine yourself on a hike or a run along a crystal clear lake, surrounded by beautiful mountains, with an endless series of trails and other recreational opportunities. Even when the temperature goes above 85 degrees F, you'll be comfortable in the 10-30 percent humidity. Jeff has averaged 20 days per summer at Tahoe for 21 years and has experienced only about 15 cloudy or rainy days, total.

If you'd like to explore this beautiful area on the south shore of the lake with a group, look into Galloway's vacation at Tahoe. After a morning run along scenic paths in national forests or on the Truckee River bike path, you'll have breakfast. Jeff and staff will then present seminars on the topics listed below. Most after-noons are spent hiking some of the most beautiful areas you'll ever experience or in other fun activities, such as swapping T-shirts, etc.

You'll meet inspiring and friendly experts such as Bob Anderson (the expert who literally wrote the book on <u>Stretching</u>), Sister Marion Irvine (a humorous and inspiring nun who qualified for the Olympic Trials at age 50), Joe Henderson (running's most prolific writer who knows just about everything that's going on in our sport), Dr. Gary Moran (physiologist and expert in biomechanics, strength, etc.), Dr. David Hannaford (sports podiatrist specializing in running injuries), and John Bingham (the Penguin from <u>Runner's World</u>).

LAKE JUNALUSKA, NC

Located just 30 minutes west of Asheville, NC, this mountain setting features a trail around the lake and lots of nearby diversions. Jeff will help you with running, nutrition, motivation and many more topics in the morning sessions. This leaves the afternoon open for exploring the Cherokee Indian Reservation, the Biltmore Estate, Maggie Valley, the Blue Ridge Parkway, the Great Smoky Mountains National Park - all within 30 minutes or less travel from Junaluska.

CANTERBURY TRAILS

Using beautifully maintained trails that have existed since the Middle Ages or before, we will run/walk between a series of quaint English villages. There will be beautiful country scenery and rich, historic heritage tours. We will eat dinner in English pubs and have oppor-tunities for sightseeing during the day. For those who don't want to walk or run (spouses, etc.), there will be transporta-tion between villages. The journey will end in Canterbury, destination of the historic pilgrimage.

TYPICAL CAMP SCHEDULE:

7:00	Group run/walk/stroll
8:00	Breakfast
9:00-12:00	Clinic Sessions
12:00	Lunch
1:00-6:00	Hiking, Sightseeing, Exploring
6:00	Dinner

CLINIC SESSIONS:

Nutrition   Mental Strength   Stretching
Getting Better As We Get Older
Motivation   Water Running   Cross Training
Marathon Training   Running Faster
Fatburning   Strengthening

CALL 1-800-200-2771 X10 FOR MORE INFORMATION.

Jeff Galloway's Weekend Retreat

Join us for a few days of hiking, running, walking and learning with the man who literally wrote the book on running. Olympian Jeff Galloway (*Galloway's Book On Running*), will help you set up an injury-free exercise routine, as you enjoy the support of others who want to get started, become more motivated, or energize their commitment to exercise.

Ski Lodge accomodations

The hotel has a fitness center, two hot tubs, beautiful pool, kitchenettes, and tennis courts nestled at the end of Squaw Valley. Meals will be all-you-care to eat, with choices, including low-fat options.

All abilities, all levels

Adult runners and walkers, especially novice and intermediate folks, will enjoy the information, the support of the group, and gentle but satisfying exercise. There will be hikes and time to socialize.

Fatburning, Motivation, Form and technique, Nutrition, Injury-free Exercise

Jeff will help you cut through the overwhelming mass of conflicting information so that you can set up a time-sensitive program for fatburning, racing, or just finishing (a 5K, 10K or marathon). Jeff's motivational style will keep you fired up for months to come.

Meet such guests as

* **Joe Henderson** - running's most prolific writer who knows just about everything that's going on in our sport
* **Bob Anderson** – the expert who literally wrote the book on *Stretching*
* **Sister Marion Irvine** – the humorous and inspiring nun who qualified for the Olympic Trials at age 50
* **Dr. Gary Moran** – physiologist and expert in biomechanics, strength, etc.
* **Dr. David Hannaford** – sports podiatrist specializing in running injuries
* **John Bingham** – the Penguin from *Runner's World*!

For more information: Call 1-800-200-2771 x 10.

FURTHER READING......
OR VIEWING....

Galloway's Book On Running (GBR)

 Experts have called this book "the standard among running books" and "the complete running information resource, written so you can understand it." In its 287 pages, you'll find just about everything you wanted to know about running: training, nutrition, injuries, shoes, stretching and strengthening, running form, 10K programs by time goal, racing, beginning, women's running, and much more. Organized so that you can easily find the segment in which you're interested, this has become the best-selling running book in North America.

"Breaking The Tape"

In two 30-minute VHS videotapes and a 30-minute motivational audiocassette, Jeff Galloway talks you through the world of running information. The first 30-minute segment includes tips on nutrition, stretching, choosing the right shoes, running injury free, and cross training. Tape Two covers form, pacing, peaking, setting realistic goals, building an interval speedwork plan for the 5K and 10K, and Jeff's six-month marathon training program. This is great for individual instruction or for group clinics and exercise reinforcement.

Return Of The Tribes To Peachtree Street (ROT)

 Since the publishing of GBR, Jeff has articulated many new concepts in the areas of mental training, motivation, fat-burning, nutrition, and speed training. His work with tens of thousands of beginners provided the inspiration for a concept called "Cruising," which has allowed almost everyone to enjoy the attitude boost, the fat-burning and the exhilaration of running, without the aches and pains. Jeff molded this new information into an entertaining format as a novel. You'll meet four people whose lives are changed for the better as they get swept up in the tribal experience of the Peachtree Road Race. You'll discover many new ideas and find that there are many more rewards in running than endorphins, burned-off fat, and T-shirts. New in 1995.

For more information or to place an order, call 1-800-200-2771.

Jeff Galloway's Training Journal—the logbook with a mission

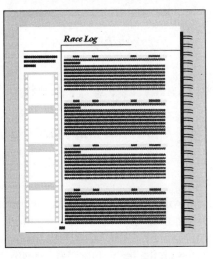

185

In this spiral-bound training tool, Jeff will lead you through the process of setting up a training program, step by step. Not only can you set up and record your progress for a year at a time, you'll be able to analyze the data in tables: logs for shoes, injuries, speed sessions. Graphs for morning pulse will help you monitor overtraining.

To order, call 800/200-2771 x 33

Let Jeff Galloway coach you at home!

proudly presents:

Jeff Galloway's Training Software

for Marathon and Half Marathon

Renowned runner, author and lecturer Jeff Galloway, whose best selling books have helped hundreds of thousands of runners, has now made his acclaimed training program available through the PC Coach software training system.

Based on the techniques Jeff uses in his Marathon programs across the country, this program will set you on the path to success, whatever your goals!

The Galloway Plan creates exciting training programs for all ability levels from beginner on up. The plan sets up a detailed training schedule for you based on:

- **Your running history and experience**
- **Your race distance (Marathon or Half-Marathon)**
- **Your personal goals (Race goal time, Train to finish, Fat burning)**
- **Your race date**

Week by week, throughout your training, Jeff is there on your computer screen to monitor your progress, adjust the training schedule, and give you tips and training advice that will keep you motivated each day, right up to your race. Whatever your running experience, Jeff's program can give you the best program for your special situation.

For more information, or to receive a free 3-week demo of the Galloway software, visit the PC Coach web site at http://www.pccoach.com
or call 1-800-522-6224

RUNNING RESOURCES AND CONTACTS

California

FORWARD MOTION
412 Hartz Ave
Danville, CA 94526
510/820-9966

PHIDIPPIDES - ENCINO
16545 Ventura Blvd
Encino, CA 91436
818/986-8686

FLEET FEET
8128 Madison
Fair Oaks, CA 95628-3756
916/965-8326

A SNAIL'S PACE RUNNING
SHOP
8780 Warner Avenue
Fountain Valley, CA 92708
714/842-2337

LOMA LINDA LOPERS
P.O. Box 495
Loma Linda, CA 92354
909/778-3200

RUNNERS HIGH
5463 East Carson
Long Beach, CA 90808
310/496-4760

RUNNER'S FACTORY
51 University Avenue
Los Gatos, CA 95030
408/395-4311

NEWPORT SKI COMPANY
2700 West Coast Hwy.
Newport Beach, CA 92663
714/631-3280

TRANSPORTS
6022 College Avenue
Oakland, CA 94618
510/655-4809

FLEET FEET
1730 Santa Clara #D3
Roseville, CA 95661
916/783-4558

FLEET FEET
161 S Hwy. 101
Solana Beach, CA 92075-1806
619/481-4148

FLEET FEET
2086 Chestnut St
San Francisco, CA 94123
415/921-7188

INSIDE TRACK
1410 E Main St
Ventura, CA 93001
805/643-1104

JEFF GALLOWAY'S
TRAINING PROGRAM
Chino Hills, Sacramento, San
Francisco, San Jose
800/200-2771 x 12

Colorado

RUNNER'S ROOST
1685 S Colorado Blvd
Denver, CO 80222
303/759-8455

JEFF GALLOWAY'S
TRAINING PROGRAM
Denver
800/200-2771 x 12

Connecticut

THE RUN-IN
2172 Silas Deane Hwy.
Rocky Hill, CT 06067
860/563-6136

JEFF GALLOWAY'S
TRAINING PROGRAM
Hartford
800/200-2771 x 12

D.C.

DC ROAD RUNNERS
P.O. Box 1352
Arlington, VA 22210
703/241-0395

JEFF GALLOWAY'S
TRAINING PROGRAM
Washington, D.C.
800/200-2771 x 12

Florida

RUNNING WILD
5437 North Federal Hwy.
Ft Lauderdale, FL 33308
954/492-0077

JACKSONVILLE TRACK CLUB
PO Box 24667
Jacksonville, FL 32241
904/384-TRAK (8725)

TRACK SHACK
1322 North Mills Ave
Orlando, FL 32803
407/898-1313

FOOTWORKS
5724 Sunset Dr
South Miami, FL 33143
305/661-3111

JEFF GALLOWAY'S
TRAINING PROGRAM
Ft. Lauderdale, Miami, Orlando,
Tampa
800/200-2771 x 12

Georgia

ATLANTA TRACK CLUB
3097 East Shadowlawn
Atlanta, GA 30305
404/231-9064

187

PHIDIPPIDES
220 Sandy Springs Circle
Atlanta, GA 30328
404/255-6149

PHIDIPPIDES
1544 Piedmont Rd NE
Atlanta, GA 30324
404/875-4268

JEFF GALLOWAY'S
TRAINING PROGRAM
Atlanta, Gwinnett County
800/200-2771 x 12

Indiana
ATHLETIC ANNEX RUNNING
CENTRE
1411 W 86th St.
Indianapolis, IN 46260
317/872-0000

Illinois
FLEET FEET
#7 S Dunton Ave
Arlington Heights, IL 60005-1401
708/670-9255

SPRINGFIELD RUNNING
CENTER
2943 W White Oak Dr
Springfield, IL 62704
217/787-4400

JEFF GALLOWAY'S
TRAINING PROGRAM
Chicago
800/200-2771 x 12

Kansas
GARRY GRIBBLE'S RUNNING
STORE
Stoll Park Center
11932W 119th
Overland Park, KS 66213
913/469-4090

Kentucky
KEN COMBS RUNNING
CENTER
4137 Shelbyville Rd
Louisville, KY 40207
502/895-3410

Louisiana
PHIDIPPIDES
6601 Veterans Blvd
Metairie, LA 70003
504/887-8900

Maryland
AMERICAN RUNNING AND
FITNESS ASSOCIATION
4405 E-W Hwy, Ste 405
Bethesda, MD 20814
301/913-9517

FEET FIRST
10451 Twin Rivers Rd
Wildelake Village Green
Columbia, MD 21044
410/992-5800

JEFF GALLOWAY'S
TRAINING PROGRAM
Bethesda
800/200-2771 x 12

Massachusetts
BILL RODGERS RUNNING
CENTER
353-T N Market Place
Boston, MA 32103
617/723-5612

JEFF GALLOWAY'S
TRAINING PROGRAM
Boston
800/200-2771 x 12

Michigan
RUNNING FIT
123 E Liberty
Ann Arbor, MI 48104
313/769-5016

TORTOISE AND HARE
RUNNING SHOP
213 E Liberty Plaza
Ann Arbor, MI 48104
313/769-9510

BAUMAN'S RUNNING
CENTER
1453 West Hill Rd
Flint, MI 48507
810/238-5981

COMPLETE RUNNER
915 S Dort Hwy
Flint, MI 48503
810/233-8851

GAZELLE SPORTS
3987 28th St
Grand Rapids, MI 49512
616/940-9888

HANSON'S RUNNING SHOP
20641 Mack Ave
Grosse Pointe, MI 48256
313/882-1325

MOTOR CITY STRIDERS
Dr. Edward H. Kozloff
10144 Lincoln
Huntington Woods, MI 48070
810/544-9099

HANSON'S RUNNING SHOP
3047 Rochester Rd
Royal Oak, MI 48073
810/616-9665

HANSON'S RUNNING SHOP
44915 Hayes Rd
Sterling Heights, MI 48313
810/247-6640

JEFF GALLOWAY'S
TRAINING PROGRAM
Flint
800/200-2771 x 12

Minnesota
JEFF GALLOWAY'S
TRAINING PROGRAM
Minneapolis
800/200-2771 x 12

Missouri
GARRY GRIBBLE'S RUNNING
SPORTS
Ward Parkway Mall
8600 Ward Parkway
Kansas City, MO 64114
816/363-4800

Nevada
JEFF GALLOWAY'S
TRAINING PROGRAM
Las Vegas
800/200-2771 x 12

New Jersey
TRI-ATHLETICS
80 Speedwell Avenue
Morristown, NJ 07960
201/292-9162

New Mexico
FLEET FEET
8238 Menaul Blvd. NE
Albuquerque, NM 87110
505/299-8922

GIL'S RUNNERS SHOE WORLD
3515 Lomas Blvd NE
Albuquerque, NM 87106
505/268-6300

New York
JEFF GALLOWAY'S
TRAINING PROGRAM
New York
800/200-2771 x 12

North Carolina
FLEET FEET
102-A E Main St
Carrsboro, NC 27510
919/968-3338

FLEET FEET
1412 E Blvd.
Charlotte, NC 28203
704/358-0713

JEFF GALLOWAY'S
TRAINING PROGRAM
Charlotte
800/200-2771 x 12

Ohio
OHIO RIVER ROAD RUNNERS
Bill Mercer
2061 Dane Lane
Bellbrook, OH 45305
513/848-2576

FASTTRACK
138 The Arcade
401 Euclid Ave
Cleveland, OH 44114
216/621-1414

ENDURANCE SPORTS
4396 Indian Ripple Rd
Dayton, OH 45440
513/426-8272

CEDARWINDS
1305 Park Drive
Medway, Ohio 45341
800/548-2388

DAVE'S RUNNING SHOP, INC.
5577 Monroe St
Sylvania, OH 43560
419/882-8524

Oregon
PACESETTER ATHLETICS
4431 SE Woodstock Blvd.
Portland, OR 97206
510/777-3214

Pennsylvania
NATIONAL SPORTING
GOODS
117 Mill Ave
Dalton, PA 18414
717/563-1620

RITTENHOUSE SPORTS
SPECIALTIES
126 S 18th St
Philadelphia, PA 19103
215/569-9957

South Carolina
JEFF GALLOWAY'S
TRAINING PROGRAM
Greenville
800/200-2771 x 12

Tennessee
KNOXVILLE TRACK CLUB
3530 Talahi Gardens
Knoxville, TN 37919
423/673-8020

FLEET FEET
597 Erin Dr
Memphis, TN 38117
901/761-0078
800/606-FEET

MEMPHIS RUNNERS TRACK
CLUB
PO Box 17981
Memphis, TN 38187-0981
901/534-6782

Texas
RUN TEX
919 W 12th St
Austin, TX 78703
512/475-3254

FLEET FEET
6034 S Padre Island Dr
Corpus Christi, TX 78412
512/993-5838

LUKE'S
3607 Oak Lawn
Dallas, TX 75219
214/528-1290

FLEET FEET
2408 Rice Blvd.
Houston, TX 77005
713/520-6353

FLEET FEET
6586 Woodway
Houston, TX 77057
713/465-0033

JEFF GALLOWAY'S
TRAINING PROGRAM
Dallas, Ft. Worth
800/200-2771 x 12

Virginia
PACERS
1301 King St
Alexandria, VA 22314
703/836-1463

JEFF GALLOWAY'S
TRAINING PROGRAM
Alexandria, Richmond
800/200-2771 x 12

189

CANADA
SPORTSBOOK PLUS
2100 W 4th Avenue
Vancouver, BC V6K 1N7
CANADA
604/733-7323

Running Room's Canadian Connections

The Running Room network allows you to connect with community running groups, events and clinics. I have visited most of the locations listed and am impressed with the staff, the selection, and the information resources. While there, sign up for the free membership in their Running club, and learn about the regular seminars: Learn to Run, Women's Running, Running Faster, and Marathon Training.

RUNNING ROOM LOCATIONS

ALBERTA

Edmonton

Edmonton Administration Office and Warehouse,
9750-47 Avenue, Edmonton, AB
T6E 5P3
Ph: (403) 439 - 3099
Fax: (403) 433 - 6433

Team Sports, 9750-47 Ave,
Edmonton, AB T6E 5P3
Ph: (403) 439 - 3099
Fax: (403) 433 - 6433

8537 - 109 Street, Edmonton,
AB T6G 1E4
Ph: (403) 433-6062
Fax: (403) 439-8465

Callingwood Marketplace, #236,
6655-178 Street, Edmonton, AB
T5T 4J5
Ph: (403) 483-1516
Fax: (403) 483-2116

Kinsmen Sports Centre, 9100
Walterdale Hill, Edmonton, AB
T6E 2V3
Ph: (403) 433 - 5901

Calgary

321A - 10th St. N.W., Calgary,
AB T2N 1V7
Ph: (403) 270 - 7317
Fax: (403) 270 - 0114

Glenmore Landing Shopping
Centre,
#118, 1600-90 Ave., SW,
Calgary, AB T2V 5A8
Ph: (403) 252 - 3388
Fax: (403) 252 - 3669

BRITISH COLUMBIA

Vancouver

1519 Robson St. Vancouver, BC
V6G 1C3
Ph: (604) 684 - 9771
Fax: (604) 684 - 4236

#001 City Square, 555 West
12th Ave.,
Vancouver, BC V5Z 3X7
Ph: (604) 879 - 9721
Fax: (604) 879 - 9731

Suite 738, 2601 Westview Drive,
North Vancouver, BC V7N 3W9
Ph: (604) 983 - 9761
Fax: (604) 983 - 3934

Unit #B, 1111 Ponderosa St.,
Coquitlam, BC V3B 7L3
Ph: (604) 945 - 1810
Fax: (604) 945 - 0042

Unit 410, 7380 King George
Highway, Surrey, BC
V3W 5A5
Ph: (604) 599 - 6001
Fax: (604) 599 - 6004

Kelowna

#115 2463 Highway 97 North,
Kelowna, BC V1X 4J2
Ph: (250) 862 - 3511
Fax: (250) 862 - 3505

Victoria

1008 Douglas St. Victoria, BC
V8W 2C3
Ph: (250) 383 - 4224
Fax: (250) 383 - 4299

ONTARIO

Toronto

2629 Yonge St., Toronto, ON
M4P 2J6
Ph: (416) 322 - 7100
Fax: (416) 322 - 7102

Unit #3, 2100 Bloor St. West
Toronto, ON M6S 1M7
Ph: (416) 762 - 4478
Fax: (416) 762 - 2848

1977 Queen St. East Toronto,
ON M4L 1J1
Ph: (416) 693 - 1530
Fax: (416) 693 - 9110

Commerce Court, #30
Wellington Street West, Toronto,
ON M5L 1E8
Ph: (416) 867-7575
Fax: (416) 867-7587

Hamilton

1457 Main Street, West,
Hamilton, ON L8S 1C9

Mississauga

Sussex Centre, #70
Burnhamthorpe Road West,
Mississauga, ON L5B 3C2
Ph: (905) 279 - 6486
Fax: (905) 279 - 6489

London

620 Richmond St. London, ON
N6A 5J9
Ph: (519) 438 - 8550
Fax: (519) 438 - 8587

Ottawa

911 Bank St., Ottawa, ON K1S
3W5
Ph: (613) 233 - 5617
Fax: (613) 233 - 1379

121 Bank St., Ottawa, ON K1P
5N5
Ph: (613) 233 - 5165
Fax: (613) 233 - 5169

MANITOBA
winnipeg

Kenaston Village Mall, 1875 Grant
Avenue, Winnipeg, MB R3N 1Z2
Ph: (204) 487-7582
Fax: (204) 487-7584

NOVA SCOTIA
Halifax

5514 - Spring Garden Road,
Halifax, NS B3J 1G6
Ph: (902) 420 - 0774
Fax: (902) 420 - 0775

For other Running Room
Locations please call our Toll-Free
Number
1-800-419-2906

191

MAJOR MARATHONS

JANUARY

Walt Disney World Marathon

This marathon is usually the first weekend in January. For further information contact:

Track Shack
1322 N Mills Ave
Orlando, FL 32803
404/898-1313

Houston-Tenneco Marathon

This marathon is in mid January. For more information, call 713/864-9305 or write:

HOUSTON-TENNECO
MARATHON
5900 Memorial Dr Ste 200
Houston, TX 77007

San Diego Marathon

This marathon is in mid January. For information, call 619/792-2900 or write to:

SAN DIEGO MARATHON
511 A Cedros Ave Ste B
Solana Beach, CA 92075

FEBRUARY

Long Beach Marathon

This marathon is in early February. For information, call 310/494-2664 or write:

LONG BEACH MARATHON
c/o Physical Education
Department
Cal State-Long Beach
1250 Bellflower Blvd
Long Beach, CA 90840

Blue Angel Marathon

Late February. For information, call 904/452-4391 or write:

BLUE ANGEL MARATHON
c/o MWR Bldg 632
Naval Air Station
Pensacola, FL 32508

MARCH

Los Angeles Marathon

For information call 310/444-5544 or write to:

LA MARATHON
11110 W Ohio Ave Ste 100
Los Angeles, CA 90025

Napa Valley Marathon

ENVIRO-SPORTS
P.O. Box 1040
Stinson Beach
CA 94970, 415/868-1829
www.envirosports.com

Maui Marathon

This marathon is in March.

VIRR
PO Box 330099
Kahului, HI 96733
808/871-6441

Shamrock Marathon

This marathon is usually the day before St Patrick's Day. This course is designed for everyone. It is an out and back course through the resort and continuing to Fort Story, home of the country's oldest lighthouse. Times will be recorded for 6 hours (12:30 pace). This is a Boston Marathon qualifying course. There is also a 8K, Masters 8K, 5K Fitness and race walk and a children's marathon (26.2 yards). For information call 804/481-5090 or write to:

JERRY BOCRIE
2308 Maple St
Virginia Beach, VA 23451

Catalina Marathon

This marathon is in mid-March. It was voted one of "the most scenic marathons" in *Runner's World* February 1996 issue.

Two Harbors, CA
California Athletic Productions
304 Stonecliffe Aisle
Irvine, CA 92715

APRIL

Charlotte Observer Marathon

This marathon is held in early April. For information, call 704/358-KICK or write to:

MARATHON
Box 30294
Charlotte, NC 28230

Boston Marathon

This marathon is in mid April. This is a qualifying race (see below). For information, send a self addressed stamp envelope (with 55 cents postage) to:

BAA
PO BOX (year)
Boston, MA 07148

You can qualify between January 1st of the year prior to the race year and mid March that race year. The qualifying times are as follows (as of 1996):

AGE	MEN	WOMEN
18-34	3:10	3:40
35-39	3:15	3:45
40-44	3:20	3:50
45-49	3:25	3:55
50-54	3:30	4:00
55-59	3:35	4:05
60-64	3:40	4:10
65-69	3:45	4:15
70+	3:50	4:20

Big Sur Marathon

This race is in April. "The most dramatic marathon in the world." You start at 210 feet and go down hill. There is a large rise in elevation from miles 9.6 to 11.9 and then you begin to run downhill again and eventually finish at 25 feet.

WILLIAM BURLEIGH
BOX 222620
Carmel, CA 93922
408/625-6226

London Marathon

This Marathon is in April.

NUTRASWEET LONDON MARATHON
Overseas Entry Coordinator
91 Walkden Rd
Walkden, Manchester
M28 5 DQ
England

or

Marathon Tours
108 Main St
Boston, MA 02129
617/242-7845

MAY

Avenue of the Giants

This race is the first week in May.
There is great scenery and ambiance among the Giant. There is also a 10K race at this event.

Gay Gilchrist
Six Rivers Running Club
281 Hidden Valley Rd
Bayside, CA 95524

Vancouver International Marathon

This marathon is in early May. One of the most scenic marathons in the world. Voted one of the top ten marathons by *Runner's World* February 1996 issue.

VANCOUVER INTL MARATHON
Gordon Rogers
Box 3213
Vancouver, BC   V68 3X8
CANADA
604/872-2928
604/872-2903 fax

193

Okanagan International Marathon

This marathon is held mid May. The flat course starts is Kelowna City Park by the sails. For further information write or call:

THE RUNNING ROOM
#115 2463 Highway 97 North
Kelowna, BC V1X 4J2
CANADA
604/862-3511

Buffalo Marathon

This race is in early May.

BUFFALO MARATHON
PO Box 652
Buffalo, NY 14202
716/837-7223

Cleveland Marathon

CVS Cleveland
P.O. Box 550
Twinsburg, OH 44087,
216/487-1402"

Pittsburgh Marathon,

UPMC
City of Pittsburgh Marathon
200 Lothrop St, Pittsburgh, PA 15213,
412/647-7866

JUNE

Grandma's Marathon

This race is in late June.
GRANDMA'S MARATHON
PO Box 16234
Duluth, MN 55816
218/727-0947

Steamboat Marathon

This marathon is in the middle of June. It was ranked one of the most scenic marathons by *Runner's World* February 1996 issue.
CHAMBER RESORT
PO Box 774408
Stmbt Springs, CO 80477
303/879-0882

Mayor's Midnight Sun Marathon

MUNICIPALITY OF ANCHORAGE
PARKS & REC
P.O. Box 196650
Anchorage, AK, 99519
907/343-4474

Rock 'N' Roll Marathon

ELITE RACING
10509 Vista Sorrento Pkwy #102
San Diego, CA 32121
619/450-6510
www.rnrmarathon.com

JULY

San Francisco Marathon

This race is in mid July. Starts at the Golden Gate Bridge, over the bridge through Presidio, Fisherman's Wharf, Chinatown, and ends inside Golden Gate Park at Kezar Stadium.
SAN FRANCISCO MARATHON
PO Box 77148
San Francisco, CA 94107
415/391-2123

AUGUST

Crater Lake Rim Marathon

This marathon is in mid-August.
Crater Lake was ranked "one of the most scenic marathon" by *Runner's World* in February 1996
CRATER LAKE RIM RUNS
5380 Mack Ave
Klamath Falls, OR 97603
503/884-6939

Rocky Mountain Marathon

Starting at Nordic Centre in Canmore Alberta, the course runs through the undulating townsite of Canmore amongst the splendor of the Canadian Rockies.
403/433-6062 or 403/483-1516

Capital City Marathon

This race is held in August.
Edmonton, BC CANADA
403/433-6062 or 403/483-1516

SEPTEMBER

Portland Marathon

This marathon is in the end of September, beginning of October. *Runner's World* called it the "the best people's marathon in the West." The motto of this race is that "all finishers are treated like winners." The course minimizes turns and narrow streets (it has less than 25 turns). For information, call 503/226-1111.or write to:
Les Smith
PO BOX 4040
Beaverton, OR 97076

OCTOBER

Fox Cities Marathon

This race is early October. Scenic point to point, USATF certified course. Community support offers participants comic along the course as runners wind through seven cities and over seven bridges. Walkers welcome. Relay Marathon and 2.62 mile run/walk round out the day's events, and a kid's race and pasta dinner are held on Saturday. For more information, please call 414/954-6790 or write to:
FOX CITIES MARATHON
835 Valley Rd
Menasha, WI 54952

Twin Cities

This race is in mid October. This marathon is known as the "most beautiful urban marathon in America" and is ranked one the nation's top marathons. There is a limit of 6,000 entrants. There are 200,000 spectators and 4,000 volunteers. There is a two-day Marketplace and Fitness Fair with Saturday family events on that weekend. For information, call 612/673-0078 or write:

TWIN CITIES MARATHON
708 N First St Ste CR-33
Minneapolis, MN 55401

Wineglass Marathon

This marathon is in early October. "One of the most scenic marathons" according to February 96 *Runner's World*.

WINEGLASS MARATHON
Mark Landin
PO Box 98
Canning, NY 14803
607/936-8736

Marine Corps Marathon

This race is usually mid to late October. Write to request information:

Marine Corps Marathon
PO BOX 188
Quantico, VA 22134
703/784-2225

Cape Cod Marathon

This marathon is in the end of October. Ranked "one of the most scenic marathons" by *Runner's World*.

CAPE COD MARATHON
Courtney and Carilyn Bird
Box 699
West Falmouth, MA 02574
508/540-6959

Richmond Times/Dispatch Marathon

This marathon is in October.

Richmond Times/Dispatch
MARATHON
Dewayne Davis
PO Box 85333
Richmond, VA 23293
8044/649-6738

Columbus Marathon

This race is late October, early November. A mostly flat clover leaf design course. Ranked second fastest marathon by *Runner's World*. Times are recorded up to 5 hours and 30 minutes. Services will be provided for runners maintaining this pace (about a 12:30 per mile). For information, call 614/433-0395 or write to:

COLUMBUS MARATHON
PO BOX 26806
Columbus, OH 43226

Detroit Marathon

This race is in October. This race starts in Windsor, Ontario, CANADA and finishes in Detroit. There is a six hour time limit. This course is USATF certified.

DETROIT FREE PRESS MARATHON
300 Stroh River Pl Ste 4000
Detroit, MI 48207
313/393-7749

Hartford Marathon

Beth Schluger
221 Main Street
Hartford, CT 06106
860/525-3435

Chicago Marathon

P.O. Box 10597
Chicago, IL 60610
312/243-0003
www.chicagomarathon.com

NOVEMBER

New York City Marathon

Marathon Entries
P.O. Box 1388 GPO
New York, NY 10116
212/423-2249
www.nyrrc.org.

Atlanta Marathon

This marathon is on Thanksgiving Day. This is the 1996 Olympic Marathon course. There is a 5 hour time limit that is strictly enforced. For more information, call or write to:

ATC
3097 East Shadowlawn
Atlanta, GA 30305
404/231-9064.

195

DECEMBER

Dallas White Rock Marathon

This race is in early December.

> WHITE ROCK MARATHON
> 3607 Oak Lawn
> Dallas, TX 75219

Tennessee Memphis Marathon

This marathon is in early December. It is an out and back course by some of the most famous Tennessee landmarks. Elvis' mansion (where you can stop and have your picture made). There is prize money. For further information, call:

> Kim Cherry
> 901/523-4726

California International Marathon

This race is in early December.

> CALIFORNIA INTL
> MARATHON
> PO Box 161149
> Sacramento, CA 95816
> 916/983-4622

196

Honolulu Marathon

This marathon is in December.

> HONOLULU MARATHON
> ASSOCIATION
> 3435 Wailae Ave #208
> Honolulu, HI 96816
> 808/734-7200

INDEX

199

NOTES